# AURORAS OF THE ZAPATISTAS

## LOCAL & GLOBAL STRUGGLES OF THE FOURTH WORLD WAR

# AURORAS OF THE ZAPATISTAS

## LOCAL AND GLOBAL STRUGGLES OF THE FOURTH WORLD WAR

SECOND EDITION

MIDNIGHT NOTES

AUTONOMEDIA

Thanks to Ben Meyers and Mike Neiman for proofreading.



Midnight Notes
P.O. Box 204
Jamaica Plain, MA 02130 USA

Website: www.midnightnotes.org

Midnight Notes Collective:
Franco Barchiesi, Michaela Brennan, George Caffentzis,
Steven Colatrella, Dan Coughlin, Peter Linebaugh,
Monty Neill, p.m., David Riker, John Roosa, Susan Street,
Chris Vance, John Willshire-Carrera

Autonomedia
P.O. Box 568 Williamsburgh Station
Brooklyn, NY 11211-0568 USA

Fax: 718-963-2603
Email: info@autonomedia.org
Website: www.autonomedia.org

Printed in the United States of America

This book is dedicated to
Fernando Lopez Isunza and Rod Thurton,
two beloved militants who died making auroras for us all.

## TABLE OF CONTENTS

## INTRODUCTION

# THE HAMMER AND ... OR THE SICKLE?
## FROM THE ZAPATISTA UPRISING TO THE BATTLE OF SEATTLE

Tyger, tyger burning bright
In the forest of the night,
What immortal hand or eye
Could frame thy fearful symmetry?
—William Blake, *Songs of Experience*

THE FOLLOWING COLLECTION of articles was entitled *Auroras of the Zapatistas: Local and Global Struggles in the Fourth World War* to make it clear that we will not be looking at the Zapatista revolution directly, but rather at its enlightening and heating effects on the struggle against the latest form of capitalism (called "neoliberalism" in Mexico and increasingly called "globalization" in the U.S.) *outside* of Chiapas. Gustavo Esteva's "Indigenous Autonomy in Oaxaca, Mexico," and the interviews with Mexican activists, "Mexican Civil Society and the EZLN," show the effects of Zapatismo on the struggles against the party-state and NAFTA in Oaxaca and Mexico City. This is followed by reports on the ever-widening impact of Zapatista ideas in Canada and Europe.

A main field for the transmission of Zapatismo has been the various national, continental and intercontinental "encuentros" the Zapatistas have sponsored from their dawning on January 1, 1994. We have reports from the First Intercontinental Encuentro (held in Chiapas in 1996) and the Second Intercontinental Encuentro (which was held in Spain in 1997) by, respectively, Monty Neill and Gustavo Esteva. We also have an account of one of the most important organizational efforts that came out the Second Encuentro, the Peoples' Global Action (PGA), which brings us directly to the streets of Seattle. In 1999 the PGA helped organize a caravan of farmers from India to cross Europe and the U.S. to protest the globalization politics of the WTO. This caravan ended its pilgrimage in Seattle on the last days of November and put the lie to the establishment view that "Third World" farmers only wanted to have easier access to markets in the U.S., and were not concerned about the environmental, moral and political sins of the WTO's policies.

The other articles in this first section discuss how the Zapatistas' politics relate to the thought and practice of the workers' and feminist movements ("Towards a New Commons" and "Questions for Ramona").

The portraits that initiate the articles in the first section, the photo essay from the film *La Ciudad*, and the digest, "The Making of *La Ciudad*: David Riker on Politics and Filmmaking," form for us in the U.S. the most important "aurora of the Zapatistas." The immigrants portrayed in the photos and in the film are the living presence of the struggles of the Zapatistas walking in our midst. Their struggles have given the U.S. working class movement a fire and resoluteness that was been missing since the crisis of the 1970s.

The "other" essays, "Victory over a Life of Living Death," "From Capitalist Crisis to Proletarian Slavery," "On Whom Do the Bombs Fall?," "Eulogy for Rod Thurton," "Eulogy for Fernando Lopez Isunza" and "Revolutionary Tygers in the Night" are indirectly related to the Zapatistas. The first deals with the struggle of Shankar Guha Niyogi in India (little known in the U.S.) which has a remarkable resemblance to the Zapatistas' effort to bring wider circles of workers and a new imagery into the anti-capitalist struggle. The next two deal with the violence of capital, which make slavery and war the defining capitalist prospects of our planet. The eulogies are for a beloved Trinidadian comrade of the Midnight Notes collective who was one of the most effective voices against neoliberalism in the Caribbean and for a young Mexican activist who was bringing together the struggle of immigrant workers with the Zapatistas in his own work. Finally, Peter Linebaugh's essay closes the circle with a short reflection on historical and revolutionary roots of William Blake's poem "Tyger, Tyger," which forms the epigraph of the book.

Together these articles illuminate the slow and often unconscious formation of an "anti-globalization" movement, increasingly confronting the rule of social capital on a global level. From the Zapatista rebellion against NAFTA (1994) to the Mexico crisis (1994/5) to the Asian financial crisis (1997) to the financial collapse in Russia and Brazil (1998/99) to Kosovo and Chechnya (1999) we see, on the one side, capital's attempt to form a new level of global superstate and economy and, on the other, an anti-capitalist struggle moving from a multiplicity of localities to large-scale confrontations like the "Battle of Seattle" in late 1999. The Zapatistas have aptly named this struggle "the Fourth World War."

The importance of the Zapatistas for us lies in their ability to open up (at great cost to themselves) a space helping all of us to resist globalizing capital. Globalization took off with the world crisis of state capitalism that reached a crescendo in 1989 both in Mexico (with the Salinas government's commitment to structural adjustment) and beyond (with the so-called "collapse of communism"). Capital's planners have attempted to make this crisis a launching pad for accumulation on an unprecedented level. "Privatization of nationalized property," "liberalization of investment and trade," "the paramountcy of private property rights," "the law of the sea," and "intellectual property rights" have become the slogans of an era of swindles, gangsterism, and plunder on continental levels. Against it, the Zapatistas, in the "forests of the night" of the mid-1990s, have articulated the existence of a commons of wealth not yet lost and, indeed, actually expanding under the very nose of the enclosers! Their willingness to fight and die for this commons has revealed its power to many in the anti-capitalist movement in Mexico, North America and beyond who had forgotten it.

The January 1, 1994, Zapatista rebellion was thus a luminous crack in a clouded sky. In previous publications Midnight Notes have theorized the "New Enclosures" and altered that concept to an understanding of the hundreds of urban uprisings against structural adjustment policies in Africa, Asia and the Americas. But these struggles, moving by a planetary circulation of anti-capitalist revolt, had not articulated a movement that consciously pitted itself against global capital and at the same time was rooted in a territorial reality.

One of the editors remembers traveling to Chiapas in January 1993 and witnessing a number of demonstrations and mass meetings of "peasants" who were speaking their grievances against the government in the whispering song of Tzotzil. Though deeply moved, he remembered asking himself, "Could these people successfully fight back the IMF's and the World Bank's plans to destroy them, their land, and their collective life? Can they show us the way out?" He left

Chiapas not knowing that, at that very time, the Chiapanacan people were engaged in the discussions that led to the January 1, 1994, rebellion against the PRI government, NAFTA, and the IMF/World Bank.

The Zapatistas gave many the hope that a new kind of anti-capitalism was in the making, one capable of inspiring the deepest commitments in people, but not locked into the losing game of "taking state power" at the very moment capital has created systems that would immediately render powerless such revolutionary states.

After the uprising, along with thousands of other anti-capitalists around the planet, some of the editors went to Chiapas to learn first-hand from the Zapatista movement. And, in the process of meeting the Zapatistas, we met each other! The audacity of the Zapatistas was to open a clearing in a forest heavily patrolled by the Mexican Army and allow others to come speak with one another about capitalism and revolution. People who would not normally have talked to each other at home found that they had to, in the pressure of meeting literally in the midst of a battleground. Anarchists, NGOers, Marxist-Leninists, autonomists, pacifists, and indigenous peoples' advocates came together in the rainforest of the Lacandon to "help" and "know more about" the Zapatistas, and ended helping and knowing more about each other. The Zapatistas, humorously and generously, become something like the armed matchmakers of a new international movement against globalization. Many of the people who at the time were dismissed by sober media commentators of both left and right as "revolutionary tourists" or "throwbacks to the '60s" were to be found in the streets of Seattle disrupting the meetings of the WTO a few years later. Indeed, the militants who joined arms to block the entrance of the WTO were often consciously applying the lessons of Zapatismo by bringing the struggle against neo-liberalism home and projecting the struggle of Chiapas on a world scale.

The Zapatistas are reminding us that this is not the first time a "peasant revolution" ("the sickle") has challenged the most advanced points of capitalist production ("the hammer"). The whole problem of twentieth-century anti-capitalism is to be found in the enigma of the hammer and the sickle, and the Zapatistas have tried to answer it in a new way. In the imagery these two tools and their users were crossed together in solidarity. But though the sickle was the source of countless revolutions, the hammer claimed priority (indeed hegemony) whenever the victory was won. This had hidden an important fact of which the Zapatistas have had to remind us: *the land is the source of a tremendous revolutionary power and those who wield the sickle often instigate revolutionary change even in the stratosphere of high-tech production, because they have the capacity to subsist without capital's mediation.* This power to resist/subsist is exactly what capital wants to eliminate throughout the world. But this power has been desperately defended by workers at the cost of billions of lives since capitalism began with the European enclosures and the conquest of the Americas, Africa and Asia five centuries ago.

We in the U.S. sometimes forget this. When we think of anti-capitalism, we think of the urban industrial working class. But the history of anti-capitalist struggle in the period after WWI shifted from the city to the countryside. This move was presaged by the great Mexican revolution of 1911–17 and projected forward by the anti-colonial struggles in Asia, South America and Africa in the 1930s through the early 1960s. It is sobering for those who claim the revolutionary laurels for the bearers of hammers (made either of real steel, silicon chips, or DNA chains) to confront the fact that the bulk of anti-capitalist insurrections in the century just ended have had their bases not in the factories, but in the countryside.

Nevertheless, again and again, peasants, agricultural workers, indigenous people, rural women, the forests and the soil were sacrificed by socialist and communist parties and even anarchists in the name of "saving the revolution," "national defense," or "development" and "progress." (The "anarchist" industrial workers of Mexico City fought against the "peasant" armies of Zapata in 1915–16 for exactly these reasons!)

This harsh experience has created political antibodies in the anti-globalization movement which are expressed in imagery and theory. At the very moment when capitalism once again touts the promise of a technological future, the anti-globalization movement affirms in the streets the moral emptiness of virtual society, warns against the dangers of genetic pollution and environmental destruction, and embraces different forms of "neo-luddism" and "neo-primitivism," "subsistence perspectives" and "limits to growth." The scene has definitely changed from the period in the early 1960s when the U.S. Communist Party was putting the image of the Bohr atom on top of its hammer-and-sickle logo and European socialist parties were defined by a "more progressive than thou" politics. Some adherents to the "glories" of the revolutionary past have called this anti-globalization imagery and theory reactionary, but we see it as the sign of a recomposition of the working class internationally. The workers of the earth and of the human body are taking the revolutionary lead and refusing to be subordinated to the "needs" of production proclaimed by the wielders of the hammer, who have in the past fallaciously argued that since the sickle needed a hammer for its manufacture, hammers came first!

This recomposition requires that the wielders of hammers learn from the most humble of the earth. This volume of *Midnight Notes* contributes to this process.

The new political chemistry has many aspects. But one of the most powerful has been the ski-masked Zapatistas, whose masks represent a refusal of hierarchies, the determination to present themselves as "just another ear of corn in the common." Can we learn this nameless commonness?

What the Zapatista movement means for the U.S. anti-globalization movement is still an open question, but signs of what it could be have been illuminated in the streets of Seattle. When representatives of sea-turtles and Teamsters fought together against the Seattle police and the U.S. military and successfully blocked the WTO, a graphic image of a new social chemistry was presented to the world. This compound was first cooked up at midnight in the wet forests of the Lacandon.

# AURORAS OF THE ZAPATISTAS

## LOCAL & GLOBAL STRUGGLES OF THE FOURTH WORLD WAR

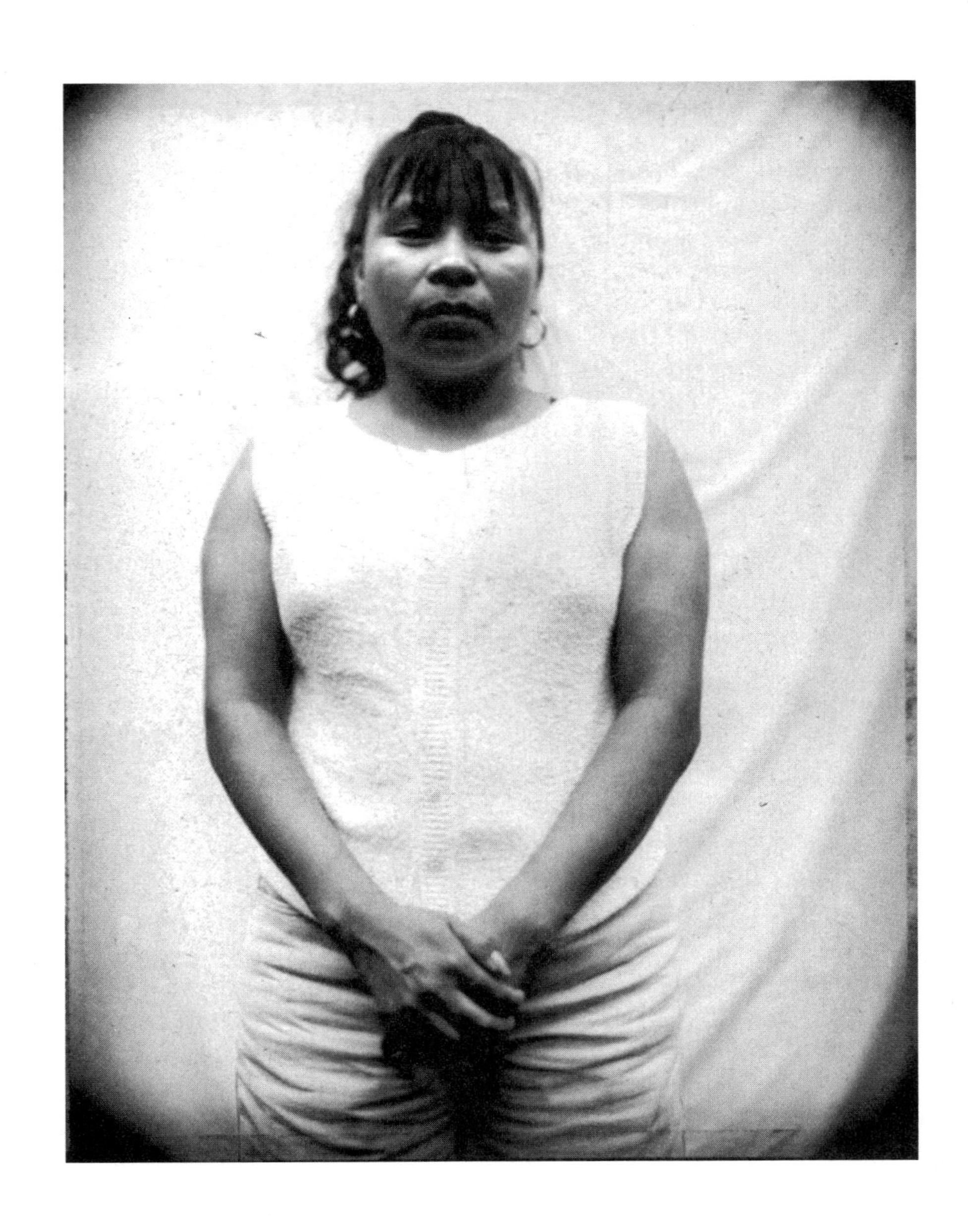

## 1
# INDIGENOUS AUTONOMY IN OAXACA, MEXICO

GUSTAVO ESTEVA

DAY BY DAY at the grassroots — in villages, municipalities, in barrios in downtown Mexico City — people are creating autonomous spaces. Within them, we see undivided societies, without social exploitation inside them. While we still live within an overall social factory, in our spaces we create contemporary forms of undivided societies.

Let me give you an example from Oaxaca. There are 60,000 coffee producers. Coffee is an imposition of capital, and coffee is grown for the international market. Over 90 percent of the land in Oaxaca is in social, community hands (this is not the case in Chiapas). Even after NAFTA and the change to the Mexican constitution which allowed privatization of common lands, almost no land has been sold to private owners.

Among these 60,000 producers, 10 different languages are spoken. After 10 years of effort, the various peoples created one organization for all the producers. This organization controls the land, the processing, and the sales to the international markets.

---

*Edited by Monty Neill and the author in August, 1999, from a presentation by Gustavo Esteva on May 26, 1998, in Boston, Mass.*

There used to be middlemen who would take the coffee and sell it on the world market, and these middlemen would keep a large share of the money. So the producers decided they would sell directly. They sent some delegates to New York to sell the crop. That year, as it turned out, was a year of coffee glut and falling prices, and they could not get a decent price.

One evening, as they sat worried and depressed in a bar, they struck up a conversation with another man in the coffee business. He asked them, finally, "What kinds of pesticides and chemical fertilizers do you use?"

"None," the Oaxacans replied. "We cannot afford to buy them."

"This is excellent. You have organic coffee. This you can sell for a good price." And they did, far exceeding their initial expectations.

Now the 60,000 producers faced the question of what to do with the higher than expected earnings. The question was posed to the assembly representing all the producers. For three months, people discussed their options. Many small assemblies were held in villages. These were real discussions over real issues as they grappled with what to do.

Finally, a consensus was reached. They uprooted half the coffee plants, the rest were kept to raise money on the coffee market. They planted corn and beans and vegetables on the land to provide for their basic subsistence independent of the world market.

"Our lives," the 60,000 producers said, "are in our hands." These producers are enclosing the enclosures after reclaiming the commons.

When they uprooted the plants, it was not that each producer uprooted half of his or her plants. Instead, among the producers as a whole, the best, most productive plants were kept, so one farmer kept all while another kept none. After this transformation, the income from the coffee does not go only to the coffee grower to use just as he or she pleases. Both locally grown subsistence crops and cash from sales of coffee circulate through the communities, through various means of distribution.

The money from the coffee is one means for improving their means. They can buy equipment, for example, to lighten the workload and increase productivity, or they can buy other goods they do not produce themselves. They are not outside the world market, but the relations of the world market are kept outside the communities. There is no exploitation of workers by owners. The Oaxacan communities are, in this sense, undivided communities. In these communities, the economy does not control life, but is subordinated to social life. Their process of improving their means is not dictated by the capitalist principle of scarcity.[1]

The forms of local government have been changed to reflect the indigenous people's assemblies. In Oaxaca, a state of about four million people, there are 570 municipalities. (In Chiapas, with a similar population, there are 115 municipalities, and a major aspect of the conflict has been the Zapatista-initiated efforts to create many more municipalities which can be controlled by, and responsive to, a local population.)

In my village, to select officers for public positions, we might begin in February with 10–15 candidates for a position. There will be lots of discussion. By May, there are five to six candidates, by August it is down to two, and in September there is only one. Then there is an assembly, which is a public recognition of what has already been agreed. Then for two days, the candidate declines the office, to represent that he or she is not seeking power.

An August 1995 state law in Oaxaca eliminated a requirement that municipalities have "simulation elections" — that is, voting by ballots for competing candidates. These elections would occur after the assembly decision. Before the new law, the PRI controlled those simulation elections and sometimes declared a new name to be the winner. This would, of course, be a mess, and sometimes violence would ensue.

Now, under the new law, municipalities do not have to hold the simulation. The new law tells the authorities to respect what the communities decide. It was changed in response to demands from the indigenous people, as the PRI feared a Chiapas-style rebellion. This concession to the two-thirds of the people who wanted their traditional means of governance did save the formal control of the state for the PRI. There still is, of course, real control by the PRI of a good part of it. Furthermore, there is an uneven application of the new law. In many communities, "post-electoral" conflicts emerged in the "elections" of 1998 due to the intervention of alien forces or internal conflicts in the communities. My own village was in the middle of a political crisis, in which the internal process was distorted and affected by external forces.

The indigenous conception of the role of state government is that it should be limited. Their democracy is similar to the original Greek definition, meaning people's power, not a form of government with representatives or parties. Rather, the people govern themselves through their discussions and assemblies. This is what the Zapatistas are trying to do in Chiapas. Let me give you a story to show you the people's idea of governance:

During a gubernatorial election in Oaxaca, 12 years ago, the leading candidate met with an assembly comprised of peoples who spoke 16 different languages. They did not let him talk, but for 10 hours speakers from the different groups addressed him, each in his or her own language. And each of the speakers told the prospective governor: How can you think to govern us if you cannot even understand us?

At the end of the 10 hours, from the back of the room, a very old man slowly walked forward to address the candidate. "We are not against you," he explained, "but we want a different kind of government. We want it to be in one place where all can see it. We do not want you trying to govern us night and day, even against our will. But in times of need, we want to know you are there. We would then seek your protection and help, like we seek shade from a tree."

Another story. A question was posed to leaders of the various indigenous peoples: if you have your way in making change in Mexico, what then will be the role of the national government? For months they discussed this issue, until finally they reached agreement on the useful role of the federal government: to name ambassadors.

In practice, I think, the new law in Oaxaca allows a juridical plurality — different forms of governing — which undermines the very basis of the nation state.

When I say that these communities are undivided, I mean in terms of class. Many of them, however, remain patriarchal, but this too is changing. Most authorities, for example, still are men. However, in Oaxaca there has been a feminization of politics as women take the lead — though even then, women may choose men to hold symbolic posts.

The Zapatistas, too, recognize that society cannot change without changes in the situation of women. The Zapatistas are trying to change both patriarchy and the sexist regime of modernity. For example, among both the Tzotzils and the Tzeltals, marriage is between two families, not two individuals. It is a several year process of development. In this process, women cannot say no, but men can. Under the new laws of the Zapatistas, women, too, can say no. But this change is not a modernity based on two individuals — it is still two families — but this change is a correction to the patriarchy.

I see, day after day, that real change comes when women step ahead. It is the opposite of Thatcherism as in Oaxaca, for the women do not do the same as the men when they have power.

However, there are still macho practices, including among women, and it is still a real problem.

Still, we see changes in economics and the relation to the market, changes in the structures and roles of government, and changes in the status of women, as people in Oaxaca autonomously act. They now are creating a tradition to change their traditions using traditional means, such as the assemblies and the processes of community discussion. These people have nothing to do with the Indians of 500 years ago, yet they are still the same. They have changed, are changing, without burying the past.

In this process of change, they are also avoiding the trap of the "individual," which is a social construction of modernity. We see in all these activities a political resistance to the construction of capitalistic individuality.

These kinds of changes are also showing up among urban workers. We see the beginnings of a new kind of union movement, but our real hope is not in a political change in the unions (most of which, in Mexico, are controlled by the PRI), but change in the workers themselves. They have discovered that defining themselves as workers in organized unions traps them in the logic of capital. So workers are changing the logic of unions and of themselves: they associate in new ways, in a logic that goes beyond capital.

**Notes**

[1] Of course, I am talking about a long and complex process that is not yet concluded. What I am trying to illustrate is the direction of these communities' initiatives, how they are reacting to capitalist domination and globalization.

# 2
# CIVIL SOCIETY & THE EZLN

## ANA ESTHER CECEÑA WITH ADRIANA LOPEZ MONJARDIN, CARLO MANZO, AND JULIO MOGUEL

THE ZAPATISTA ERUPTION on the First of January 1994 was like a lightning bolt that shook the technocratic fantasies which placed Mexico among the most developed countries in the world. It brought to light the cruelty of market forces, the inhumanity of capitalism with or without NAFTA, the human catastrophe implied in the continuation of neoliberalism and in the collective destruction that only benefits big business. For many, it also meant the recovery or the strengthening of hope and dreams of freedom, at a time of confrontation with beliefs, theories and political practices that have forced a reassessment of history. Can a revolution at the end of the twentieth century be thought of in the same manner as it was thought of during the first decades? Where are the vanguards and the leaders of the left? How can an anti-capitalist revolution be thought from the countryside and, furthermore, from the Indian populations? Is the Zapatista

---

*Adriana Lopez Monjardin, Carlo Manzo, and Julio Moguel were EZLN assessors at the Mesa 1 (Indigenous Rights and Culture) at the 1997 Dialogo between the EZLN and the Mexican Government. The original Spanish version was published in* ***Chiapas****, 4, 1997. This translation is by Franco Barchiesi, Susan Street, and John Willshire Carrera.*

*Adriana Lopez Monjardin, an anthropologist and a professor at ENAH, also participated, as a coordinator, at the Mesa on the Transition to Democracy at the Forum on the Reform of the State convened by the EZLN and COCOPA.*

*Carlos Manzo also participated in the Indigenous National Congress and the First Encuentro. He is a Zapotec from the state of Oaxaca.*

*Julio Moguel, a Professor in the Faculty of Economics at UNAM, is an editor for both the* ***Jornada del Campo*** *and the journal* ***Economia Informa****.*

movement a revolution? What does the recovery of the "national" accomplished by the Zapatistas mean? Does such a movement have any chance of advancing?

Many things have changed since that January 1, 1994. Many thoughts have matured, but so have many traps. Dignity creates paths and develops networks of expansion. Power already has its networks charted and it is constantly working to develop them even futher.

The difficulties of the path being followed, whose goal it is to build a new world through dialogue, are those posed by the possible real limitations of democracy, which have become apparent after the nullification of the San Andres Agreements by the Mexican government. In a context of growing social insubordination, of destabilization and competition between ruling groups, where social decomposition appears to take place much faster than recomposition, the loss of sovereignty in relation to the aims of an insatiable neighbor, of militarization of civilian power and of politics itself, a great fragility seems to characterize the possible scenarios and, with them, the prospects for a just, respectful and dignified society.

For this reason, the construction of a different future requires the best efforts, ideas and experiences, and honest, careful, sharp and critical reflection, from all of those who think this is possible. With the following, we start a series of interviews that will allow us to enrich our reflections with the opinions of social actors from different sectors, with different histories, and who come from quite diversified movements and communities.

*Question: Returning to the moment when you first heard of the Zapatistas, their actions and ideas, what attracted you to them? How could such diverse realities find common ground with or even embrace the Zapatista cause?*

MONJARDIN: My discovery of Zapatismo took place, as it did almost everywhere else, through television. During the first days of January 1994, I was surprised various times by images of young women who looked at the camera, laughed and talked to each other. Their faces were hidden, in part, by their kerchiefs, they wore embroidered shirts from the Altos (highlands) of Chiapas, and other things in their behavior puzzled me. I knew Tzotzil women and I knew that they did not usually look like that, or laugh like that. There was something different: pride, joy, defiance and self-confidence. Like many others, at first I thought they couldn't be the same indigenous people I had come to know living in the Altos. And, in fact, they were not. There was something new in their body language because they had learned to march like insurgents, militia-women or support groups of an army they knew as theirs. And they had taken San Cristobal de las Casas for the first time in five hundred years.

At the beginning of February 1994, I and another colleague traveled through several municipalities in the conflict zone. In those days, journalists were reporting that everybody was locked in their houses saying they did not speak Spanish. However, I suppose that two women driving a Volkswagen did not intimidate anyone, as the indigenous people received us in their neighborhoods and ejidos. When we arrived in their communities and explained that we wanted to learn more about their agrarian problems, they proceeded to ring their bells and call for people to come and to talk to us. We ended up chatting for several hours. We never asked if someone was Zapatista, we just talked about landlords, farms and the supporting mobilization in Mexico City.

Having gone from community to community, one day we were informed that the Zapatistas were having a meeting nearby where they were going to elect delegates for the Dialogue at the Cathedral. We started inquiring as to how we could get to the meeting, and things happened initially the way they always happened: they told us that if we went that way, further down the road, we would come to it. Well, we drove for a ways until a young man came by on horse back. He wore no uniform and carried no weapon. He was very young, between sixteen or seventeen. I will never forget the way he looked at me when we asked him how we could get where we wanted to go. He replied: "Why?" We explained to him that we were collecting information on agrarian problems to make them known in Mexico City. Very serious, the indigenous horseman looked at us leaning out of the window of the car and just said, "No."

Well, we went on and finished our tour. During that period, I remember the women I saw on TV during the capture of San Cristobal. Only later, did I really understand that a revolution had in fact begun and that it was very deep. Clearly, I should have been aware of it from the beginning as it was, from the very first days, written all over the faces, the bodies and the voices of indigenous people of Chiapas.

MANZO: In some ways it was about questioning our identities and realizing the existence of long-standing unsatisfied historical demands, in a country that was being presented by its government and its politicians, both to itself and to the world, as the "waiting room of the first world." It was also the confirmation of enduring historical continuities of cultural elements in the mentalities of broad sectors of the population, in this case of the indigenous people in Chiapas; the rediscovery of new revolutionary ideas arising from the interaction between academics, writers, intellectuals, social activists, and the indigenous people: as Antonio Garcia de Leon has declared, the "return of history."

On the other hand, what some of us called "el Zapatazo" came to mean for us a recovery of history, its re-evaluation and contextualization, its living presence, against the "end of history" that was being preached by neoliberal doctrine between the end of the eighties and January 1, 1994.

Since then, many of us intellectuals, academics, thinkers and social activists have discussed the exhaustion of the dominant paradigms of a globalizing Western perspective, and from that moment forward we have been gaining supporters in our dialogues. Zapatismo has confirmed with blood and fire for both the country and the whole world the real possibility of a direct and radical questioning of neoliberalism; of its body of ideas, "values, principles and reasoning." It also provides a challenge to our very political and cultural identity. UNAM (National Autonomous University of Mexico) itself has been left as a silent witness to this challenge as it has been perpetuating and pursuing a traditionalist curriculum of study which has lost much of its sense of criticalness at all levels of its programs of teaching and research. This has been an age of academic and intellectual camaraderie between the university's administration and researchers, and the Salinas government.

The "Zapatazo" was accompanied by a message between the lines: "My life, why should I want you if you are not dignified?" and then it is up to you to decide.

In my particular case, as a Zapotec indigenous from the Isthmus [in Oaxaca], as with other Isthmic comrades, we have been meeting since before 1994 to reassess our regional history in order to try to recover our rebelliousness and autonomist historical identity. Our efforts have greatly coincided with most of the Zapatista proposals and spirit, so that some have even stated that: "They anticipated us."

This great end-of-the-century rebellion comes to inaugurate the 21st-century Mexican modernity, reflecting a new living and vibrant history, understandable to our eyes as investigators of our capacity as historical subjects. It is the new historical subject that is going to change the world, however weird and utopian that might sound.

Zapatismo came to confirm what it had proposed in 1992, at the watershed of the fifth century: *that the indigenous are an innovative historical subject.* This was the recognition of the potential existence of a new civilizing matrix arising out of an indigenous worldview and in its interaction with the "rest of the world" (the national and international civil society), a process that has begun to define a planetary revolutionary proposal.

MOGUEL: My first steps towards Zapatismo took place during the first days of 1994 when I, as did many others, became aware that the capture of six or seven municipalities on January 1 in Chiapas was the concentrated expression of a veritable indigenous insurrection, rather than being a mere armed propaganda action by some guerrilla groups. The confirmation of my wholehearted and open support and solidarity with Zapatismo took place when I came to understand, or I came to believe that I understood, the basic meaning of its discourse. I would like to summarize what I then came to understand by quoting a section of my article "Images of the Future, From the Jungle," which appeared in *La Jornada* on March 28, 1994:

The future that the Zapatistas were referring to "was not perfect, nor did it have the ideal roundness of utopia." The warrior discourse of the Zapatistas was not expressed in an intention to "seize power" or to defeat the "enemy army": it was not a question of carrying forward a "prolonged popular war in order to get close to the cities and to impose the might of a red and ruthless militia; knives would not talk louder than the voices of the Indian people, those of real human beings. We soon came to know that the Zapatistas thought of themselves as one (and not the most important) among many forces prepared to transform this country from below...." In my article I reported that the Zapatista discourse "had been shaped through a complex process of political and ideological influences," and "out of different currents," but no one should doubt that the "filter" and the actual contribution of an original and secular culture of Indian communities had given to "this convergence of ideas its coherent... defined structure."

The Zapatista claim of a right to popular rebellion against "misgovernment" — explicitly raised by them on January 1st under Article 39 of the Constitution — reflected the foundation of their insurrectionist "model" which gave rise to a political program that was aimed at establishing the foundations of a new democratic regime, including apparently simple demands such as those of jobs, land, housing, food, education, independence, freedom, democracy, justice, and peace. This list of issues showed or confirmed in the current Mexican social and political reality the idea that demanding real democracy and the conquest of basic rights is deeply radical and subversive to the reality of capitalism at the end of the century.

*Question: What was the impact of Zapatismo on the struggle in your sectors? What have been the most important changes in the national political landscape in these last three years, and how has Zapatismo influenced them?*

MONJARDIN: What has changed in the past three years? Well, for example, who still remembers a guy called Constantino Kanter, who as a landlord of the Altamirano municipality [in Chiapas] had headed the farmers' backlash? In 1994, he promoted the mistreatment and harassment at San Carlos hospital, the attack on a students' march, and a prolonged picket in front of the Angel in Mexico City.

At the end of 1993, the indigenous of the Chanal and Altamirano municipalities used to go to work for farmers like Kanter, the Urbinas, the Zunigas, Santiago Robledo, Manuel Albores, Hector Culebro, Luis Espinoza, and Livorio Varela. Daily workers received wages of four to five new pesos per day, only paid after they finished with the tasks that their supervisors imposed on them. If they did not finish, they had to return the following day to finish in order to get paid. Sometimes they were paid 50 cents per hour, and were surveilled by a foreman so that they would work faster, with no time allowed even to take their Pozol. Other times, they were employed as daily laborers and made to wait up to one week before being paid. If an animal died, the owner gave the meat to the laborers instead of paying them their daily wages. The worst was when a cow had been dead for several days and the indigenous workers had to compete with the buzzards for the rotten meat.

Although the landlords did not disappear, after 1994, Constantino Kanter has now exhausted the possibilities of group-based political action: he and his people have lost their legitimacy and social support. They have lost the ability to use words to claim their "right to defend their properties." However, their actions are now being disguised behind the bumblings of the Secretariat for Agrarian Reform and in the "deals" with the federal and state governments. In the middle of a spectacular million-dollar dance, which was used to siphon public resources to finance the official party's [Partido Revolucionario Institutional — PRI] electoral campaign in 1994, they were compensated for the lands that were taken from them through invasion.

They have now also hidden themselves behind the clandestine, unaccounted for actions of the "white guards," and not only in Altamirano. In the northern region of the state, the Setzer family exemplifies the new methods of exercising power. After Elmar Setzer lost the interim governorship inherited from Patrocinio Gonzalez, Carlos Setzer, protected by his bullies, found himself in the painful necessity of personally hitting a campesino in public in order to defend his legacy. In Palenque, Manuel Huerta, a paradigmatic example of the region's landowners, has various properties under his sons', his wives' and his ghosts' names. Two of these properties were seized in 1994 by the Xi'nich indigenous, who founded the new communities of Plan de Ayala and Emiliano Zapata. Then, on March 7, 1997, they were violently evicted by the police. The following day, the Jesuit priests Geronimo Hernandez and Gonzalo Rojas and the indigenous leaders Francisco Gonzales and Ramon Parcero were detained and tortured under the false accusations of inciting peasants to self-defense during the eviction.

Although the landlords lost their words, they have kept their jails. They have lost their use of justice, but they continue to rely on the law. What then has changed since 1994? Nowadays, the Altamirano municipality is governed by indigenous campesinos. In that zone, there aren't many daily laborers left working on the farms for a few pesos per day. The landlords, who are always in agreement with the modern neoliberal officials, complain that "jobs have been lost." They, however, do not convince anyone. What we have always called oppression, they are now trying to reduce to a "disequilibrium between the demand and supply of labor."

MANZO: One of the important effects and changes facilitated by Zapatismo, favorable at both a national and international level, has been and continues to be the constant reformulation and advocacy of new elements in the wide, slow and sometimes piecemeal process of articulating a new political culture.

This phenomenon, most perceptible in Mexico, can be largely explained by the recovery of cultural elements fundamental to the indigenous worldview and their recreation in the political norms and attitudes of broad sectors of the civil society. Those political norms, traditional patterns of a traditional polity — read, parties and institutions — had never been questioned prior to 1994, even by those commonly interested in the analysis of the political processes at a national level.

Unquestionably, the demand for a charter for dialogue constitutes another important element of a pivotal instrument for the solution to situations of conflict and crisis, and, through it, the search for consent, as well as the rejection of any imposition of decision making on the part of the Zapatistas, of civil society and of some political parties.

The eruption of Zapatismo brings to the forefront, in the case of Mexico, the decomposition of a system of immoral and corrupt political loyalties that continue to persist inside the ruling elite, characterizing most of the Mexican political system.

From 1994 to the present, the acceleration of the processes of political and social decomposition and recomposition have been quite apparent as a large unfinished trajectory, in front of which, invariably, governors, officials and members of the cabinet and of the militias have been parading, making evident a system of exchanges in the power group, mostly linked to international drug-trafficking cartels.

Most of the negative effects of the process of decomposition hereby described are: a) The over-militarization at every level, including the police forces; b) An increase of more than three-hundred percent in the budget of the militia (SEDENA); c) An increase in the impunity exhibited both by officials and by notables; d) The flagrant violation of human rights, especially in indigenous regions; e) Finally, the crystal-clear evidence of state legitimated violence as the ultimate condition for the permanence of the elite.

MOGUEL: The EZLN dared to raise in its political discourse the notion of "going beyond capitalism," expressing its desire through the broad idea of the "threshold." This position, which to some resulted in some programmatic limitations of Zapatismo and for others exhibited a mere variation in its disguise, held for me the virtue of opening a channel to a non-excluding process — or excluding only in a limited way — of social and political alliances undertaken in the complex tasks of struggle and political change.

How can the Zapatistas' aims be summarized? The making of a democratic revolution (according to the meaning Habermas gives to the idea of revolution) leads to a "new relation between governments and the governed," where the former rule by obeying and the latter build or rebuild their forms of ruling and collective instruments for ruling.

This proposal is inscribed today in the struggle of broad social sectors against the party-state system. This is taking place at a moment when this struggle and the combination of mechanisms and instruments of formal political representation are experiencing a deep crisis. The debates being proposed by the Zapatistas are very directly linked with issues of power and legitimacy, as well as an evaluation of the naturalness and the substance of current political institutions.

*Question: Considering the initial ideas of the EZLN and their subsequent evolution, what are the main contributions of Zapatismo to the revolutionary movement? Has the initial proposal been modi-*

*fied? In what sense? How is its idea of a new world related to how the Zapatista struggle has developed during the last three years? Can we say the construction of such a new world has begun?*

MONJARDIN: While the landowners lost their words to speak on the public scene, the indigenous peoples recovered them. This they did for themselves and for the "everybody" to whom they directed their movement. The construction of the Zapatista new world started with having found the words to designate the bad life, in order to rediscover the sense of what needed to be changed.

This is because to break up the monopoly of the land and power in the hands of the Kanters, the Huertas and the Setzers, neoliberalism's monopoly over words had to be first destroyed. In 1994, in the darkest moments, after the collapse of the socialist world and under the Salinista totalitarian discourse, it was indeed necessary to say that Mexico was not in a "process of transition to democracy and the First World." That was what the Zapatista Army of National Liberation said on January 1, 1994. It said that with its words, its actions and its name.

Certainly many, nearly all, Mexicans knew this. But it also true that few had the words to project a future where ejidal and communal lands were not to be privatized and where large estates would not be the 21st century's alternative for agriculture, cattle and forestry. Not many would imagine a time when workers and the unemployed, the exploited and the excluded could demand a social policy that was not suffocated by narrow limitations imposed by the stigmas of "paternalism," "statism" and "subsidies," or a world where they were not just condemned to being "brilliant myths" or victims of "extreme poverty."

Before January 1, few remembered the hopes necessary to imagine a world where democracy need not be reduced to pretending that oppressors and oppressed were equal at the moment of depositing a piece of paper with colorful symbols in the ballot box in order to choose between different political parties. Before this date, few dared believe in a world where competitiveness and globalization were not the manifest destiny of Mexico, at the cost of its inhabitants.

MANZO: To talk of the "beginning of a new world in construction," as the question asks, would be like denying the influence of historical processes that are entirely feasible today. That is to say, one must look to the historical experiences in the everyday struggles of the people in order to detect the role redefined social relations are playing in the political, economic and cultural contexts at a global level. In this sense, the break with traditional patterns in everyday political and economic activity, at an individual, communal, national and international level, must necessarily undergo an objective analysis of the interrelated, long-term and contingent processes. We should do this in order to demonstrate to ourselves that there indeed exists a whole combination of historical decisions inherent in these social processes that proves these processes to be truly revolutionary. For example, the permanence and/or existence of dictatorial or neo-fascist regimes historically roots their political and economic programs in experiences of domination. Such experiences are felt by the elites in power as legitimately theirs as they try to socially defend or validate their model of rule on the predominance of the individual over and above the social or the collective, in a sense.

Zapatismo offers a universe of elements that break with the traditional logic of the many lefts. It advocates the social and cultural viability of "a world that contains many worlds," recommending in some way for themselves the "sacrifice" of individual benefits in order to secure the collective ones. "Everything for everyone, nothing for us" means putting horizontality and dialogue before political verticalism and individual decision-making. Power relations are to be rethought following a number of ideas contained within the slogan "rule by obedience": "look down, not up," "propose, not impose," "convince, not destroy to win," "obey, not order to rule." These principles constitute, in synthesis, a new political, social and organizational model that essentially questions, at a universal level, the existing power relations as they have traditionally been conceived from a Western perspective.

MOGUEL: Three years after its emergence on the public scene, Zapatismo has already changed some basic patterns of the political culture of the several lefts and of many social sectors. Or at least it has established solid bases for doing this. Not only has it conquered the heart of the national indigenous movement and become its indisputable political and moral leadership, it has also gained the hearts and minds of broad sectors of the youth and other "excluded" and "marginalized" groups. And this is not to mention the huge presence of Zapatismo on the international level, at the places where the struggles and the efforts of left-wing movements are played out, in social and political movements of those condemned by neoliberal capitalism to a hard life in the cellars of its crumbling edifice.

In Zapatismo we see the "recovery of the ethical dimension of politics." But not only that: the EZLN has been able to show an extraordinary novel way of "subject construction" which, at the same time, includes a way of constituting discourse. The form in which this took place in the national indigenous movement clearly illustrates the "method" to which I refer here. Consider, for example, all the elements that entered into play during the negotiations in San Andres Sacamch'en, a process that articulated social and political forces of very different natures and origins.

One of the most relevant products of the San Andres Dialogues on Indigenous Rights and Culture was that, for the first time in the country's history, an organization opposed to the established order included society as a whole in a negotiation that sought a transition to democracy as its end result. An important and intense moment in this process came when the National Indigenous Forum was created in the first week of January [1996]. This not only gave new direction to the discussions at Mesa 1 [Indigenous Rights and Culture], it clearly framed and set forth the organized forms and the fundamental programmatic policies of a new indigenous movement in the country. [Mesa means literally "table," the reference is thus to a space to dialogue, as in sitting around a table.]

Do we know of any more successful or original strategy of construction and reaffirmation of collective identities — the construction of new political subjects — than the one that started with the indigenous mobilizations in 1992 and carried through until the National Indigenous Forum in January? Had there ever been before, and without the intervention or mediation of political parties, such a negotiation with the state capable of advancing our understanding of fundamental aspects of the social and political fields of "the popular"?

Zapatismo has constructed a new way of understanding politics; more precisely, of "seeing" political power, with the intention that such a view would "produce another way of doing politics" (Marcos, *La Jornada*, January 10, 1996). In my opinion, the point is not to reject the polls and the system of representation, nor to eliminate the party system and destroy the state, but instead it is to "create a new relationship between rulers and the ruled."

*Question: The existence of the EZLN as an armed movement is legitimized by the absence of civilian forms of struggle and by its reclaiming demands for fundamental rights as stated in the thirteen points. Nonetheless, the struggle of the EZLN has been for the construction of peace, but not of a peace that disguises the violence of the state, but instead a peace where the weakest and the smallest ones have all their rights and live with dignity. The EZLN has repeatedly shown that it does not want war; unquestionably, it is at war. The presence of the Mexican army in the Zapatista areas reminds us of this all the time. How do you evaluate, in such a context, the Zapatista's intention to shift to civilian struggle? Could the constitutional recognition of the San Andres agreements open up such a possibility? Why? What are the risks implied? Is it possible to defeat state violence in this way, or at least to sufficiently limit it? Could the political conditions in the country allow for a struggle like the Zapatista one on the civilian terrain? Would that imply a change of perspective in the initial project of the Zapatistas? In which ways could this contribute to solving their demands?*

MONJARDIN: The Zapatistas declared war on the mighty government. At the same time, and as loud as their "Ya basta!," their call to civil society started to be heard: "Brothers, don't leave us alone." This call met its first echoes among the indigenous in the mountains of Guerrero, who replied: "You are not alone." Thereafter a dialogue started between the EZLN and a multitude of people and organizations: in the National Democratic Convention (CND), in the National Consulta, in the National Forum on Indigenous Rights and Culture, in the Special Forum for the Reform of the State, in the Intercontinental Encounter for Humanity and Against Neoliberalism, in the Dialogues of San Andres Sacamch'en De Los Pobres. Since 1994, tens of thousands of us have participated in these spaces where our words met. We have marched the streets of towns and navigated across the nets of virtual communication, warding off silence and loneliness.

We *mestizos* needed the indigenous peoples to recover our voices because all our words had been spent, blown away by the wind, or simply stuck on paper. Power continues to impose a sort of treason of the word. But, over time we have learned that when the Tzeltales and the Tzotziles give us their words, they are giving us the most valuable thing they have. This is not because they have few "things," but because they back up their words with their lives.

When, at the Intergalactic [Intercontinental] Encounter, Commander Ana Maria said that behind the masks "there is us," she was saying that the recovered words already are everyone's heritage, not only of the indigenous of the Southeast, not only of the Mexicans. The word rescued by the Zapatistas and delivered to society has been the main contribution of the Zapatistas to the revolutionary movement. For this reason Zapatismo is not only in Chiapas and it is not only an armed movement.

The San Andres Dialogues have been, formally, a space of negotiation between an armed group and the government. However, there is much more: the Dialogues turned out to be a privileged space of encounter between the EZLN and civil society. This feature has been dramatized from different perspectives. For example, in October 1995, during the first sessions of Mesa 1 on Indigenous Rights and Culture, many of the indigenous persons invited by the government, members of the PRI [Institutional Revolutionary Party] or of the CNC [the PRI's Confederacion Nacional Campesina], started their interventions "acknowledging the sacrifice of the Zapatista brothers, who made possible for us at last to be heard."

From a different space, from the height of power, at Mesa 2 (Democracy and Justice), no way was found other than to impose isolation and silence on the officials of the Secretariat of the Interior, given the real possibility of confrontation as each side presented its proposals. This Mesa 2 encounter did not result in an agreement signed by the EZLN and the federal government, as happened at Mesa 1. Mesa 2 was canceled because the governmental delegation decided to ignore its guests and experts, as well as their words and reasons. This situation led directly to the suspension of the Dialogues.

In March of 1996, in a meeting with EZLN leadership, an insurgent called Brusli (or Bruce Lee) clearly explained what the Zapatistas expected from the people invited to be their consultants. He recounted the history of the insurgents who had been preparing to fight for many years to ensure never to wound a comrade. In the same way, he said, those who are going to fight with the "weapons of intelligence" must be very careful not to hurt a comrade. By that time, what one of the consultants (Ricardo Robles) called "a low intensity fraternity" had begun to develop.

In these multiple spaces of encounter with civil society, the Zapatistas are building a new form of political participation. They have placed the process of negotiation with the government at the service of this encounter. Several times, in San Andres Sacamch'en De Los Pobres, the Zapatista commanders explained to their guests that they really had no "demands," because their demands could only be those fought for by the whole society. For this reason, they could only negotiate with the government those proposals based on a consensus reached among their consultants. They kept their word.

MANZO: The Zapatistas' intention to move toward a civilian form of struggle is already a fact of everyday knowledge. Since January of 1994 up until now, the national and international diffusion of the process started in Chiapas has outweighed other political initiatives and organizations working toward the same goal. In formal terms, since January of 1996, Civilian Committees of Dialogue have been set up throughout the country — in response to the Fourth Declaration of the Lacandon Jungle — and now more than three hundred committees exist in Mexico. Separate events called for by the EZLN (the CND, the National Indigenous Forum which became the National Indigenous Congress, the Special Forum for the Reform of the State, the very process of national dialogue started in San Andres Sakamch'en and the First Intercontinental Encounter for Humanity and Against Neoliberalism) have given ample evidence of the organizational and political potential that, at the initiative of the EZLN, has been developing and permeating broad sectors of the political and civil society at a national and international level. In the international sphere, the guerrilla movements in Central America and the establishment of national and international networks of communication (internet and other media), have made possible the coordinated action of diffusion and support of the Zapatista proposal.

In another sense, the social, political and economic conditions of the country continue to appear as a reflection of the causes that originated the EZLN. In this case and under this logic, the possible transformation of the EZLN would not depend upon a decree or the signing of an agreement verified by international organs, as in the case of the Guatemalan guerrillas. Zapatismo is, therefore, a historical process that, in terms of political strategy, exceeds the temporal and sociopolitical patterns of the current regime in power, and even of the political parties in Mexico. It is quite likely, although not desirable, that this process will not mature and be resolved during the current six-year term. To no longer be a reflection of the critical conditions that the country currently faces would imply the disappearance of these conditions, and with that, at some stage, the disappearance of the EZLN itself. The demands of democracy, freedom and justice become nearly impossible under the rule of the group that has kept power in Mexico during the past ten years. Analyzing formally and with a cool head the entire process of dialogue established since February 1994 between the EZLN and the federal government — in particular the part that refers to San Andres — that process has practically taken two years after San Miguel (April 1995), up to the present moment of crisis. The first theme in the Dialogues' agenda (Indigenous Rights and Culture) took nearly six months, and as we all know, the Agreements have not been respected nor in the least bit fulfilled by the federal government, making its option for a military solution to the conflict quite apparent.

Given this experience, even changing the agenda and the format of the process of dialogue, in the face of the non-existence of a dialogical culture on the part of the government and of the lack of honor in the fulfillment it promises, we should expect that the transformation of the EZLN into a civilian political force exceeds the expectations of the current six-year term. This is so even considering the instability of the country's contingencies: spring of 1996 will be defined in winter of 1997; probably 1997 will be resolved in 1998. Nothing is previously written or defined. In relation to the constitutional recognition of the San Andres Agreements, their complete accomplishment appears unfeasible; certainly it exceeds the expectations and the capacity of the current Congress of the Union and probably of the next one to be convened at the end of 1997. In synthesis, the peace process goes hand in hand with the key role of civil society in the sphere of national political relations. That is to say, at the national level, the opening of a democratizing process that could fulfill the demands recently expressed at the Mesa on Democracy and Justice would then be able to play a catalyzing role in generating the necessary social conditions for peace.

MOGUEL: The Zapatistas' intention to adopt the form of civilian struggle is the logical or natural consequence of what has been heretofore affirmed. Without a doubt, the constitutional recognition of the San Andres Agreements would make real such a possibility. The risks involved in taking this road are incalculable, but perhaps not greater than the ones the Zapatistas have already taken on in its emergence as a political armed force. Obviously this would not guarantee that state violence would be defeated once and for all, but it would definitely imply the possibility of setting limits.

But an important question arises here: "Would the current conditions of the country allow for a struggle such as the Zapatista one to be played out on a civilian terrain?" Everything seems to indicate that this is highly unlikely in the short term, not at least in this 1997. Mexico has entered a spiral of violence and political disorder — to say the least — that does not allow us to anticipate any positive political exit for Zapatismo, for the national indigenous movement or for the democratic forces in general.

*Question: The constitutional recognition of the rights of the indigenous* pueblos, *established in the San Andres Agreements represents a very important step in the construction of the peace that the Zapatistas seek, although it supposedly does not represent the solu-*

*tion to all their demands.. What would the importance of this recognition be and how is it related to the principle of "for everyone, everything"? [*Pueblos mean, *in some sense, peoples; an historical cultural group usually linked to territory and goes beyond community.]*

MONJARDIN: The San Andres Agreements, signed by the EZLN and the federal government in February of 1996, were built during a process of dialogue where hundreds of people participated directly. Organizations, communities and traditional authorities of the indigenous peoples were represented alongside specialists, media people and members of non-governmental organizations. All of them have in common a tradition of reflection about the indigenous world.

The Agreements crystallized the consensus achieved during the Dialogues and also reflected the balance of forces established between the national indigenous movement and the government. The Zapatistas' proposal oriented the process, not in the sense that it predefined its contents or the demands included, but by opening the negotiations with the government. This was a service for civil society, one to which the lives of many indigenous people in Chiapas were given. During and through this process, the National Indigenous Congress was formed.

Based on the San Andres Agreements, the Conciliation and Pacification Commission elaborated a proposal of constitutional reform concerning indigenous rights with the help of consultations — with the participation of both representatives of the federal government and of the EZLN, its consultants and guests as well as the National Indigenous Congress. For the first time a legislative initiative was built from below, involving various social actors and with the consent of representatives from all political parties present in the Congress of the Union. The flexibility and the political will of all these subjects dramatically contrasts with the regime's authoritarianism and with the federal government's betrayal of their word.

The importance of the constitutional recognition of indigenous rights implies, therefore, in the first place, opening a channel to start to repay the historical debt that society has with indigenous peoples. But it cannot be reduced to that. It also implies the possibility of strengthening a new form of political action, by integrating new organizations and by changing the laws. It calls for mestizos to reflect on the issue of autonomy and to question the racist and exclusionary assumptions that have been imposed on the nation by the rulers. And, finally, it puts the political will of the federal government to the test:

the government must fulfill the agreements with the EZLN and create the conditions for achieving a peace with justice and dignity.

MANZO: The recognition of the San Andres Agreements, in relation to the issue of indigenous rights and cultures, is a demand from wide sectors of the civil society, and of parts of the political society, including, of course, the indigenous peoples. Expressed in the Agreements, one finds a combination of elements that together constitute alternative proposals — in the political, juridical, social and economic spheres — to the neoliberal model imposed by the current regime. If we look beyond the indigenous peoples, many other sectors active in struggles regard the fulfillment of the San Andres Agreements as the satisfaction of their own demands. They also see the possibility for solving by peaceful means a whole nexus of national problems that in other ways would keep taking more lives and keep producing guerrillas throughout the land. In this sense, the lack of implementation of the Agreements could mean, as it is already meaning, a hardening of the arrogance, of the impositions and of anti-democracy in Mexico.

In particular, for the indigenous people and for the independent national indigenous movement, the San Andres Agreements, when linked with the repeal of the 1992 amendment of Article 27 of the Constitution [which eliminated the Constitutional basis of the indigenous ejido land control], already constitute a political program of struggle that has led us to consolidate our internal organization and also led us toward the search for alliances with different sectors of national and international society. This in turn has allowed us, leaving aside the approaches and the will of the government, to develop a process of dialogue and organization unparalleled in the history of our country.

Historically the indigenous peoples were left at the margins of the social and constitutional pacts that have defined the relations between society and the state. The lack of fulfillment of these and other agreements could be a catalyzing factor for defining a new constitution and a new and truly inclusive model of society or social pact.

MOGUEL: The EZLN concentrated most of its political energies in the process of debate and negotiation on the issue of indigenous rights and culture. We all know that this process had one of its most significant moments when, after four and a half months of discussions, the Agreements of San Andres Sacamch'en were signed on February 16, 1996. What would the meaning of this recognition and implementation of such agreements be?

A first aspect, which is absolutely crucial in the San Andres Agreements, is the recognition of the right of self-determination of the indigenous peoples, and as an expression of this, of their autonomy "as part of the Mexican state." This substantiates the idea of multiculturalism (while undermining the culturalist meaning of the concept) and establishes a principle line of rearticulation of national unity based on a concept of "difference."

In this perspective, autonomy is an essentially "integrationist" concept. Nonetheless, some people believe it to be "segregationist"; it is problematic because of the way in which the line of (re)integration is projected. The concept of autonomy in the San Andres Agreements breaks with the homogenizing logic of the perspective which views social subjects (society, civil society, and so on) not as fabric(s) of inter-subjectivities (obviously different and revitalized by their own interactions), but instead as joints of a mechanically existing body, whose reproduction is regulated "from outside" by the market.

"Society" as it asserts or re-asserts itself in this process of national (re)integration, is not, as a consequence, a mere sum of individuals inside the above-mentioned trend to homogeneity, but a relation constructed by individuals and groups or collective subjects for whom both individual and collective rights are recognized.

This is why self-determination — and autonomy as its expression — is mentioned in the San Andres Agreements as "rights of the indigenous pueblos." What this speaks to is the possibility that the indigenous peoples:

a) Decide on their own forms of coexistence and organization.
b) Apply their own normative systems in the regulation and solution of internal conflicts.
c) Elect their authorities and exercise their forms of internal governance.
d) Reinforce their political participation and representation.
e) Have access in a collective way to the use and valorization of the natural resources on their lands and territories, "taken to mean the totality of the habitat that the indigenous peoples use and occupy."
f) Maintain and enrich their languages, knowledge and all the elements that configure their culture and identity.
g) Acquire, operate and administer their own media.

The idea of "difference" is expressed fully in two lines of thought contained in the San Andres Agreements: the possibility that the indigenous systems of regulation and solution of internal conflicts could be articulated to normative systems at the federal level; and the possibility that the indigenous *pueblos* could define, "in accordance with the political practices corresponding to the traditions of each *pueblo*, the procedures for the election of their authorities and representatives and for the exercise of their own forms of internal governance, in a framework that ensures the unity of the national state."

What is decisive in the San Andres Agreements (and in the COCOPA document [Comision de Concordia y Pacificacion, formed with members of national legislature to negotiate with Zapatistas]) is the idea that the exercise of self-determination should not be restricted to isolated communities, but is to be established in the framework of "one or more indigenous *pueblos*, in accordance with the particular and specific circumstances of each federal entity." In this perspective, the communities, "as entities of public law," would be in a condition to co-ordinate actions and associate freely for cultural, political or developmental goals or interests.

A (re)articulation of national unity based on this indigenous notion of "difference" depends on a particular idea of state distribution of powers and functions, one that is quite different from that which characterizes the current process of deconcentration or "decentralization" promoted by the ruling powers today. (The decentralization underway currently tends to segregate or balkanize the country by route of the transnationalization of its parts or regions to benefit "globalization.")

Moreover, the idea of autonomy derived from the San Andres Agreements does not even presuppose a design of decentralization ("to delegate" or devolve pre-existing powers and functions from a center to a periphery). It does house a proposal to recompose the national (economic, political and social) body by rearranging its communities, municipalities and regions. For this reason changes are framed in the establishment of a new pact between the state and the indigenous *pueblos*, as well as in ideas or proposals to reconstruct the regional spaces, starting from their consistent social subjects (such as the indigenous peoples themselves). This means that the proposal to articulate intercommunitarian relations — or what defines the possibilities for a re-municipalization — is of particular relevance.

*Question: Contrary to previous revolutionary experiences, the Zapatistas do not aim to seize power, or at least don't plan to do so in the traditional terms. Unquestionably, the Zapatista struggle is facing the most powerful enemy in the world: international capital.*

*Is it necessary to destroy this power to build a new world? Can this power, which is first and foremost political and military, be destroyed starting from a struggle like the Zapatista one? How? Where are the limitations?*

MONJARDIN: Since the uprising on January 1, 1994, the Zapatistas have managed to sustain and develop a "symbolic guerrilla that disturbs the current conformism," to use Pierre Bourdieu's words. What follows? Will it be necessary to destroy the power of international big business to build the new world? Well, yes, I suppose so. But, for now, what about changing the question?

Shouldn't we ask ourselves how we can build new powers from below? How can we create a new common language to define injustice and to imagine the new world? How can we recover trust in our words? How can we call for participation in a new political project that is not on its way to replace the palaces of power, but that can change lives, so that common and ordinary people start making decisions? Is it possible to exchange answers and certainties for a few shared questions?

MANZO: The Zapatistas have not dedicated themselves to the seizure of power, nor do they aspire to be the vanguard of a revolutionary process that leads to the transformation of this country and the world. In the same way, I believe that the Zapatistas have taken one of the most respectful approaches towards contrary political or economic experiences. Consider the Zapatista postulates known until now; expressions such as "for everyone, everything," "build instead of destroy" and "for a world that contains many worlds" constitute, from my point of view, a call for tolerance in different spheres of life. These elements are lacking in the most fashionable neoliberal proposals, including, of course, those of international capital. The problem is planetary and goes beyond the possible effects of transnational capital on particular political-economic systems. At a socio-political level, the rise of the right and of neo-fascism in Europe, against which broad sectors of the European civil society have demonstrated — see, for example, the silent march by more than 120,000 people in February [1996] — corresponds to a socio-cultural historical effect that is not directly determined by the impact of transnational capital. The right and neo-fascism constitute, undoubtedly, a face of the neoliberal monster, just as international capital does.

The Western civilizing matrix has shown its own self-destructive and intolerant capacity to survive and it has done so at the cost of the disappearance of the smallest and the weakest — most of us — of the different and the diverse, which is, as a matter of fact, what enriches cultures. The possible sudden death faced by the Montes Azules (Blue Mountains) in the next three years, with or without international capital, is presented as an unsolvable problem. If this is repeated in Central and South America and in Africa, it would inevitably lead to the destruction of all of Mother Earth. We are therefore facing a problem of exhaustion of the Western civilizing vision which encapsulates all those forms of social, economic, political and cultural relations among ourselves and with nature.

From the indigenous world view, re-evaluated and reappreciated since the emergence of Zapatismo, we can build new paradigms, promoting and producing in the simplest of our actions a new political and economic culture. We can re-establish the whole combination of possible relationships among ourselves, in the individual, communitarian, national and international spheres. We can respect, recognize and reproduce the sphere of community without diminishing, perhaps, individual and private rights. We could, finally, construct the groundwork for the next seven generations to build a world that contains many worlds.

MOGUEL: Certainly, the Zapatista struggle is facing the most powerful enemy in the world: international capital. But the war is not between the EZLN and this gigantic enemy; it is between international capital and the growing masses of marginalized people whose future is nothing but hunger, sickness and death. The EZLN is just one among many millions of voices that are rising from this new field of pain and struggle. Can big business win in its crazy race against these growing masses of marginalized and impoverished groups? Or, to put it differently, what would a more or less sustained and coherent victory of neoliberalism mean? To build islands of economic power and wealth in the middle of an eternally angry sea of poor people?

This is not the place to evaluate the social and political forces that in Mexico and around the world raise their fist against the neoliberal horror, nor is it the space to reasonably think through their possibilities of success in the middle or long term. But these forces are not few and they are not asleep. Zapatismo is such a source of inspiration and of living hope that it has been capable of enlightening paths that until a short while ago were thought by some of us to be nonexistent or inaccessible.

# 3

# ENCOUNTERS IN CHIAPAS

MONTY NEILL

*Here we are, the dead of all time, dying once again, only now with the object of living.*

*You have to get out of yourself to save yourselves.*

*What we seek, what we need and want is that all those people without a party and organization make agreements about what they want and do not want and become organized in order to achieve it (preferably through civil and peaceful means), not to take power, but to exercise it.*

— EZLN/Subcommandante Marcos

THE BUSES, slowly moving down the 60-mile dirt road to La Realidad, stop again. Why? We, participants in the Intercontinental Encounter against Neoliberalism and for Humanity, get off and walk around. The word filters back: a bridge is out and we have to fix it. Arriving on the scene, I see that the bridge is made of iron piping, the kind used to keep cattle from crossing, and it is lying on the road next to the gully it used to span. Campesinos are digging in the gully. Using trimmed limbs of trees as rollers, braces and levers, dozens of us, women and men, including Superbarrio in his flamboyant red costume, slowly maneuver the bridge into place. We are applauded by many more, bus riders and local folk, who are too many for everyone to put a hand on the bridge.

Between bouts of lifting, we wonder how the bridge got moved. One rumor is that the local campesinos moved it so they could charge our buses a toll. But this makes no sense: the campesinos are pleased to see us helping them replace the bridge. One of them, together with a few men from our caravan, takes leadership in directing the replacement. Ideas flow from the working group, are considered and often used, in a democratic process.

A joke circulates that the Zapatistas moved the bridge so we would have to learn cooperative physical labor. But really it seems that the gully was partly blocked so the rainy-season water was not running properly. The bridge had to be moved so the gully could be dug out and then the bridge set properly. That's when our caravan, the early stages of perhaps 40 buses, arrived. Anyway, the activity is a pleasant break in a 14-hour trip, and it is not raining anymore and the ground is no longer muddy.

### *In the Circle*

Encircled by the armed women and men of the Zapatista Army of National Liberation (EZLN), people from over 40 countries meet in an Intercontinental Encuentro in the rain and mud season of Chiapas in southeastern Mexico. The EZLN hoped people would come, though Subcommandante Marcos said they had vacillated on this idea, initially thinking only a few would come. But we are here in the thousands. Mexico, Spain, France, Italy, and Germany provide the largest groups. The U.S. delegation is unfortunately small, and smaller delegations have arrived from other European countries, Japan, and the rest of the Americas with a few from Oceania, Africa, Asia and the Caribbean.

Our diversity is not just our continents and nations, or our gender (perhaps 40% women) or age (mostly young rather than veterans of the sixties), but our experiences and ideas. These we are to share and reshape through the experience of the encounter in the forest, striving toward a new possibility.

It is not quite the whole world, with too few from the South of our planet, and it is not likely that the kind of work, paid or unpaid, that the participants do accurately reflects the work done across the planet. But has there ever been such a gathering? We are not a party, nor party representatives to a Comintern. Indeed, we are not representatives but simply ourselves, though we are labeled "delegations." Many are activists from various forms of community and workplace struggles, such as the Argentinean mothers of the disappeared.

We certainly are not the owning class, who meet in fancy hotels with fine wines and fancy foods. Rather, we sleep on the ground or in hammocks under plastic roofs, or in tents, and eat tamales, enchiladas, beans, and soups. Alcohol and drugs are prohibited in the rules we each signed as a condition of attending. This gathering is, after all, in a war zone.

Thus, security concerns are real. At the start, in Oventic, not far from San Cristobal, everyone is thoroughly searched. Divided in two lines, women and men, standing behind their packs, a Zapatista empties each pack, feeling for weapons. Even Swiss army knives are taken, a receipt given to pick them up when leaving. A quick pat-down, then the Zapatistas carefully re-fill each bag. It is all done with care and respect for our belongings and our persons.

In the beginning and at the end, in La Realidad, southeast toward the Guatemalan border, the Encuentro meets as a whole. In between, it separates into five mesas (tables) to discuss politics, economics, society, culture, and identity. Each table divides further into sub-mesas.

The additional three village sites, all in or near the Lacandon forest, are Roberto Barrios (near the great Mayan ruins of Palenque), Morelia, and La Garrucha. To arrive at the villages requires traveling past the Mexican army, which has set up a base next to each community that has declared itself a Zapatista community, and past the immigration checkpoints set up to harass us all, both Mexicans and non-Mexicans. Getting to Roberto Barrios required walking through the army base then fording a stream.

At each locale, the mesa is within a circle, within the protection of the EZLN. At Roberto Barrios, the site of the economics table, some 3500 local people, among the materially poorest on the planet, have spent four months constructing a space for the encounter: a hall to hold 400 (with rented chairs and an excellent sound system), a kitchen and a dining hall, sleeping areas, a space for the press and to house the omnipresent computers and to recharge batteries, showers and toilets. It is a huge, overwhelming and humbling gift.

### *Discussions*

Cooking is done by the community. Every day the local people, mostly Mayan of various groups (Chol, Tojolabal, Tzeltal, Tzotzil), clean and repair and take care of our physical needs. We do wash our own dishes. Some do not do this well and are sent back to do the job correctly.

The EZLN does not participate in the mesa discussion. At each sub-group, two commandantes sit and listen. They greet us at the start, thank us for our work at the end. They have provided the space for us to dialogue, but choose not to participate verbally. Still, the words and practice of the EZLN, the physicality of the rain and mud, and the space provided by the local community, surround and support the discussion.

I attended the economics mesa subgroup whose task was to define the economic dimensions of neoliberalism. Other mesas in economics focused on alternatives, on "progress" under neoliberalism (narcotrafficking, financial speculation, and deteriorating health care), and on work and the dictatorship of the market. There was a plenary one night with five papers presented. Amidst a range of cross-cutting issues, we talked intensely for two-and-a-half days, emerging, as did all the sub-tables, with a short paper, each of which was presented at a closing plenary of the mesa.

In each discussion group, papers were presented and discussed. In the one I attended, papers were grouped and summarized in clusters of four, followed by an hour of interventions and debate. This enabled a building process which greatly strengthened our final paper.

Neoliberalism, our group said, is the current phase of capitalism. It has many names: structural adjustment, Reaganism, Thatcherism, the new world economic order, austerity. It is the immiseration of the many, caused by accumulation by and for the few, who back up their efforts with control of the state, the gun, the media. People's talks portrayed in detail the human faces of misery: loss of land, rising unemployment with no social wage or safety net, overwork, declining wages, increased homelessness, growing racism and attacks on immigrants/migrant workers, no health care, and in too many places not even running water or electricity.

Privatization, untrammeled rule of the market, globalization of the reserve army of labor, increased competition among workers, commodification of all kinds of social relations and of the body and mind, mad cow disease as a sign of the mad destruction of nature in the name of profits, financial speculations that shatter entire national economies in a few hours, slavery restored, the more intense attacks on women and children, reassertions of patriarchy, mobile production processes, debt, death squads and militarization within nations, and the leading world organizations of immiseration — the

World Bank, the International Monetary Fund, the World Trade Organization, NAFTA and Maastricht: The economy and social life have been re-shaped since the early 1970s, with an eye to extracting greater profits at the expense of working people around the world. However, the core of the problem is not just the neoliberal phase of capitalism, but capitalism itself.

Disagreements were voiced. One strong view (which I share) is that neoliberalism emerged in the 1970s as the capitalist response to world-wide class and social struggles which broke apart the planetary capitalist phase often labeled "Keynesianism" or "Fordism." Others, however, pointed to the mechanisms of capitalism, such as the falling rate of profit, as the source of the crisis which provoked neoliberalism.

Is neoliberalism itself in crisis? Some thought yes, others no, a discussion complicated by political ideas and experiences being transferred across languages and cultures. One position (again which I share) is that struggles have provoked crises and reshaped neoliberal practices, such as the austerity plans of the World Bank and IMF. Yet clearly the cycles of struggles have not stopped the neoliberal process of driving down wages and multiplying divisions and borders within the working class of the world, waged and unwaged, landed and unlanded.

The sub-mesa also discussed population, technology, the role of nations and the state, and the effects of social atomization. Its report recognized that neoliberalism could not be reduced to the economy, but controlled politics, used culture, dominated social institutions, and destroyed or reshaped identities, all in the search for profit and accumulation. Thus, though the group focused on economics, it saw struggles and alternatives across all these social terrains.

### *Breaking out of Circles*

Traveling from town to town on long bus rides through spectacular, lush mountainous forest, deep valleys, innumerable fields of maize climbing steep hills, small villages, and areas clear-cut by a former governor for his personal enrichment, the Encuentro mapped a political geography that transcended the circles which held the discussions. Our movements crossed the enclosures of the Mexican army, our presence broke the enclosures of the Mexican state.

Relations between encuentristas and the Zapatista communities also broke through some circles. On the first night in Roberto Barrios, local musicians and dancers performed. Outside the hall stood local community people. As the rain began, a few inside shouted for them to join us under the roof. A Zapatista announced that the community had decided not to come inside because, for security, they wanted to have a cordon of people around the hall; that decision could not be overruled by the Encuentro.

Two nights later, as delegations from the various nations sang songs of resistance and liberation, and again community members danced and played, and a traveling troupe, "Arcoiris" (Rainbow), joined the festivities, the community of Roberto Barrios came into the hall. The women mostly sat in a group in the rear, the men stood by the entrance, the children moved about most freely, in a partial dissolution of another boundary, if not a complete break.

The discussions broke circles inscribed by language. Spanish was the language of the Encuentro, but many participants did not speak Spanish. Translation was arranged informally, with bilingual people from different nations sitting in clusters as translators who sacrificed their involvement in the discussion in order to keep others involved. And of course translation broke down at points, especially with some of the more complex presentations, leaving monolinguists with only rough approximations. Still, new connections transcended old borders.

For my submesa, it was not enough to begin to identify neoliberalism. We also asked ourselves, what do we want for humanity? What are we doing in practice to create the new from within the old?

We looked often at the emerging practice and dialogue surrounding us in the Zapatista army and communities. The EZLN has proposed a range — perhaps a contradictory range — of ways of living and doing politics and economics that build from the practices of the historical left and those of the Mayan people. In the EZLN command structure, the community is at the top, with the leaders charged with obeying the will of the community. Politics is the process of dialogue, of coming to new understandings and practices through bottom-up social transformation. To create this space for change, as well as to warn the Mexican state that people facing death will not go peacefully, the EZLN has needed to use its guns.

People brought a myriad of practices to the submesa — equal exchanges, development of new forms of community, international solidarity actions and new forms of international links (such as is happening with dockworkers), and collective production processes. There was not time to explore what all these possibilities mean, where they cohere and where they contradict each other; where they can support fundamental change and where they may fuel capitalist growth or act to patch up a system which our sub-table thought was not salvageable for the benefit of humanity. I sensed new forms emerging of a long-standing division on the left, between reforming the system and replacing it with something radically new. Still, different perspectives and practices were together, offering material for debate.

Central to all the alternative proposals was the idea of stronger networks of communication and support. Survival and victory depends on coordinated action beyond the level of the nation. This need not mean centralized planning of struggles, but rather voluntary cooperation across a wide variety of situations and actions. Yet this formula has only an embryonic content: activists are just beginning to learn how to cooperate quickly and effectively so as to intensify, broaden, and deepen struggles.

At the final event, in La Realidad, as the Encuentro came back together, each sub-table from all five mesas presented summaries. These told us something of who we were and were becoming, yet they were incomplete, a first step in a process of producing new relations of struggle.

Marcos' speech at the closing was not a summarizing of the Encuentro, but a verbal contribution from the EZLN to the discussion. He reinforced the idea of breaking out of enclosures, remarking that even as neoliberalism globalizes the market it constructs more and more borders within countries and divisions among the people. He, too, emphasized the need to develop networks.

### *Leaving the Circle*

At the time of the Encuentro, armed struggles were expanding across Mexico. The Mexican army was militarizing all of southern Mexico, attacking all forms of popular organizations as the devastating consequences of neoliberal austerity deepened. The EZLN is now attempting to build the Zapatista National Liberation Front (FZLN) and seeks to move beyond the armed struggle, but they are not sure it will be possible. Soon after the end of the Encuentro, the EZLN broke off negotiations with the Mexican government, accusing the government of failing to negotiate in good faith, failing to implement existing accords, failing to release Zapatistas held prisoner, and militarizing Mexico.

The heart of the Encuentro was to begin to create a new "we." I don't know if this new we will grow, expand, deepen, learn, and act with increasing capacity against neoliberalism and for humanity, but I did detect a few positive signs:

We leave with a sense of urgency — to support the Zapatistas and to find new ways of combatting neoliberalism across the globe — and of patience. By now we should know, from historical experience such as the Mexican revolution, that a revolution is not simply a moment in time, but a protracted process. As Commandante Tacho explained in the final plenary, everything can be done, but even small things can be hard to do. We need a practice of urgent patience. In this practice, we might include local and regional encounters to try to forge new ways of thinking and working together across the borders the system continuously erects. Another intercontinental encounter is being planned for next year in Europe.

We leave with more questions than answers, but at this stage of recomposition that is a healthy acknowledgement. New networks were proposed, one for building and circulating struggles, the other an alternative communication network, both to be decentralized — but how will these really work to strengthen and expand the struggle against capitalism? We oppose neoliberalism and have perhaps sketched its definition, but what actions do these analyses impel us to take? The care and respect we received from the Zapatista communities was certainly a working practice of "for humanity." Still, our conversations barely touched on what it means to be "for humanity," what "humanity" means in a world of class exploitation, or how we can free ourselves from the tortures and expropriations some humans have created for the rest.

We leave with great hope, having seen the capacity of the Mayan people to build structures and provide a space for thousands of visitors from around the planet. Much indeed is possible. Lightly-armed guerrillas held off a modern army, creating new spaces. How surreal is it for thousands of people to bathe in the mud in the mountain jungles and discuss economic and political theory and dare to imagine we can win a new world? Is our hope crazy, or is it our only chance?

The deepening crisis in Mexico will have powerful ramifications in the U.S. The left in the U.S., such as it is, ignores Mexico at its peril. The U.S. government and transnational corporations continue to supply the Mexican state and capitalists with billions of dollars and, often under the guise of the drug war, new sophisticated weaponry. If, as some analysts suggest, Mexico breaks apart, as it did in its last revolution, the U.S. government is sure to intervene to protect the interests of capitalism. And more than stopping U.S. intervention, U.S.-based activists need to help a new Mexican revolution succeed.

Creating a new "we" means, in part, building bridges across the Rio Grande. The bridges enable travel in two ways: the Zapatistas' words and actions show that we in the U.S. need them, for from a supposedly isolated corner of the planet comes not only a challenge to neoliberalism that has yet to be contained, but comes also a challenge for us all to rethink ourselves and act anew against the misery created by the capitalist system. It is not them and us working on the bridge, it is us.

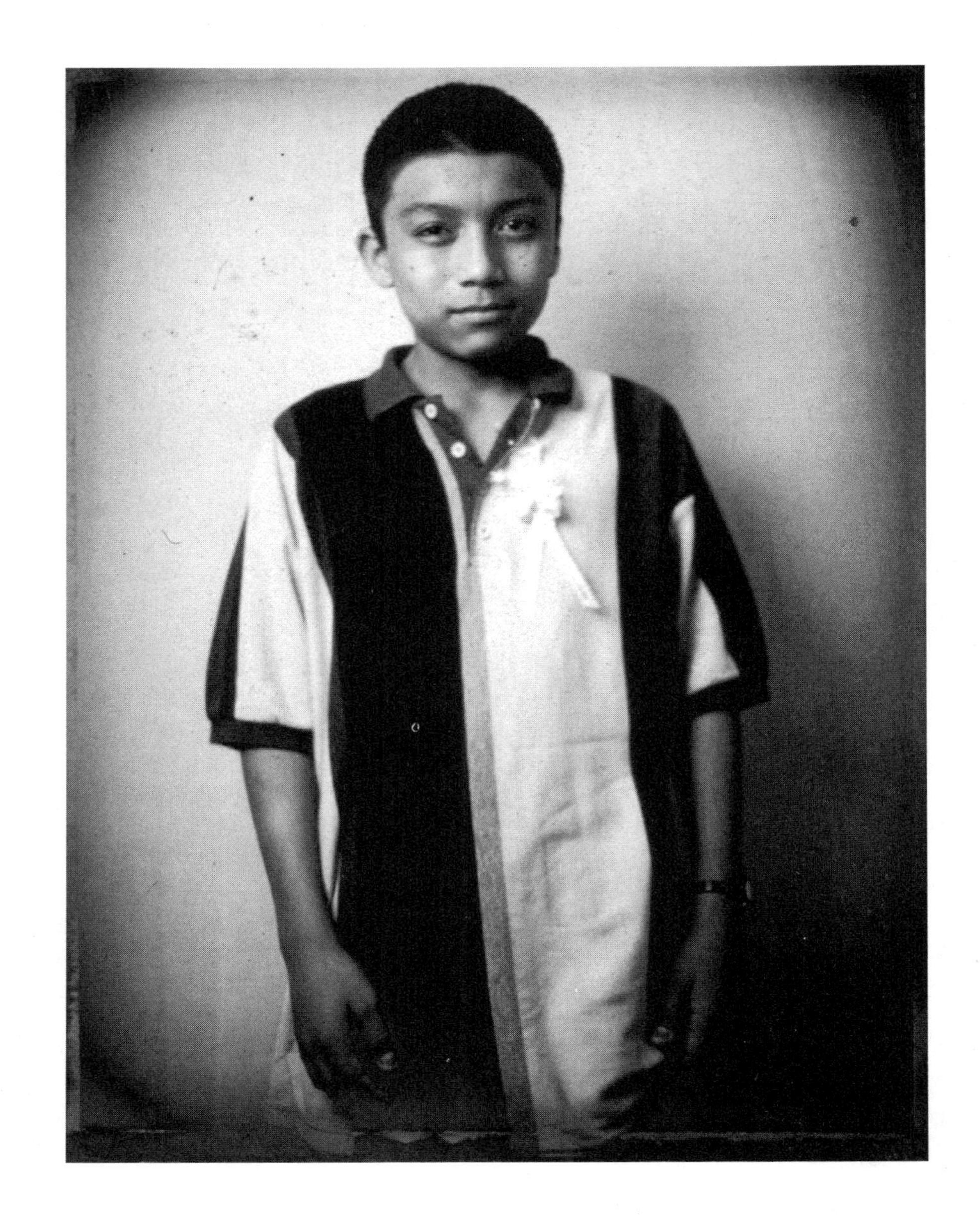

# 4

# AN ENCOUNTER OF DISCOVERY: THE TRADITIONS OF PEOPLE OF REASON & THE REASONS OF PEOPLE OF TRADITION

## A REPORT ON THE SECOND INTERCONTINENTAL ENCUENTRO

GUSTAVO ESTEVA

WE MET AGAIN.

We came from many places, with a diversity of motives and purposes, and holding different views and positions. We were many in number, and our common denominator was not clear or well defined; our intent to define it provoked conflict and opposition rather than agreement.

And yet, we came together. We combined the ancient meaning of the word "encounter" (to meet as an adversary, to dispute) derived from its etymology (in and against), with its contemporary meaning: to go to meet. In my view, from the threads of our diversity we wove together a fabric of our opposition and resistance. In doing so, we created opportunities for liberation, preserving the contours of our negative common territory.

In Spain I heard complaints, disagreements and discontent with regard to the "encuentro" itself, the organizers, the participants, and even those who were not present. I continue to hear these complaints. I will not examine them here. Some are basically irrelevant. Others are not, but are now incorporated into the general conscience. It is not necessary to elaborate upon them. The sharpest and most ferocious critiques against the organization, for example, I heard coming from the organizers themselves. To my understanding, this signifies that we learned about unfruitful paths. We will try not to fall into them again. Instead of belaboring these mistakes, which would be tiring and irritating, I present an elaboration of my own experience in the Encounter, concentrating on those aspects that still perplex me and, I believe, require further discussion and reflection. I do not synthesize nor draw conclusions. I do reflect on the issues that remain open or whose exploration was deepened during the course of the encounter.

### The Means and the Ends

It was not easy for us to meet. In addition to the physical, ideological, and linguistic distances and the organizational and logistic difficulties, we were separated by cultural distances. For some cultures, the proposal for an encounter of this kind means to meet one another, to share with one another. The encounter is an end in itself: an opportunity to practice hospitality when confronted with the otherness of the other. For other cultures, a meeting is only a means to reach certain ends. If these goals are not reached the encounter is considered useless.

This has not been a secondary issue in the logic of our encounters. From the beginning, during the first encounter, the tension arose between those who fully enjoyed the opportunity to meet and share with others like them and those who sought and pushed for a specific outcome: a manifesto, an organization, a political platform, a show of strength, a massive support for a specific agenda, a solid step towards the world unification of the struggles or the construction of a common ideological, political, or organizational denominator...

The first group was enthusiastic, given the direct and lively contact and the richness and variety of the debate. And later, they dedicated themselves to learning from the others, to arranging specific forms of interaction, to building bridges, to clarifying agreements and disagreements, to appreciating differences, all amidst the thousands of tasks imposed by the Encounter. The second group traveled from frustration to frustration, encountering obstacles and resistance when they tried to push their ideological, political, or organizational agendas. Among them there were some who discovered along the way the intrinsic sense of "encounter," the reason for doing it, and they saved the plans and mandates they had brought for a more appropriate occasion. Others maintained their impulses until the very end and returned to their countries of origin with the frustration of their "un-encounter."

For some, to distinguish and separate means and ends is indispensable. Rational behavior and reason are defined by them as pursuing coherent ends and using means appropriate for achieving them. For others, this operation is impossible — the means are only the counterparts to the ends. Their arbitrary and abstract separation is the source of confusion and often violence. The tension between these two concepts was manifested in the second Encounter, just as it was manifested in the first.

**Universe, multiverse**

This tension frequently set up another one, heightened to moments of complete contradiction: the temptation or even compulsion to become attached to a supposed or real Zapatista orthodoxy and the conscious intent, open and generally healthy, to avoid this attachment. The pretext for expressing this tension, not always admitted, was the exploration of where to hold the next Encounter. Opinions regarding this matter were wildly and violently expressed from the very first day of the Encuentro.

The exploration itself was a sign of inspiration and hope. It reflected the general conviction that, independent of what could happen during the second Encounter, there would be a third. That is to say, there was the insight that one was taking part in a process of lengthy duration, of which each encounter was episodic and not an end point or an ephemeral event, closed onto itself.

This underlying convergence of views disappeared upon the examination of the possible sites for the third Encounter. The explicit proposal to hold it again in Mexico, this time in Mexico City, met with as much support as resistance. I did not hear anyone opposing the Zapatistas or denying the need to maintain and deepen solidarity with them. But I did hear, in varying forms, the argument that it was convenient to give to the "movement" other images and dimensions: to support with our presence other specific struggles, in the Sahara or in Brazil, and that by doing this we would demonstrate our diversity and prevent others from thinking that we came together only for the Zapatistas, or, even worse, that they were directing the "movement."

There was increasing consensus about the non-existence of a "Zapatista orthodoxy." This conviction became an issue or at least a source of concern or distress for those who had hoped to find in Zapatism a new true doctrine. It also was evident that there exists a singular and unique Zapatista style. It is the style of specific cultures, well rooted in their own spaces, that can open up to others. No doubt, it is possible to learn from them. But the attempts to imitate or reproduce this style fail — among other reasons because they are out of place, and uprooted, when adopted by others in other places.

Where to hold the third Encounter is not such an important issue. The Zapatistas have not expressed their own opinion on this matter, and their situation and that of Mexico is highly uncertain. In any case, there was no need to take a decision about this during the Encounter, and no decision was made. This specific discussion, however, was only the tip of an iceberg, that represented a much more profound issue.

The idea of the "enlightened vanguards" has lost weight and foundation. This does not imply, however, the abandonment of the idea that the processes of transformation should be lead by a small elite group which possesses the "historical truth" and the appropriate capacity to lead the people. For those adopting this concept, several social groups (organized workers, above all) continue to be the central protagonists for change. They should head the corresponding processes, particularly in industrialized countries, where the initiative, or at least the main responsibility, would still reside. Each of these points is motive for intense debate. And it does not generally lead to a consensus, but to the proliferation of groups which organize themselves around one of the points of contention, with the ultimate goal of "seizing power" and leading the changes "from the top down."

In the face of this collection of different positions, another one, considered sterile or counterproductive in the traditional debate among the vanguardists, has been gaining prestige. This stream of thought and action focuses on the ways in which ordinary men and women can create political spaces in which they can have, maintain and exercise power in order to organize and implement a transformation "from the bottom up." Above all, the outcome of the transformation in the forms of social and political organization is maintained in a horizontal condition — the power remains in the hands of ordinary men and women — and open to changes. There is no need for a leading elite and there is no search for it, although obviously there is leadership as well as forms to practice, and control it and to take initiatives.

For the first collection of positions, the priority of the political agenda continues to be the unification of all world struggles around a common doctrine. In fact, those holding this view believe that in the era of "globalization," this attitude has more validity than ever.

For the second stream of thought, what matters is to connect and to articulate the struggles of resistance and liberation, starting with their common opposition to the so-called "Neoliberalism." Each of these struggles, which respond to many diverse forms of social and political grouping and classification, have their own motives and reasons for wanting to link themselves with others. There is no need to homogenize or create hierarchies among them. None of the struggles or the "truths" that define them would have priority over the others, except in terms of the immediate requirements for solidarity when faced with specific "crises." According to this position, the class analysis or class content of the struggles remains relevant, but they are conceived in a different way and with other practical implications.

The dialogue between those still immersed in a universe — who consequently convey a universal conception — and those who recognize themselves in a multiverse and defend pluralism, is not impossible. It requires an escape from conventional universalism without falling into cultural relativism.

The historical vision that sustained the image of a future integrated world, ruled by reason and well-being, is ready for a museum, along with the ideology of progress which offered a guarantee of unity. These dogmatic positions, encased in a body of rigid and closed doctrine, have become more and more untenable in the current circumstances of the world. If they do not seek refuge in fundamentalism, refusing any possibility of encounter, they are forced to open themselves to other concepts. But it is not easy to encounter conditions that truly facilitate the formation of consensus among these different or opposite positions. The encounters stimulated by the Zapatistas clearly favor such kind of interaction, among other reasons because they resist the totalitarianism of logos. The participants in the encounters consist mainly of men and women directly involved in specific struggles, within their own political spaces and communities, dedicated to resistance and confrontation with the forces of oppression, in its multiple forms. They convey a vital and concrete experience that nourishes a common substance, and upon which the dialogue can begin — as was anticipated already in Chiapas. The outcome of the interactions during the first Encounter, which continued throughout the year, could be seen clearly in Spain.

**One "No," Many "Yeses"**

Without a doubt, the will to encounter was a robust motor for the encounters convened after the initiative of the Zapatistas. But that very will, with its many diverse motives and reasons, is the cause of innumerable dis-encounters.

The interminable discussion about the "web" to be created by the pockets of resistance is a good illustration of this point. All of us want to remain linked, and we employ many efforts to construct mechanisms for articulation. Given this common desire, however, the temptation emerges all the time to build a global and integrated web that will oppose the gigantic organized forces of capital with a force of equally gigantic resistance. The impossibility of building such a web does not constrain those who are obsessed with its construction. They are not satisfied with the effectiveness of the many webs already in operation, that owe much of their effectiveness to the sensible recognition of their own limitations and thus avoid the arrogance of all-encompassing pretensions. Some suspect that the efforts towards global integration have been insufficient, so they persist in them. Meanwhile, the majority seems to be concentrated in multiplying the initiatives which articulate ideas and actions.

I have the impression that a way for reconciling opposing and contradictory positions proved its worth during the second Encounter. Increasingly there is explicit recognition that to say "no" may be the most complete and vigorous form of self affirmation in political actions aimed at implementing collective ventures for the common good. The unifying "no," which expresses a shared opposition, always contains a "yes": the radical affirmation of one's own being, of what is desired. Keeping such affirmation at the level of the "no," rejecting what is not desired, condenses the many affirmations of all those sharing an opposition. It becomes an affirmation of plurality, accepts plurality as a condition of reality itself , and thereby defines the world as it really is: a plurality of peoples, cultures, ideologies, religions, environments, etc. The potent political strength of the rejection and its capacity to protect the initiative of those affirming their own spaces mutually supports the "no."

Politicians and parties, always in need of followers, assume that it is impossible or ineffective to concentrate political action in negative proposals. They continually look for or try to create affirmative projects, expressing shared ideals across broad groups — that is, one common "yes." Inevitably, they thus betray people's real hopes. This carpetbagging gives people abstract promises that cannot be fulfilled.

The motives of those opposing a dam or nuclear plant may be highly diverse. There will be some trying to protect the space in which they live. Others participate in the struggle in the name of general ideals. In general, it is impossible to achieve consensus among them about what they want, for themselves or the society. But this does not mean that they lack alternative proposals. It only implies that they give free rein to the richness of their diversity in order to nourish their common articulation of a specific rejection.

Recent history is particularly rich in examples of social and political movements that have been successful in their efforts to stop, to reject, to limit. They have been capable of effectively and sensibly saying "No, thanks." Each success became an effective affirmation of the diverse initiatives of those making a common cause in a specific struggle.

Too often, these movements start to fail or are dismantled when their inner dynamic compels them to formulate their proposals in affirmative terms. They inevitably lose their consensus, thus weakening their driving forces and tending to disperse. Many movements, which looked vigorous in their initial conception, were not able to take off or rapidly lost their spirit or luster, due to this propensity to give an affirmative shape to their political proposals.

The "globalized" phenomena are real. There are concrete entities promoting them, such as international institutions and transnational corporations. It makes increasing sense to foster coalitions of discontented and diverse people and cultures, who share opposition to this phenomena but may lack enough strength to stop it at the local, regional or national level. For coalitions to have a unifying force, and retain their strength and vitality without betraying their original impulses, it may be best to remain at the level of what they do not want.

The Zapatistas provide reliable proof of the effectiveness of this approach. From the first day of January 1994, they spurred into action millions of discontents, who were capable of rapidly forming effective political coalitions with a single word: Basta! Wide segments of the population, unsatisfied with the dominant regime for many diverse reasons, felt affirmed in this expression of dignity and they began to mobilize themselves. The Zapatistas demonstrated their additional savvy to resist the temptation to lead all of these movements, to unify them around one single ideology, a common ideal of life or a single political proposal. In this way, they allowed the affirmation of multiple conceptions to give force to the common rejection. Enough! became a vigorous political position, widely shared by millions of Mexicans. They now face the challenge of articulating and making compatible their diverse goals and tasks, to move forward in the dismantling of the regime which still is in power and to construct a new society in which all have a place.[1] To say no, with sufficient firmness and conviction, may be today the best form of saying yes.

The "no," enriched through the encounters, nourished in multiple ways, is not the fruit of shared reflection nor does it assume full consensus. "Globalization," for example, is not the same as "Neoliberalism" or "new international division of labor."[2] To the encounters come participants who have conceived their strategies of resistance and confrontation from very diverse characterizations of the oppression and its agents against which they rebel. This gives rise to interminable debates about the validity and truth of each point. Old labels reappear. New ones are invented to define and disqualify the ideological adversary. The participants start to perceive that the insufficiencies or weaknesses of old labels or "truths" cannot be overcome by any simplifying abstraction that pretends to reduce the condition of the world to one singular version.

What arises also, with growing clarity and without doctrinaire pretensions, is a double impulse. One is the impuse to replace the effort of homogenizing unification, with its classic protagonists and now conventional doctrines, with an articulation which promotes concerted action for struggles of resistance. This recognizes beforehand its diversity and resolves contradictions and counterpositions in its very process. This can be seen as an impulse from local to global: coalitions, alliances, articulations, without homogenization. The second impulse is to recognize that in each struggle for liberation that began as resistance there are differentiated forms and destinies. Each struggle defines its conditions, realities, and hopes. The world that each conceives and wants to put into practice is a world which encompasses many worlds. Contradicting capitalism, which is by definition a world system homogenizing everything as it creates one world, this second impulse accepts the outcome of a world of many worlds, not one world. This is, perhaps, the most radical of the anti-capitalist conceptions. It is the option which seems most capable of articulating local and global forms of resistance and liberation in the International of Hope.

San Pablo Etla, March 1998

**Notes**

1 I recognize that this construction goes beyond saying "no." Rather than try to oversimplify here, I think it best to address it later through the examination of concrete instances of such construction.

2 C.f., Introduction to Midnight Notes No 12, *One No, Many Yeses,* also available on the Midnight Notes web page, http://www.midnightnotes.org.

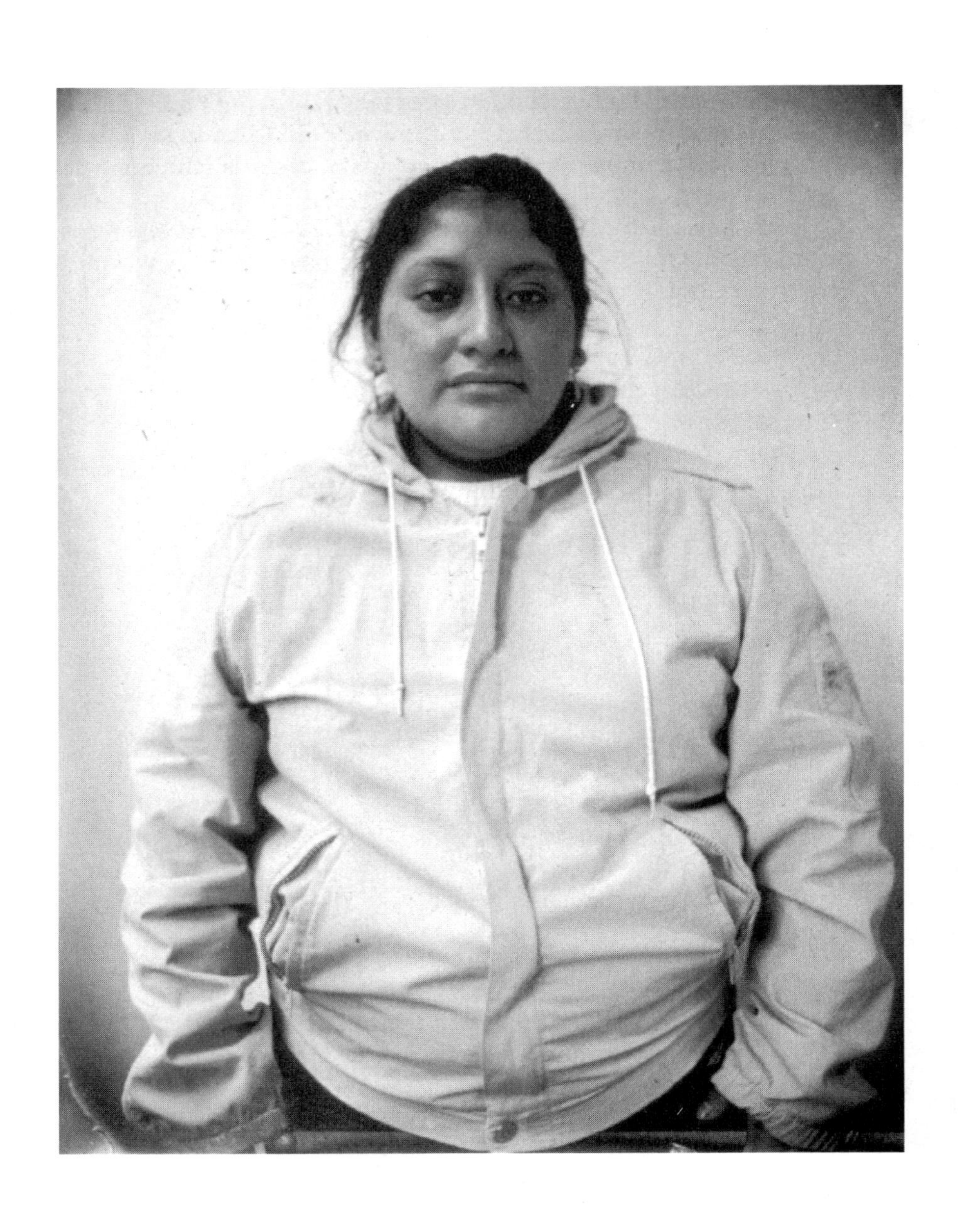

# 5
# CANADA AND ZAPATISMO

## CHRIS VANCE

I'm right in the clutches of the colonial system, where they cage us like animals, they feed us like dogs but they count us like diamonds.

— O.J. (James Pitawanakwat),
Ts'peten Defender in 1997,
on being a political prisoner

THE ZAPATISTA MESSAGE from Chiapas is familiar to the vast majority of people up here in the north. "Democracy, Liberty, Justice!" is variously demanded by farmers, feminists, the homeless, indigenous peoples, migrants, prisoners, sex workers, students, unionists, and everyone else forced to sacrifice labor and land for capital. Still, a crucial problem remains: How might this diverse working-class fulfill its revolutionary hopes? Stories of recent conflicts between indigenous nations and the Canadian state — in a context of widespread resistance to neoliberal austerity — offer a few suggestions, which might be, in turn, familiar to Zapatistas.

The armed "standoffs" in Canada during the summers of 1990 and 1995 involve land title and privatization; that is, original colonial problems of capitalism and recent tensions over how the economy is restructured. This combination provides a radical basis for unifying indigenous and non-indigenous struggles and then most effectively reclaiming our lands and labor against the state and capital. Connecting the peoples and nations in Canada with Zapatistas in Chiapas respects the continuity of common lands and rejects the divisions of nation-states, militaries, and commodities. It is relatively easy to dismiss the nation-state of "Canada." Its very name is merely an appropriation of an indigenous word for "village" (as Toronto, its biggest city, is named for "gathering place"). This reflects Canada's territorial conflict with surviving indigenous nations — an infamous yet official map of Canada even presents its surface area as literally hundreds of overlapping indigenous national borders. Indigenous struggles in these northern climes are noteworthy for their powerful advancement of sovereignties as a strategy for popular independence. Canada is routinely embarrassed before United Nations bodies investigating remaining colonial state formations, although the lack of any other UN member supporting indigenous independence repeatedly prevents any direct resolutions or charges. This situation clarifies how Canada, like many nations, rules more by its complicity in global colonial capitalism than respect for international laws including self-determination. Within Canada, the extent to which indigenous movements threaten the status quo may be viewed in light of the Zapatistas' revolutionary coming-together of indigenous and other laborers. The emergence of such a Zapatismo in the north is still in formation, but ongoing anti-neoliberal struggles are bridging previously competing sectors of labor, and to succeed, this need only ground itself more deeply alongside the persistent indigenous promise to reclaim land from colonial capital.

The opening quote reminds us: the prison of colonialism fundamentally degrades and extracts. Likewise capitalism. In each case, we prisoners perpetually work the chain-gang — our living energies tortured to maintain and expand the prison. The colonists focus on forcing land into property and the capitalists on forcing labor into work. Yet we still possess our lives, our humanity, and our memories of past freedoms and dreams of future liberations. These are our powers against all shackles, bars, guards, and fences — and our strengths with which we are able to replace exchange with giving and property with commons. First we must recognize and abolish the prison.

**Mohawk 1990: "The people lead"**

On July 11, 1990, the Quebec Police approached a barricade erected by Mohawk people on the border of their Kanasetake lands. The people's blockade served to protect their pine forest from a golf-course expansion. Police demanded another male authority. "You are talking to our spokesmen," replied a Mohawk woman. "There is no leader. The people lead," a Mohawk man agreed. Within hours the police assaulted the barricade with tear gas and hundreds of bullets, retreating only when they shot down one of their own.

This conflict is typical of first contact encounters as the metropole commands absolute conformity to its rules and the people assert their own different practice. For example, the force which would evolve into the Royal Canadian Mounted Police was established in 1873 to violently destroy trading independent of chartered corporations. Police immediately targeted the extensive circulation of gifts and ceremonial gatherings of people (known on the west coast as potlatches). At that time the Metis (mixed indigenous and French) defended their provisional government in the Red River Valley of the prairies up until 1885 when their leaders were militarily defeated and hanged in the capital city of Ottawa. Similarly, the Mohawk's own social structures of longhouses and councils of decision-making were outlawed by force of arms in the early 1920s. Many have since revived these traditions.

"The people lead" was also a hopeful saying for the entire working class which by 1990 in Canada was forced into job training and welfare wages by the hundreds of thousands. "Free" trade with the United States was restructuring the economy after an election on this issue in which the overall majority voted against the pro-free trade party but enough of that party's individual candidates for Parliament were elected to form the government. Indeed, a majority of people polled in Canada also supported the Mohawk people but the state's orders stood for 3,500 soldiers to surround the barricade for 150 days. The land in question is used by Mohawks for ceremonies, especially burials and caring of graves. A neighboring resort town, Oka, was supported by capitalists, politicians, and judges in its effort to expand a golf-course over the pine forest. The basic practice that the land is part of an unceded commons is precisely what the Mohawk could reclaim only through intense struggle. Canada's gluttony for the labor and lands of the commons is so great that in 1867 it attempted to unilaterally sever the nation-to-nation relation between Britain and the indigenous peoples by proclaiming itself a "Dominion" with power over all people, indigenous and otherwise, delegating provinces to administer the Crown (really common, indigenous) lands. Indigenous victories always involve an effective counter to this enclosure of the commons. The state's reaction in co-ordination with capital is to negotiate final surrenders of these commons through new treaties between colonial indigenous agents ("Band" and "Tribal" leaders), provinces, and the federal government.

The circulation of struggles in 1990 confronted the state with enough pressure to recognize the Mohawk use of the pines. Throughout August and September, tens of thousands of people in the downtowns of many Canadian cities turned banking districts into centers of popular education and noisy agitation. On September 4, in Ontario, anonymous actors brought down five enormous electrical towers. Three days later, in Alberta, Milton Born-With-A-Tooth and other Peigan Lonefighters repelled dozens of armed officers guarding the destruction of the Lonefighters' diversion of water from an unpopular dam. By September 26, the Mohawks reached an agreement with the state over the pines and crossed their own barricades to face a deflated Canadian Army.

### 1492–1992: The 500-year-old aurora

In 1992, the original aurora of resistance to capital's enclosure of the Americas turned 500 years old. This strengthened the popular imaginations of pre-capitalist life, but meanwhile capital projected new forms of exploitation into the future. The struggles against new enclosures in Canada connected diverse sectors of the working class but have not yet created a lasting alternative and common space. This challenge to create another wave of coherent resistance still frustrates activists in Canada today.

Solidarity between indigenous groups around 1992 interrupted the colonialist celebrations and connected neoliberalism to the genocides which preceded it. As sloganeered about the U.S. attacks on Panama and Iraq: "new world order, same old shit." New coalitions convened tribunals on genocide, conferred about 500 years of resistance, and declared opposition to the commodification of life forms. A flotilla of ships headed by a Gitsk'an indigenous leader even intercepted a replica of Christopher Columbus' boat as it re-enacted the infamous 1492 sailing. Notice how these actions reveal certain vulnerabilities of neoliberalism. Overall, the marking of 500 years of resistance at once reminds people of struggles otherwise forgotten and places neoliberalism within the genealogy of invasions and enclosures. This reveals neoliberalism's offer of new marketplace freedoms as nothing but another extension of servitude.

In 1995, an Americas-wide gathering of indigenous representatives declared themselves against the Human Genome Diversity Project. The collection of genetic samples is popularly known as the "vampire project" for sucking indigenous blood into pharmaceutical laboratories under the guise of providing medical care. "We hold that life cannot be bought, owned, sold, discovered or patented," the declaration asserts. This discloses the logical extreme of neoliberalism's plans as the total annihilation of life independent of capital. If only non-indigenous people had opposed the North American Free Trade Agreeement (NAFTA) with the equivalent forces of labor's histories of resistance and refusals of commodification. People in Canada lived through an economic recession for years after the Canada/U.S. Free Trade Agreement went into effect in 1989. In response to demands for alternative policies against austerity, capital and the state threatened that even worse impoverishment can follow conditions of social democracy (New Zealand) and socialism (Eastern Europe). This logic concluded that problems generated by free trade required solutions furthering free trade. In 1993, NAFTA was enacted by the federal governments of Canada, the U.S., and Mexico. Furthermore, neoliberalism required changing the constitution of the state as it related to capital. Provincial social democrats reconstituted regional deals in rapid progression. Social contracts in Ontario corporatized government workers' unions; annual budgets in British Columbia replaced priorities of social welfare with bond ratings; privatization in Saskatchewan severed state commitments to social services and public control over uranium; and the commodification of "Crown Lands" in Britsh Columbia created new proposed treaties with colonial indigenous governments. The federal politicians' success in resolving the national constitutional crisis was less direct.

In 1993, proposed amendments to the constitution, including clauses about land widely interpreted as deepening possibilities for exploitation, were defeated in a referendum. However, Canada's inclusion in the World Trade Organization in 1994 effectively superseded the earlier referendum by committing Canada to the rules of the latest global capitalist authority. People resisted these advances in various ways which are still not unified although they led into subsequent struggles. The largest feminist organization, for example, exemplified its opposition to neoliberalism with a report on "new reproductive technologies." The National Action Committee on the Status of Women effectively defined capital and patriarchy as an enslavement of human bodies and reproduction. This focus on slavery informs current feminist organizing around indigenous "self-government," poverty, pay equity, migration, and the World Bank and International Monetary Fund.

Unionists in Ontario rebelled against the new conservative government which generalized the austerity of the preceding social democratic "social contract." Workers organized "days of action" (general strikes) against structural adjustment and funded radical anti-poverty coalitions of unemployed workers. The Ontario Coalition Against Poverty asserts a political practice familiar to the Zapatistas by gathering in egalitarian assemblies to reflect on their experiences and deciding on this basis how to organize. Consequent direct actions include finger-printing politicians who (threaten to) so catalogue the unwaged, self-reducing rents and food prices, and creating open urban spaces of protest and popular education. [For an elaboration on self-reduction of prices see Bruno Ramirez in *Midnight Oil*; on opening spaces recall the popular assembly in Quito of strikers workers and thousands of recent indigenous migrants which declared its negation of the Ecuadorian government in January 2000.]

The Ontario Coalition Against Poverty also joins Mohawk warriors for demonstrations at the federal Parliament. These unionists, anti-poverty activists, feminists, and indigenous anti-colonialists are similarly radical in rejecting the condition of their subordination: workers refuse their exploitation (work), the poor refuse their exclusion from resources, women refuse the appropriation of reproduction, and the indigenous refuse dispossession.

Consider a few particular, historical experiences of subjection in Canada. An increasingly efficient state, re-militarized through the First World War, attacked at once indigenous people and other laborers. The government expanded registries of "Indians" into police dossiers for violent assimilation (dispossession of lands and outlawing of traditions) and standardized measures of work and productivity (national accounts of wages useful to correlate with accounts of strikes). Entire generations of indigenous youths were individually tracked through Residential Schools of state and church torture. On a slightly smaller scale, up to 6,000 Quebecois orphans and thousands of people deemed physically or mentally different were also catalogued and systematically abused by their "protectors."

Today, workers in neoliberalism are quantified and analyzed by capital and the state to match the concrete divisions and competitions which allow austerity (citizenship, income level, place of residence, etc.) The state even created Human Resources Canada to encourage the coordinated corporatization of labor increasingly freed of social welfare.

The point here is to remember both some facts of material expropriation as well as some methods of social control. Our collective memories clarify what needs to be abolished for the sake of our common liberation (colonies and capitals, at least). How popular movements struggle for and then maintain such abolition involves keeping our diverse living energies autonomous from exploitation. indigenous uprisings have been the most militant expression in Canada of this kind of struggle.

**Ts'peten 1995**

Well, everybody is on Indian land, does that make you Indian?
— Rosalee Tizya, Fourth World Documentation Project

Uses of land contrary to colonial expansion and capitalist accumulation are generally suppressed in Canada, occasionally with as much intensity as at the site of a sundance ceremony in British Columbia in the summer of 1995. The Ts'peten Defenders of the sundance are significantly similar to the Zapatistas. The Defenders presented themselves after years of organizing, demanded recognition of their own territories ("sovereignty"), and articulated popular opposition to global capitalist planning. Absent from the sundance struggle, however, were Zapatista-style bases ("autonomous municipalities") and a circulation of struggle among various sectors of the working-class. Nonetheless, the military attacked each in like fashion, revealing the coercion which rules neoliberalism.

Beginning in 1988, various people, mostly indigenous, reclaimed the sundance at annual gatherings on parts of Ts'peten land which the state and capital recognized as a cattle ranch settlement, even though none of the 450,000-acre ranch was ever ceded by the indigenous Shuswap. The sundance subverted the colonial pattern of settler forts enclosing lands reserved for Indians. Now, a center of indigenous life recreated a commons against the settlement of the area. Before, the chartered corporations assumed ownership of all lands. Now, the sundancers reminded all that the expanse of unceded lands remained their sovereign indigenous territories.

Twenty years before the Ts'peten sundance, the Dene and Inuit of the far north attempted their own end-run against colonial death on the far northern frontier. A massive oil pipeline in the Mackenzie Valley was proposed to finish off what trading post settlements began only a few generations before. The past and proposed development projects threatened the fertility of common lands and the free movement of hunters and trappers. In unified resistance, dispersed people asserted their livelihoods and thus defeated the pipeline and their frontier status.

Significantly, in the course of this struggle the Dene and Inuit specified how their traditions of noncoersion rejected colonial/capitalist development. "No one can decide for another person...when working, for instance, a person should not be forced into anything." The opposed roles of indigenous/settler continued in and around Ts'peten while their respective leaders forged desperate deals in the face of threatened neoliberal crisis.

In 1993, after the defeat of a national referendum on Constitutional amendments including Aboriginal self-government, indigenous leaders (largely paid by the federal government) promoted negotiating new treaties, especially in British Columbia where the newly governing social democrats promised expedient agreement. Meanwhile, an altogether different indigenous movement named itself "sovereigntist" and charged colonial courts with "fraud, treason, and genocide" for refusing to rule who had legal jurisdiction while enclosures continued.

As for non-indigenous people, settling Canada was as little rewarding as ever during the economic recession which followed the 1988 Canada/U.S. Free Trade Agreement, including the withdrawal of wages from over 500,000 lost manufacturing jobs and widespread austerity by all levels of government. Unions offered only austere contracts and the left party only socialist cutbacks. In BC, the state and some colonial indigenous bodies negotiated land use agreements and treaty proposals. Non-indigenous people perceived a lack of deal-making with themselves, but any connection between them and similarly disenfranchised indigenous sovereigntists has yet to be made. Honourable instances of indigenous/settler solidarity remain exceptional, for instance in a 1914 trial of indigenous people for holding a potlatch when the defense of the right to give food freely was supported by a jury of settlers.

In June 1995, on Shuswap territory, an armed ranch owner and a few of his workers violently disrupted the sundancers' preparations, threatening to burn down their lodge and stating that federal police were planning a raid. The Ts'peten Defenders formed immediately. They repeated an earlier demand to the Queen of the United Kingdom for an "independent and impartial tribunal" respecting territorial borders and encroachments. The Defenders thus placed themselves among the seven "Tribal System Natives of the Sun-Dance (Central), the Potlatch (Western) and the Feast of the Dead (Eastern) Traditions" who authored the original demand. An indigenous federal police officer who documented a history of Ts'peten concluded, "It's a big rip-off. It's genocide," and was promptly re-assigned off the case.

The police implemented a "smear and disinformation campaign" as a sergeant then said into a videotape later played in court. They labeled the defenders "terrorists" after seizing weapons from an unrelated group of fishermen and accused the Ts'peten of shooting officers after displaying a fatigued bullet-proof jacket. A corporal said at the time, however, "This is not the first time we've had to take flak-jackets to the firing range." The police also covered-up their relations with the military, which involved their importing machine guns, 50-caliber barrels, and Armored Personnel Carriers. The police even requested the paramilitary Joint Task Force 2, a secretive arm of the Canadian military reportedly experienced in Somalia, Haiti, and Bosnia. A Superintendent warned, "Once the APCs come out of the package, there will be a war," and the commanding officer noted, "There are six hard-liners in the camp who will require killing."

The Canadian military was interrupted by a murder at the Ipperwash park in Ontario. On September 11, an unarmed indigenous protester, Dudley George, was assassinated by the police charging a barricade defending a burial ground. The police continue to evade even a state investigation, reinforcing how the police are themselves a most tyrannical criminal racket. The specifically racist character of police operations is shown by the fact that 50 per cent of those killed by the police since 1980 were indigenous, and the murders of 200 indigenous women since 1969 remain unsolved and under investigated.

Back on Shuswap land, the Ts'peten were attacked once more on September 11 when their supply truck was blown up by a land mine and shot at with tens of thousands of bullets while an indigenous negotiating liaison group drove into the sundance area (one liaison member suffered a heart attack from the explosion). After another week of military harassment, the defenders vacated the sundance ceremony and were arrested.

A useful definition of Zapatismo is the combination of indigenous and other anti-capitalist approaches together creating a common space to assert revolutionary autonomy based on "democracy, freedom, justice." In Chiapas, an indigenous tradition of "command by obeying" replaced the left strategies of the "vanguard" and "foco" while "communities in turn broke with their centuries-old isolation, to comprehend the function of the state under neoliberalism, and to see themselves as part of the world of labor" (Lorenzano in *Zapatista!*, p. 129). Then what of Canada and Zapatismo?

Up here in the north, the hands of militant indigenous groups and radical popular organizations are open and full of Zapatismo offerings. Gatherings of gift-giving, however, are few and far between. The renewals of these common spaces which are occurring require broad circulation of, for example "council fires" held in the St'at'imc nation on the topic of logging: "places where people can come to talk together and ask questions and to seek answers. Council Fires are a way of raising awareness of who we are, where we are, and what our visions are for the future."

Imagine indigenous reclamations of land combined with popular reappropriations of labor. Such a revolution is as close to us as the grounds we walk upon and the bodies we live through. Let us remember and revive the creation of spaces for reclamation, for instance as developed by the Ontario Coalition Against Poverty and the Mohawk nation.

**Sources**

Howard Adams (1989). *Prison of Grass: Canada from a Native Point of View*. Saskatoon: Fifth House Publishers.

Valerie Alia (1994). *Names, Numbers and Northern Policy: Inuit Project Surname and the Politics of Identity*. Halifax: Fernwood.

Anti-Colonial Action Alliance, http://www.web.ca/~acaa

Somer Brodribb (ed.) (1999). *Reclaiming the Future: Women's Strategies for the 21st Century*. Charlottetown: Ragweed.

Bruce Clark (1999). *Justice In Paradise*. Montreal: McGill–Queen's University Press.

Claire Culhane (1991). *No Longer Barred from Prison*. Montreal: Black Rose Books.

*Dene* nationals to Mackenzie National Pipeline Inquiry (1977). *Dene Nation: The Colony Within*. Toronto: University of Toronto Press.

Connie Fife (ed.) (1993). *The Colour of Resistance: A Contemporary Collection of Writing by Aboriginal Women*. Toronto: Sister Vision.

Fourth World Documentation Project, http://www.cwis.org/fwdp.html

John Holloway and Eloina Pelaez (eds.) (1998). *Zapatista! Reinventing Revolution in Mexico*. London: Pluto.

Rolf Knight (1978). *Indians At Work: An Informal History of Native Indian Labour in British Columbia, 1858–1930*. Vancouver: New Star Books.

Craig MacLaine and Michael Baxendale (1990). *This Land Is Our Land: The Mohawk Revolt at Oka*. Montreal: Optimum Publishing.

George Manuel and Michael Posluns (1974). *The Fourth World: An Indian Reality*. Don Mills: Collier–MacMillan Canada.

Lee Maracle (1990). *Bobbi Lee: Indian Rebel*. Toronto: Women's Press [first published 1975]).

Midnight Notes Collective (1992). *Midnight Oil: Work, Energy, War, 1973–1992*. Brooklyn: Autonomedia.

J.R. Miller (1996). *Shingwâuk's Vision: A History of Native Residential Schools*. Toronto: University of Toronto Press.

Alanis Obomsawin (1993). *Kanehsatake: 270 Years of Resistance*. Toronto: Studio B/National Film Board of Canada.

Bryan Palmer (1992). *Working-Class Experience: Rethinking the History of Canadian Labour, 1800–1991*. Toronto: McClelland and Stewart.

Eric Robinson and Henry Bird Quinney (1985). *The Infested Blanket: Canada's Constitution — Genocide of Indian Nation*. Winnipeg: Queenston House.

Settlers In Support of indigenous Sovereignty, http://kafka.uvic.ca /~vipirg/SISIS/SISmain.htm

**Contacts**

Canadian Alliance in Solidarity with the Native Peoples
PO Box 991
Kahnawake Mohawk Territory
(Quebec, Canada) J0L 1B0
450 632–6926 (tel)
450 632–8914 (fax)
casnp@cyberglobe.net
http://users.cyberglobe.net/~casnp

Indigenous Peoples Council on Biocolonialism
PO Box 72
Nixon, NV
USA 89424
775 574–0248 (tel)
775 574–0259 (fax)
ipcb@ipcb.org
http://www.ipcb.org

League of Indigenous Sovereign Nations
PO Box 131
Accodeek, MD
USA 20607
301 490–1879
lisn2000@lisn.net
http://www.lisn.net

Leonard Peltier Defense Committee
PO Box 583
Lawrence, KS
USA 66044
785 842–5774 (tel)
785 842–5796 (fax)

National Action Committee on the Status of Women
203–234 Eglington Ave. E
Toronto, ON
Canada M4P 1K5
416 932–1718 (tel)
800 665–5124 (tel)
416 932–0646 (fax)
nac@web.net
http//www.nac-cca.ca

Ontario Coalition Against Poverty
239 Sherbourne St.
Toronto ON
Canada M5A 2A2
416 925–6939 (tel)
416 925–9681 (fax)
ocap@tao.ca
http://www.tao.ca/~ocap

Prison Activist Resource Center
P.O. Box 339
Berkeley, CA 94701
USA
510 893–4648 (tel)
510 893–4607 (fax)
parc@prisonactivist.org

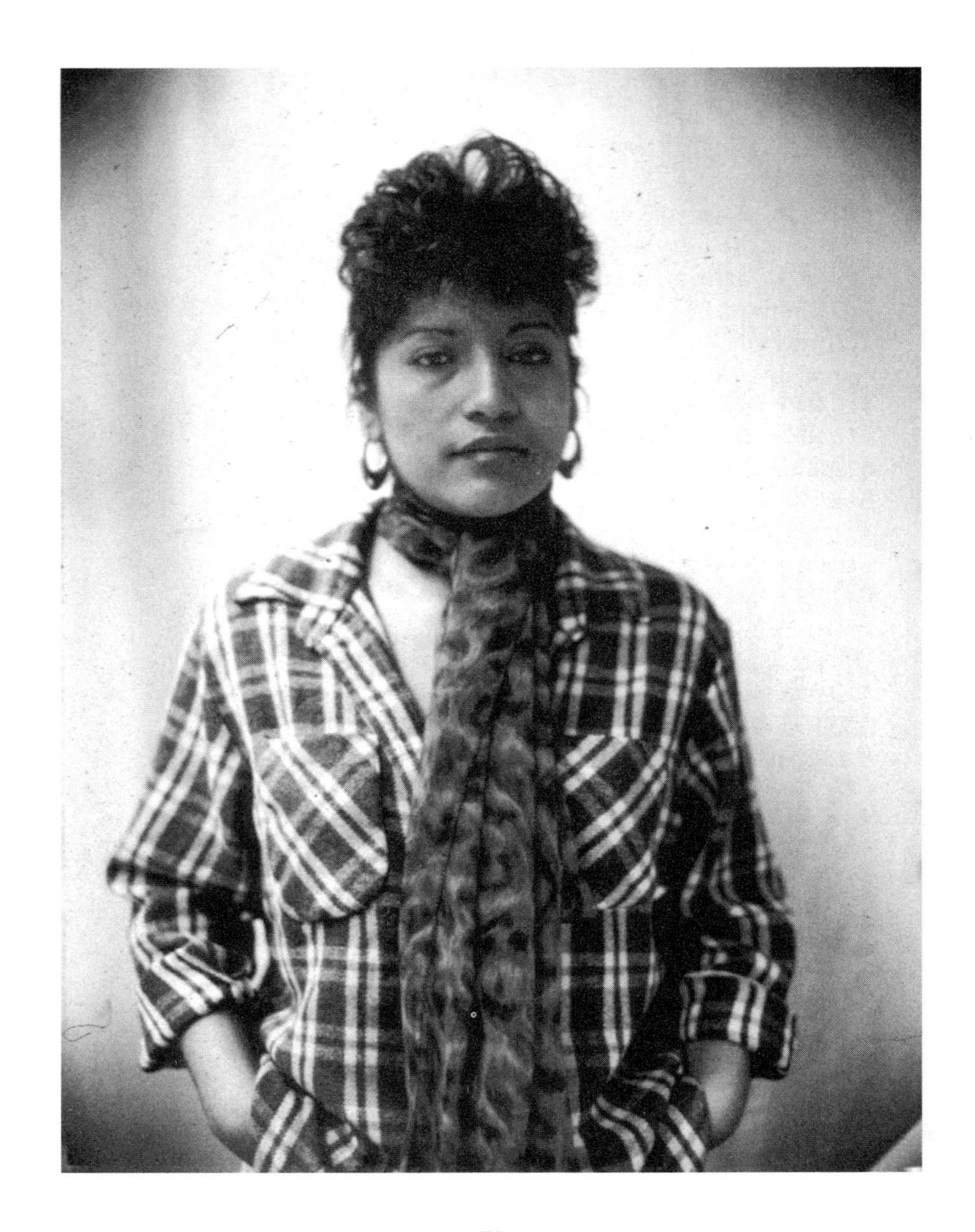

# 6
# ZAPATA IN EUROPE

ANA ESTHER CECEÑA WITH ADELINA BOTTERO, LUCIANO SALZA, FRIEDERIKE HABERMANN, MARC TOMSIN, MASSIMO DE ANGELIS & ULRICH BRAND[1]

*Introduction by Ana Esther Ceceña*

ON JANUARY 1, 1994, three years ago, when the majority of the world's population was immersed in a most profound desperation brought on by the neoliberal reorganization of society, when the armed struggle in Latin America appeared to have proven its uselessness or inefficiency, when the dismemberment of the Soviet Union and the fall of the Berlin Wall showed the semi-occult face of the other version of power, when most people tried to adapt themselves with resignation or enthusiasm to the technocratic modality of mediocrity and submission, and when very few still hoped for freedom and a spirit of rebellion — an indigenous community, a community that only appeared as nothing more than a trace in the census tracts of neoliberal demography, rose up armed with dignity and brandishing flags which suddenly gathered new meaning, having lost it in the past, calling for democracy, liberty, and justice.

---

*Translated by Scott Rowe, Susan Street and John Willshire-Carrera. Edited by George Caffentzis and Monty Neil.*

In an unusual way, the *true word* of the Zapatistas traveled throughout the world. In only a few days, men and women of the most diverse cultures, social sectors, languages, and historical contexts learned of their goals and made them their own. In just a few days, the Zapatista word became fundamental to a universal struggle against a system of universal domination.

These past years have become the scene of multiple experiences and reflections for all who have listened to the *true word*, for all who made possible the beginning of an international debate which is unstoppable, for those who believe that it is possible to create a world founded on the principles: *Directing by obeying, and for everyone — everything.*

The non-recognition by the Mexican state of the San Andrés Accords — an agreement signed by the Mexican government and the Zapatistas in 1996 guaranteeing cultural autonomy to the indigenous — denotes a node of reflection with multiple outcomes. A retrospective analysis of the experiences of these three years can be of great use to all of us in our joint efforts to reflect on and build a road to utopia, within the communitarian spirit that the Zapatistas have conveyed to us. With the goal of contributing to this process, we interviewed via the internet social activists and/or critical thinkers from diverse parts of the world. The responses we received coincide with the search for new forms of political organizing which involves the rejection of (and on occasion the horror of) any sign of authoritarianism. It also involved the rejection of parties and other, older forms of political organization, systems of domination, and, generally, any type of intolerance, imposition and submission. From the most enthusiastic optimism to a desperation that is never defeated, from praise to doubt, there is a shared agreement concerning the virtues of direct democracy and the thought-bridge of the Zapatista communities of Chiapas, as well as a clear interest in the collective building of a new world. May these interviews serve as testimony of unity within diversity and an acknowledgment of the word and actions of the Zapatista, which are still in process and not completed.

*Question: Returning to the moment when you first heard about the Zapatistas and their actions, what attracted you to the Zapatistas? What caused you to realize that you shared their ideas? Coming from such different realities, what caused you to take on, or reject, the Zapatista cause?*

MASSIMO DE ANGELIS[2]: I have a distant memory of January 2, 1994, when I first heard through the newspaper of this new Latin

American group which had taken several cities in an unknown region of Mexico called Chiapas. I remember my double reaction: on one hand, I was absolutely happy that someone was taking on and creating trouble for the military and government of Mexico exactly on the day that Mexico had become a member of the North American Free Trade Agreement (NAFTA) club. On the other hand, I never thought that those involved in this uprising could be like the Zapatistas that we would later come to know, and implicitly I thought that this involved a traditional guerrilla force, with all of its limitations and with all of its déjà vu. Then the news began to flow as my friend Harry[3] began to email me from the United States about the rebellion and other people began commenting on its novel character.

In fact, I did not need any convincing about the Zapatistas' methods of the struggle and ideas for two reasons. First, I never felt indoctrinated. An indoctrination takes place when someone tells you what you ought to think and how you ought to subordinate your life and your actions to the indoctrination. Like in a classroom, you have to repeat what the teacher tells you in order to obtain a good grade. As in the old model of "revolution," when we were supposed to subordinate our thoughts and needs and act and think just as the party dictated. No, the Zapatistas were honest in this respect from the beginning. They told their story and they told it their way. There was so much dignity in this! And they told us that it was not the complete story, but rather a fragment. It was our turn to talk, with humility as a tool and as a catalyst.

Second, I would like to be able to say that in some respects I was already a Zapatista before the Zapatistas emerged (of course I called it something else at the time), but in theory I was a Zapatista. I "knew" that what we called, in the old western radical tradition, the "working class," was not only, in fact, made up of victims of exploitation and misery but also was a dignified group of human beings in perpetual struggle. I "knew" that the "working class" did not constitute a homogeneous force, but rather it was a hierarchy divided by sexual, racial, and national differences. I "knew" that the creation of a new world could only come about through a process of transformation, and not "after the revolution." I "knew" that for that to happen, we could not unite ourselves before we, in fact, became united without subordinating the dignity, the necessities, and the aspirations of a group of people (women, Blacks, campesinos or whomever) in search of the "greatest good." I "knew" that all the struggles were important and that they would have to find a means of expression in the process of constructing a new world. And I also "knew" that the traditional form of doing politics was extremely boring. But I believe that all of this "knowledge" was only good for writing articles and participating in exhaustive debates about how we could change the world and which model of transformation and political organization we would adopt. The Zapatistas were able to catalyze so much social and human energy that now we can begin to talk about that which we are changing, when we are to change it, and how we are to change it. Unfortunately for the Marxist parties, the Zapatistas returned to life that marvelous phrase that says: "Radical criticism is that which takes things by their roots."

I believe that explains why so many people, from so many distinct places and diverse ways of life and struggle, are fascinated by the Zapatistas. They opened a space. And they have already said that they do not have a program for us to follow (we have to fill this space with our own imagination). They accept solidarity but by being in solidarity with our own struggles (here we ought to fill this space with our struggles and networks of communication). Let us take, for example, the first Encuentro. Let us imagine an international meeting organized during a revolutionary moment of the past, any revolutionary moment, where invitations to attend would have been extended not only to the members of the party but to everyone: people of the popular sectors, militants, women and men who seek change. And where the meeting had not been called to ask for solidarity with the insurgents, but rather to try to address and answer the following questions: How does the power against which we rebel affect you? How do you experience people who come from so many different places? What are your life experiences with respect to contemporary economic strategies, the preeminence of the market, war, and cutbacks of social spending directed to satisfy basic needs? How do you struggle? In which struggles are you involved? What are the barriers which you have encountered, and what are your possibilities of transcending the conditionalities of the markets, the factories, the politics of the state and the politics through which international organizations try to subdue you?

How do we reconstruct our human dignity in the face of the degrading conditions of dependence in which money works to permanently subdue us to the authorities, the market, the boss, and the party? What are our hopes? What view do we have of the world? What is our vision of needs and the manner with which to satisfy them with a new human meaning? Do we dream? What is the common ground we share? In what manner can we relate to our mutual hopes, struggles, needs, aspirations, desires, and lives? These are all huge questions which do not have easy answers and, as far as I know, have not been put forth since the Soviet Revolution, not in China, Algeria, Cuba or Nicaragua. However, they were posed in the first Encuentro for Humanity and against Neoliberalism which took place in the summer of 1996. The answers did not come easily, and perhaps many were never answered. The historical importance of the Encuentro consists in having raised these questions and in the fact that there was, and among many people continues to be, the determination to keep repeating the questions until answers are found, not only in theory but also in practice.

FRIEDERIKE HABERMANN[4]: What initiated my rapprochement to Zapatismo were the words of the Sub and having found people within the Zapatista movement with whom I am willing to struggle to change the world. Outside of Zapatismo, there are many people with conceptions of revolution which do not appear to me as being emancipatory, and in those cases I would rather refuse than participate.

Many times I have had (and still have) the impression that it was difficult to find people outside of my particular circles with the same leftist political ideas; the majority of leftists sustain very structured, hierarchical, dogmatic, Eurocentric and, not least of all, sexist ideas. And then I discovered that in another part of the world there is a movement with the same emancipatory political comprehension which even creates the essence of an international network of resistance. That is why I decided to participate in this movement.

Of course, conditions are very different in the Lacandona Jungle than in the metropolitan European jungle. But there also exist common elements since neoliberalism, that is to say capitalism, penetrates our lives and determines them — in distinct ways and on levels that comparatively can seem more or less privileged, but always with economic pressure and emotional violence. Neoliberal capitalism universally forces all of us to sell a good part of our lives, our emotions, desires and aspirations.

COLLETIVO INTERNAZIONALISTA DE TORINO[5]: We were attracted due to our interest, sympathy, and solidarity with all who "move in opposition." It was also in reaction to the lies and the rage with which the Italian media, including those of the "left," labeled the Zapatistas as terrorist, leftovers of obsolete struggles "destined to fail."

More so now than in the past, we believe that it is during the present period that material conditions for the internationalization of struggles and solidarity have matured. The globalization of the market and misery, the violence with which neoliberalism imposes an increased impoverishment of the living conditions of people, always becoming more extensive among the subordinate classes of different countries, leads them to be more easily united against the common enemy. The 1st of January of 1994 marked in this sense an emblematic moment, perhaps the beginning of an era: on one side NAFTA, with all that it represents, and on the other side, the EZLN and solidarity.

Furthermore, the Zapatista experience finally brought to an end a long period during which entire peoples and subordinate classes at the international level had accumulated defeats and resignation (we are referring to the Nicaraguan and Salvadorian experiences, the Gulf War, the wars disguised as "ethnic wars" in Yugoslavia and other countries, and all those struggles which the European proletariat has been rapidly losing after many long years of prevailing). The EZLN and the indigenous people of Chiapas represented a new symbol of hope, possible rebellion, a beacon that need not be turned off.

In particular, they brought with them important new elements both in content and methodology. In their communiqués, the EZLN expressed with vigor and strength a message that transgressed local barriers, directed itself to the peoples of the world, fomented struggles wherever and however they were expressed, and called out for unity.

ULRICH BRAND[6]: I learned of the Zapatista's actions through the media on January 2, 1994. Then beginning in February of the same year, international magazines began to publish information, and in the magazine *Links (leftist)*, where I work, we also translated articles and commentaries from *La Jornada*. For example, in February we published articles, one by Javier Garrido, as well as the first Declaration of the Lacandona Jungle and other news. Due to a lack of a collective undertaking of these issues in my city, I integrated myself into such coordinating efforts at the federal level.

Furthermore, by mid-1993 I had already begun to plan a trip to the United States and to Mexico because of my interest in studying the integration of the most powerful country in the world with a peripheral country, and the realities and the opportunities of resistance which that generated.

What determined my approach was, of course, solidarity with any emancipatory movement. However, due to my own history, knowing more about some parts of Latin America than parts of other continents (the movement of international solidarity in Germany is very oriented towards movements of liberation in Latin America) also played a role. Furthermore, I was also fascinated by the fact that at the "end of history," a group of women and men in Mexico and Chiapas were showing their concerns for the concrete conditions in the world, shouting so strongly and intelligently, "enough already!"

I share their ideas because of my fascination with all emancipatory struggles and solidarity with human beings who resist power, the destruction of life, profits, and stupidity. And then, on the other hand, the great strength and attraction of Zapatismo, in my opinion, is its capacity to reflect on world changes, especially the disappearance of the Soviet Union. There are no clear concepts to elaborate on revolutionary social politics. However there exist some preconditions that many emancipative movements have not seen: that concrete contexts of struggles are fundamental and departing from them one can find diverse confluences. (I would say that presently these take the form of resistance against neoliberalism and the need to improve on the perspective of liberation at a national level.)

I cannot say if the Zapatistas deliberately did it (though, I would like to know), but references which are so inclusive of particular concepts of bourgeois society (justice, democracy, and liberty) from a time prior to that of authoritarian socialism was an incredible stroke of luck. I am convinced that a precondition for a society profoundly humane (I would still say socialist) is the radicalization of these values instead of their negation, as has occurred in the case of authoritarian socialism with respect to democracy and liberty. Paradoxically, communities that did not have rights in a bourgeoisie society are those that are now promoting these rights.

On the side of freedom, justice, and democracy, the concept of dignity is fundamental. There is no dignity in a patriarchal and capitalistic society, and even less so in its neoliberal phase.

I believe, personally, that our connection with the "Zapatista cause" was in the beginning only about concrete solidarity with a liberation movement. But throughout these last three years, by means of many discussions and readings, many of us have begun to understand what the "Zapatista cause" could mean for us. It continues to be in process. In times for us of low combativeness, of so many defensive or even reactionary struggles, the low level of affirmative impetus behind the movement, that is to say that of attacking power and capitalistic and patriarchal structures, pains me deeply.

MARC TOMSIN[7]: My curiosity and sympathy for the Zapatista uprising in Chiapas was immediate on January 1, 1994. For an anarchist, "Land and Liberty" immediately brings to memory the Mexican Revolution of the beginning of the twentieth century (Flores Magón, Villa, and Zapata) as well as the revolution of the Ukrainian peasants from 1917–1921 (Nestor Makhno), and, of course, the memory of the CNT (National Workers' Confederation) and the FAI (Anarchist Federation of Iberia) of the Spanish Revolution in 1936, and the agricultural collectives of Aragon (whose history I heard directly from anonymous survivors exiled in France).

I had ignored almost everything about Chiapas until then, and so I found myself obliged at that point to review my geography. I found a good guide in Bruno Traven, who under his first pseudonym, Ret Marut, also referred me to the ephemeral Republic of the Councils of Bavaria (in 1919 with the German anarchists Muhsam and Lanauer) and to the American "Wobblies" (Industrial Workers of the World).

It was then, simultaneously reading Traven and the first declarations of the insurgents from Chiapas in 1994, that I began to understand the EZLN. At the time, the first actions of the Zapatistas in 1994 spoke for themselves: the opening of prisons, the destruction of municipal, juridical, and police registries.

I also need to add that since May 1968, when I was eighteen years old in Paris, I do not remember having heard a revolutionary social movement proclaim so clearly, as has the EZLN, that it does not have as an objective taking power. This, in conjunction with their practice of direct democracy in the communities, is undoubtedly the essential reason for my active solidarity with the Zapatistas.

Concerning the obstacles created by my ignorance of the reality of Chiapas, or better yet, the Mexican reality, I soon overcame it starting in the summer of 1994 through meetings and "discussions" with companions from Barcelona who know Mexico, and later with Mexicans who became companions in their travels through Paris. Here, I ought to enthusiastically and with great gratitude mention Amado Avendaño Figueroa, whose explanations, patience, humor and modesty were very illuminating.

*Question: There has recently been talk, above all when dealing with the constitutional recognition of the San Andrés Accords, of the EZLN becoming civil political organization. Taking advantage of the vision you have from a distance, how do you evaluate this proposal? What risks in your point of view does this imply, given that the existence of the EZLN as an armed movement is based up to now on a lack of any alternative civil means of struggling for the vindication of the fundamental rights of indigenous people.*

MASSIMO DE ANGELIS: As you have said, I find myself too far from the reality of Mexico to make such a delicate analysis concerning the power relationships among the different forces, as well as the possibilities facing the indigenous people in that context. But I do know that one of the strengths of the Zapatistas is their continual rejection of and refusal to assume the form of the traditional political party. Nonetheless, I think that the EZLN is conscious of the risk of going from an organization of indigenous communities to a purely representative organization of the indigenous peoples' interests. If the latter occurs, the dream of the EZLN and the Zapatistas will come to an end, and the indigenous communities will be the center of the electoral haggling. But where is it going? How will it develop? Obviously, I cannot respond to these questions, I only know that ahead is not behind. Here again, the future of the indigenous communities in this context will depend greatly on the ability of social movements around the rest of the world to develop their struggles. Outside of Mexico, we have the capacity to do exactly what the Zapatistas did for us: open a space for ourselves, and by doing this open up space for them as well.

COLLETIVO INTERNAZIONALISTA DE TORINO: We will follow the political evolution of the EZLN with great concern.

On the one hand, it feels like returning to old situations we have already lived through, although they must be different. The Peace Accords (signed without the causes of the conflict being substantially changed), in exchange for the consequent dismantling of the guerilla forces and their integration into the political sector, is a strategy that has been institutionalized in Latin America and in other countries in the world. It is a strategy integral to the implementing of anti-subversive plans and strategies designed and fine tuned by imperialism and its reactionary and puppet governments, being themselves the only beneficiaries of this type of "pacification." The examples abound, and the risks that this path brings are there for everyone to see.

On the other hand, it seems that the decision to convert themselves into a civil political force can be seen as a natural continuation of the political trajectory followed by the EZLN up until now. We share the content of the call to action made by the EZLN directed to civil society asking them to mobilize and organize horizontally, and recognize their efforts towards unity, but we observe some contradictions. We bear in mind that unity cannot be affirmed by a unilateral decision. It must develop through a democratic process, the coming together of those for whom it is necessary that the conditions be created. A network engendering connectivity, understood as a non-hegemonic and non-hegemonizable space, based on civil society in its totality and not on a particular group, can demonstrate how advantageous it is for all to establish relations of mutual solidarity. We fear that the EZLN has come to think that it could give form to unity through means which are fundamentally unilateral. At least with the MLN [Movimiento de Liberacion Nacional], and still with the Zapatista Front for National Liberation (FZLN), we believe we have observed a plan of unity planned from above, and therefore still in agreement with the old ways of doing politics, instead of referring to the work of bringing together the archipelago of realities to learn, to respect, and perhaps to stimulate a relation of mutual support and strong solidarity.

MARK TOMSIN: This question for me is the most difficult. It seems to me that I have already responded to it partially during the 1995 Encuentro. I believe that the participation of the EZLN in a civil political organization is already a reality in the life of the communities in struggle from where they come. That is to say that it is not about an isolated practice, as if all the aspects of social life were split up. That was very well explained by the Sub himself in a frank interview with the Uruguayan magazine *Brecha* about democracy, community, and politics. In the Zapatista communities there is "another political culture" that mixes history, memory and communication of the past with communication of the present, the struggle, the collective experience, and community resistance. This practice and this thought are a critique of politics as a separate activity. (I do not think, here, only of the political caricature of the electoral processes going on in Mexico or in France, but rather what the Sub stated in *Brecha*: "The parties divide the community and create fractures on all sides.")

This critical reflection is not new nor is it specific to the indigenous peasant communities. In 1920, a sector of the revolutionary German working-sector movement proclaimed that "revolution is not a party issue" and proposed a collective form of organization, founded on the experience of "councils" of factory workers, of soldiers, of neighborhoods that could not be governed from above but rather were determined by the will of their members. One can also remember that Traven, who came from the same German revolution, counseled the proletarians of the West, since 1930, to be inspired by the communitarian practices of the indigenous people of Mexico, particularly their chiefs (and this also holds for the Sub).

In this same manner, today in France there cannot be a "political translation" of social movements, such as that from the Fall of 1995, or of civil disobedience to the laws, or the racist and xenophobic logic of the State, without the recognition of the sovereignty of those movements and their organizations, supported by the assembly of their participants.

I do not see a possible alternative for the EZLN if it transforms itself into a "civil" organization, than that of immersing itself in the social movement while affirming its sovereignty against the logic of the parties, of power — that which Pierre Clastres denominated "the society against the State."

FRIEDERIKE HABERMANN: From my perspective, I do not believe it is possible to judge this as a transformation into a civil movement. I see the danger that the EZLN may lose its clarity, its authenticity and as a result, its strength of fascination. There are no truthful politics in false politics and it is not possible to overcome a system using its own rules. On the other hand, I do not see another way of getting out of the situation. I admire its courage and bravery, but I do not want dead martyrs.

ULRICH BRAND: Of course, I am in favor of radical change in Mexico through popular civil struggles. Of course, I hope that the "Enough Already!" weapon of the Zapatistas is more than a symbol used to wake up and strengthen the progressive forces. I lamentably suppose that the system of the PRI will not let go of power without violence as has been the case with Eastern Europe. In a capitalistic society like that of Mexico, which is also quite tied in with U.S. power, the elite has much more to lose than the elite of authoritarian socialism (who are themselves in power under other slogans). Nonetheless, I would like to be wrong about this.

*Question: From the beginning, the Zapatistas exhibited substantial differences from earlier armed movements in rejecting the role of the vanguard in the revolutionary process. They openly point out that the creation of a new world corresponds to all of humanity and that they represent only a part of this humanity. They call for everyone to struggle for their own demands from their own spaces, using their own means (rather than joining the armed struggle). This allows each person to assume his or her responsibility in the struggle, not in other people's struggles, but in one's own. From your perspective, what would be the main criteria behind what we could call an international Zapatismo? Is it possible to talk about an international Zapatismo? What are Zapatismo's ties with other struggles?*

MARC TOMSIN: My effort to respond to the second question seems to anticipate the third question, at least in reference to the possible convergence of struggles around the world. Regarding international Zapatismo...the famous phrase "Zapatismo is not, does not exist. It is only as useful as are bridges, to cross from one side to another." International Zapatismo would be yet another ideology that one would have to combat, or at least criticize (neither does anarchism escape this danger, from my perspective). No one can doubt that the Zapatistas handle paradoxes with virtuosity and that, in the words of the emissaries of the EZLN in France in November of 1996, the term Zapatismo was mentioned incessantly. If it is about a magical formula to express the inexpressible, let it be. But, repeated in front of a culturally and politically-oriented audience, the formula is not effective; it produces instead confusion and even reinforces the Parisian intelligentsia's confusion (so well represented by the article in *Le Monde Diplomatique* in January 1997: "The About Face of the Zapatistas"). Those same Parisian intellectuals were frightened upon seeing the theater of Odeon invaded on November 11, 1996, by hundreds of people from the *Sans Papiers* or "No Papers" movement from Africa, Asia and Europe, who with their friends and children joined the Zapatistas and thus occupied for a couple of hours this sanctuary of culture. Listening to each other and understanding each other, the words of the exploited Chinese, Africans, or Turks connected with the words of two EZLN messengers. In the transgression of the cultural character of the theater, given this occupation of its space and above all of the scene reserved only for renowned comedians and intellectuals, one may find the answer to the question about what binds these groups' struggles with Zapatismo. This meeting can only take place when they confront the powers that be. This happened only a very few times during the Intergalactic Encuentro celebrated last summer in Chiapas, and unfortunately, it seems even less possible as Europe's "Intergalactic II" is being organized. It is rebellion itself that binds our struggles with Zapatismo, with the indigenous and campesino community insurrections in the mountains of Southeastern Mexico.

FRIEDERIKE HABERMANN: For me the boundaries and bases for imagining a community of struggles are given by radical democracy — necessarily anti-capitalist, anti-racist and anti-sexist because if everyone participates it would not be possible for a group to dominate all others. I believe that a network of international Zapatistas does exist along these lines. Nonetheless, we are still not sure that we all agree. For example, when we talk about neoliberalism, are we against this phase of capitalism (that is to say, do we want a politics like that of Keynes and import substitution) or are we anti-capitalist? When we talk about patriarchy are we all understanding the same thing? Do we consider capitalism to be a phase of patriarchy or do we believe that patriarchy is but one contradiction within capitalism? What does feminism mean?

It is necessary to pursue many more collective discussions in order to express and review our ideas in much greater depth. The ties of Zapatismo with my own struggles are actually quite extensive. Through the collective REDaktion and Zapapares, I am directly trying to deepen the idea and to extend our networks. Indirectly, the people with whom I struggle and participate are people with a knowledge of Zapatista politics, even when they do not identify themselves as such and even when they are unaware of this identification.

MASSIMO DE ANGELIS: There are three elements that ought to be taken into account when we talk about the international struggle. First, the circulation of world struggles, second its amplification, and third the constitution of a new world, that is to say a new human world. The struggles circulate by means of the communication and coordination of actions, but they do not necessarily expand by the same route. The circulation of struggles can occur solely as solidarity. For example, a rally can be organized in front of the Mexican embassy in London, as we did in solidarity with the indigenous peoples of Chiapas. Of course this is important, but it is not sufficient. Only when we convert the Zapatistas' struggle into our own struggle, when we move from the Mexican embassy to Downing Street (headquarters of the British government) do we contribute to amplifying the struggle. And only if we ask ourselves, how are we to substitute our world for this? May we advance our demands and make our struggles really constitutive of a new world? These three pillars can be forged in our struggles in only one way: "By asking, we may walk," just as we have learned from the Zapatistas. We need to ask ourselves the questions and then find the answer in one and many meetings. The first

Intercontinental Encuentro for Humanity and against Neoliberalism was one such meeting. The following meeting will be better because we have the experience of the first and we know what can be improved. And one thing that would push the struggles to circulate, expand and constitute a new world is to make sure that in the next meeting there will be representatives of popular movements from all over. This implies that the national organizers must ensure and promote their participation.

These are the principles under which we can talk about an international Zapatismo. It means a series of international meetings where the participants aren't simply supportive of the Zapatistas and where they don't recognize the Zapatistas as the only worthy combative subject, but as one of many subjects involved in the struggle. International Zapatismo is constructed when industrial workers, students, women, office workers, teachers, the unemployed, peasants, indigenous peoples, health care workers, all over the world recognize each other as human beings confronting a common enemy. When acknowledgment of "the other" is a necessity for oneself. When, in any part of the world, those who organize against neoliberal politics recognize the Zapatistas as one of them. When these same people become aware that without the freedom and aspirations of the indigenous peoples there may be no solution to their own problems, in any country where they might be, and vice versa. When this acknowledgment bursts from any struggle over any issue being dealt with, the humanity that we are constructing is going to be as solid as a rock because the proposals that we are pushing cannot turn against us. As a matter of fact, it is in the acknowledgment and recognition that every person is necessary for every other person that we can define our humanity, and when that occurs, the power of money cannot be used against us, as an instrument of division.

In this context, the only meaning that I can attribute to international Zapatismo is that of being a crucial space of struggle, dignity and hope created by the Zapatistas out of a neoliberal world of despair and inhumanity. But the word "Zapatismo" is destined to disappear in the mixing the many names of the "local heroes," and along with it will go the local aspirations, needs, desires. In one word, Zapatismo is the struggle for a human world, in the context of our confrontation with a power organized to snatch our dignity and our humanity from us in the name of money.

The enclosure of the Zapatistas' own struggle depends entirely on the international coordination of civil society's struggles in Mexico and especially in the world. We have the ability to break the circle and to open more space for the Zapatistas and their struggle and thereby to amplify their impact. Again, the international meeting is the most important priority of this project.

COLLECTIVO INTERNAZIONALISTA DE TORINO: We believe that there is some risk in making good theory and bad practice (or a contradictory political proposal). As a matter of fact, the unitary process presents on the international level some of the same problems and possible errors as on the national or local levels. We need not confuse unity with unification, that is to say, the intent to put everyone under the same flag, when different realities have the right to exist and enjoy a deserved autonomy.

There are multiple individuals, groups, organizations and villages struggling and resisting neoliberalism on behalf of humanity, each one with its own history and culture. It is necessary to discover these realities, bring them to light by creating physical spaces (newspapers, bulletins, web sites, radio, meeting places and meeting occasions) where they are not threatened by oblivion and isolation, in an international network space that would allow them to connect on a horizontal level, without the burdens of hierarchies and centralized decision-making centers. These spaces would include everybody and be for everyone, with equal opportunities. A network to gather and amplify denunciations, to receive and to spread information and experiences, to solicit and give support, to accumulate and concentrate strengths, with no other links than honesty in this common intent. In our opinion, these are the ideas that would permit progress and the convergence of struggles throughout the world.

And the role of Zapatismo in this network? Evidently the role is that of one point of reference, a very active point, but always one among ten, a thousand, or ten thousand. Trying to make Zapatismo a reference point for everyone (for the Palestinian people, for the Nigerian unions, for the independence movement of East Timor, for the African immigrants in Europe, for the Italian workers fired from Olivetti) would be artificial and useless. It wouldn't make much sense even to create a civilian Zapatista base in foreign countries, recruited on the basis of solidarity with the EZLN. Other myths, cults and ideologies do not work for us; what does work for us is being able to look at the EZLN as the beginning of a new era.

ULRICH BRAND: I have been studying the emancipation struggles in Argentina and Uruguay. I believe that the biggest error was, and is, the position of the revolutionary vanguard (armed or not).

Emancipation is an individual process, and at the same time a social process, that ought to be lived as a learning process (errors are not to be denied) and not as the adoption of the truths of a vanguard. Without knowing the Zapatistas' reality in a profound way, I believe that the Zapatistas do it like that. Probably now it does not seem to be a radical democratic process, but Zapatistas' practices are just that and that is what I like about them.

I agree that a new world is not created with revolutionary arms. The armed struggle in a capitalist society is not the same thing as an armed struggle in an almost feudal society, as was the case in Cuba, Nicaragua and in many more countries in Africa, Asia and even in Russia in 1917. Armed struggle in a capitalist society with its variety of powers (including patriarchal power) is a defensive struggle, and though legitimate, as in Chiapas, to defend their needs, it can never be an offensive measure in the difficult march toward radical changes. (In many cases, including West Germany, the armed struggle has been counterrevolutionary).

Concerning the issue of the convergence of struggles, the great bond between Zapatismo and our struggles is definitely the resistance against neoliberalism. I do not see a convergence on the grounds of a struggle to destroy a State Party, necessary as it may be in Mexico, because in many countries, political power is not so easily identifiable.

A problem with the idea of convergence until now is that neoliberalism has not been well understood. Some refer to neoliberalism as being responsible for every evil. Others see it as an economic policy of the conservative parties that could be abolished with social democratic politics. These are very limited perspectives. I believe that we must understand that behind neoliberalism there are powerful interest groups, that neoliberalism is the result of certain dominant strategies, and a weakening of the subaltern classes, that neoliberalism is the cause of globalization. The governments and their intellectuals want to make us believe that globalization is something "natural." But those same governments, together with business, constructed globalization by opening the national economies, and deregulating the financial markets. The principal cause of globalization is the change in the relations of force in favor of the dominant classes, along with the recuperation of high profit rates and the destruction of workers' rights. Globalization is not something "natural." Globalization is class struggle. It is something very real while at the same time an ideological argument used to justify any policy against the interest of humanity. The big problem is that on a global level, forms of resistance do not exist, not even for the Zapatistas. But the great merit of the Zapatistas is that, as a national liberation movement, they understood the global context of their struggle (not only by asking for solidarity). They also realized that it is necessary to enhance all forms of struggle on a global level, and they even organized an Encuentro to promote this process. But it would be a great mistake, very arrogant and in disagreement with Zapatismo itself, to see the Zapatistas as the first ones and as the only ones. Many efforts already exist to internationalize emancipation struggles on the regional and world level.

Yes, I do believe that it is possible to talk about international Zapatismo. It is ambivalent because many companions have an almost romantic perspective on the Zapatistas. They do not understand the "lead by obeying" idea; instead, they obey the supposed directives announced by the Zapatistas. A Zapatista International would have to be carried out independently of the Zapatistas in Chiapas, at the same time include them as a very important and innovative part, and I believe that this is what is beginning to happen. For this reason it could be difficult to use the term "Zapatismo," but it is something that is yet to be defined.

With respect to Germany, I believe that the solidarity movement with Chiapas is very weak and at the same time very strong. From the quantitative point of view, during the revolution in Nicaragua, thousands of comrades organized in Germany and did a good job. But in many cases, their cause was very limited because it was still about "exporting" revolutionary desires from here to there. But with the victory of Chamorro, thousands abandoned their militancy; the adored object of solidarity had disappeared.

Today there are few who organize solidarity groups, even though the interest in Chiapas and the EZLN runs deep among those who do, but I would say that these groups are more sustainable. Militants tend to see more of the ambivalent nuances in Zapatismo, for example, in their reference to the nation or to civil society. In Penumbra, the group in which I am active in Germany, we are aware that direct solidarity is necessary, but that we also have to integrate ourselves in the struggles here. Few intellectuals, party militants or unionists in Germany are interested in Chiapas or Zapatismo. The victory of neoliberalism leaves the defensive struggles in a national(istic) frame, yet another paradox in times of globalization, but there it is.

*Question: What are the principal contributions of Zapatismo to the other movements and processes of emancipation in the world?*

*What are these movements' contributions to the Zapatistas, or what could they be?*

MARC TOMSIN: Taking into account what I said earlier about the term "Zapatismo," the principal contributions of these communities fighting for emancipation consist in having known how to maintain their unity as they move forward, questioning, for example, some aspect of domination deeply set in the hearts of their communities (evidently that which men exercise over women, with all of its consequences for their children, education).

The second principal contribution concerns the fundamental acknowledgment of that direct democracy where everyone's word ought to be spoken and heard. This liberation of language, of critical thinking and imagination, that I felt in May 1968 in France, I found again in the Zapatistas at the end of the twentieth century, as they have succeeded in making themselves heard throughout the world.

The world's "contributions" to the Zapatistas also has to do with the word. When people find the strength and the courage in themselves to rebel, the patience to organize and the richness of their memory, the bases of a planetary solidarity exist. Therefore, the creation of networks of mutual help, of dialogue and of reflection, where criticism and respect ought to come together, becomes a real possibility.

There is another thing to point out: the insurgent communities of Chiapas have exposed a world economic logic, whether it be called private capitalism or state capitalism, as in countries that were called "socialist." This also is valid for the social movements in Europe or Asia; we know less about what goes on in Africa, but if we consider the self-organized struggles that are developing among the immigrants in western Europe, the hope is great.

FRIEDERIKE HABERMANN: It seems to me that the principal contribution of Zapatismo to our movements is the knowledge that it is not necessary to conquer the world, but rather that it is necessary that we remake it. This is the most difficult thing to do, because to make a new world implies that we also renew ourselves. But if we continue together along this path (alone we can do nothing) we can create, at the same time, distinct pieces of the world we want.

The world's major contribution to the Zapatistas was the awareness that they are not alone, and I hope that this cannot be militarily destroyed.

MASSIMO DE ANGELIS: The Zapatistas' biggest contribution is that the impasse we faced was overcome. It was an impasse in which hope did not exist, human necessities were replaced by the needs of the market, and the past, the present, and the future could only be understood in the manner that bankers understand life and time, using the formula of a compound interest rate.

They also made two crucial methodological contributions which concern the method of social transformation. First, with their idea of "leading as obeying," they united in political practice two centuries of Western literature about direct democracy, together with two thousand years of indigenous experience in direct democracy, to the extent that, presently, anyone who reflects on political practice has to consider the Zapatistas' experience. Second, vindicating their "by asking, we walk" maxim, they not only established the correct priority as far as questions go, but they also brought about an understanding that in order for these questions to be the correct ones, they must be set forth by the people struggling. A movement based on the maxim, "by asking, we may walk," can only be a movement sufficiently humble to be able to ask questions and sufficiently firm not to allow the answers to come from some authoritarian and mystical leader. And in the process of asking we move forward and confront the problems as they arise and as they really are. And in the process of asking, we fight to overcome the obstacles that spring up. And in the process of asking, we also dance and sing to unmask politics from its alienated professional seriousness. Politics becomes a human issue. Their concept of politics is just as simple as that announced in Marcos' August 29, 1996, letter to the EPR [Ejercity Popular Revolucionario, a guerilla movement in Guerrero state]: that people without a party or organization should agree on what they want and the way in which they are going to achieve it. But such simplicity is in reality the point of entry to a number of essential questions that have no easy answer. Only people who are involved with common exchanges and struggles can formulate these questions with the hope of finding answers. The Encuentro was simply a moment in which these issues could be formulated.

There are three things that the world can give to the Zapatistas: space, solidarity and respect. The first one, space, would come through our own struggles against neoliberalism. Solidarity can come by helping them to deal with the federal army and the commodification of life under tremendously difficult material circumstances. The third one, respect, would come through stories, and an appreciation of their ways of enacting collective decisions.

COLLECTIVO INTERNAZIONALISTA DE TORINO: For many, Zapatismo has meant the definitive overcoming of an old way of doing politics, the expression and the example of new practices, just as much a question of content as of form. At the ground level, the demand for all of this has always been more felt. Nonetheless, this is still an incipient process. In fact, if the experiences of Zapatista indigenous communities and their theoretical contributions have, in part, allowed us to define the ideas with which to begin, a great effort is necessary from everyone in order to find the most appropriate forms for their realization. The impacts are numerous and represent a true revolution.

Predefined ideologies housing useless divisions are replaced by confronting the real situation and by joining struggles based on concrete and unifying objectives: democracy, freedom, justice, land, housing, work, and the like.

Lack of communication is replaced by an effort to reach every corner of the earth, using all possible channels and directing them to people's hearts with a language that leads to dialogue, and not only with the "specialists."

The vanguards, the leaders and the bureaucrats are rejected in an effort to include entire sectors of the population, to develop the "civil society" (its organizations and its individuals), and to open participation to all those who are honestly interested in change and in democracy from below. We must begin with our own organizations and avoid propagandistic figures and concentrations of power.

Historical experiences, past and present, have shown us how little reliability there is in a revolutionary process that lacks democracy. It has been one of the fundamental causes of the failure of revolutionary processes in Latin America.

The idea of the "conquest of power" is substituted by the idea of the development of a civil society organized to exercise power, according to the principle of "leading as we obey." Nonetheless one should not forget the other part of the issue: how to resolve the problem of the existence of the class enemy, in a society in which the division of classes remains a determining element? How, if not by conquering power? Perhaps we can think about convincing and not destroying "the enemy."

ULRICH BRAND: I have already mentioned some of the principal contributions of Zapatismo. The Zapatistas have already made it clear many times that they do not want to, nor are they able to, lead international struggles or conduct an international Zapatista organization, even though many still try to assign them this role.

The world's contribution to the Zapatistas is direct solidarity: sending material goods, informing, protesting and participating in peace camps. This is crucial, though it seems to me that this solidarity could be more intense. Concerning the concrete struggles in Mexico, I believe that "the world" cannot contribute much because it does not know the circumstances. Until now the Zapatistas' struggles remained necessarily a national one, and probably it has been difficult to listen to many outside voices; we must not forget that they are acting under conditions of war. I share the Zapatistas' perspective that the most important contribution from outside Chiapas is the struggle to radically change the international social conditions that cause poverty and uprisings.

*Question: Briefly, how do you evaluate the last three years of struggle, in terms of its impact on a revolutionary conception in the world?*

MARC TOMSIN: The "Mexican alarm clock" made itself heard even in the hearts of those Parisians who thought they knew almost everything regarding the social and revolutionary issue. It also touched the hearts of the old Spanish anarchists who never gave in and who have survived all the various repressions. The free world returned with the practice of sovereign assemblies; the criticism of the separations (political, economical, cultural and social) should intensify much more; the self-organization of the struggles of resistance to economic domination should still affirm itself. Personally, all of this has put me in touch and in harmony with the younger generations of dissidents. Meanwhile, within the solidarity movement with the Zapatistas, the old centralist and vanguard-like schemes continue to operate, the militants of revolutionary politics attempt to reconstruct their virginity. We should not hesitate about putting them on their heads, just as happened with the intelligentsia of the Parisian left in Odeon.

The social movement has returned to find, in these three years, the meaning of the Word, of the Assembly, and of Direct Democracy. It is now necessary for us to gather confidence in ourselves and to proclaim our sovereignty.

FRIEDERIKE HABERMANN: The Zapatistas demonstrated that after the "end of history" (Francis Fukuyama) one could still say "Enough is enough!" This movement began in Chiapas, but it also occurred in almost every part of the world. The Zapatistas demonstrated that there are human beings who do not live according to the established rationality, i.e., thinking only in their own interest. Instead, they were crazy enough as to risk their lives in order to realize their dreams, following the possibility of a life based on dignity and community. The network of a "globalization" — global and local at the same time — of the struggles and dreams still further extended. The Zapatistas in Chiapas are not alone.

MASSIMO DE ANGELIS: The last three years have seen a resurgence of struggles around the world. Beginning with the generalized revolts in Africa and Latin America against structural adjustment policies, the revolts in one of the Asian "tigers," South Korea, those of other Southeast Asia economies such as Indonesia, and even those of the northern part of the world such as the struggles of General Motors' workers in the United States, of the railroad workers in France and of the dock workers in the United Kingdom, among others. What appears to be happening is a reversal of the tide. Not only are the struggles becoming more extensive, they are also tending to connect among themselves. The global politics of neoliberalism are stimulating struggles in all parts of the world that tend to resemble each other, presenting similar characteristics. The effects of struggles in one part of the world are already felt in another part of the world and not only on a material level. People are rebelling against a way of life that is trying to sell us everything in the name of economy and competitiveness. As another example, one of the recent events that has contributed most to showing that the pillars of power are not so strong (and, indeed, appear to be made of cardboard) is the struggle of workers in South Korea. Only fifteen years ago, when in Italy the first neoliberal policies were introduced into the labor market, South Korea was one of the great models supposed to show us how happy workers could be in a land oriented toward exports. Now the global executors of the rules of money and indignity have lost even this model. Everything was a lie!

COLLECTIVO INTERNAZIONALISTA DE TORINO: It is difficult to evaluate the real impact of the EZLN in terms of the struggles or of the revolutionary conception until recently fashionable worldwide. The lines of alternative communication still have many defects, that is, when they are not totally absent in the first place. But despite censorship of the means of information, one fact seems obvious: struggles all over are coming alive, and these struggles involve more extensive strata of the population and often break the dikes of union and party control. It is a sign of growing social malaise resulting from the universal application of the neoliberal doctrine, in addition to the accumulation of desires for change. Nonetheless, it is difficult for us to evaluate whether the events in Mexico over the last three years have had an influence on these struggles, either because, in fact, the emergence of the Zapatistas has yet to produce concrete results demonstrating that they are an example to follow, or because the information diffused officially has been scarce and unobjective. Solidarity and alternative communications reach but a limited part of the population.

Regarding the atmosphere of solidarity which has grown around the EZLN, we observe that, even though positive examples do exist, there is still a long road to follow from good theory to effective democratic functioning. Frequently, what goes on has been more about a brush stroke of color, exterior and superficial, instead of a profound change in the way in which people relate to each other and work together.

Another thing is the level of the institutional left: several politicians, who are directly responsible or co-responsible for the neoliberal politics carried out by the Italian government, have used a relationship with the Zapatista command or a meeting with the "Sub" to adorn their own public image. But, naturally, nothing has changed in their political action.

ULRICH BRAND: With respect to the struggle or the revolutionary conceptions (I would prefer to speak in the plural) in the last three years, I am at the same time pessimistic and optimistic. Pessimistic because the real struggles in many parts of the world are not very emancipatory, but instead are reactive. The economic wars and the military are growing, and so is the destruction of the environment and the tendency toward authoritarian politics.

But I am optimistic because our consciousness about the limits within the neoliberal system is developing slowly. I am convinced that during the struggle, the general limits of the capitalist and patriarchal system are also evidenced, that is to say that it is not possible nor desirable to return to the Fordist phase of the welfare state which for a great part of humanity did not mean well being. (One aspect of the struggle in Germany consists of convincing the movements that still want to return to that phase to give up this conception.) But it is necessary to see that the system is not self-confining; we must set its limits. This is, of course, a tremendous job because the mechanisms of power are well developed, dynamic, and in many cases, extremely subtle.

For example, for the Zapatistas it is crucial to open social spaces for discussion. In a country like Germany this is also a problem, but the reason in this case is not an authoritarian party like the PRI that tries to control all public spaces, but rather subordination of more and more public spaces to the logic of profit. The great majority of the means of communication are independent of the State or of the political parties but live on advertizing revenues.

Many people are dying and are going to die, the conditions of life are becoming worse and the economic, political and cultural powers are becoming stronger. But, in general, there is no alternative to the process of self-learning about the democratic process, even though in some cases counter-violence seems necessary to me. We still have to learn practically and theoretically the possibilities and limits of a revolution, or better yet, of revolutions. Until now, resistance means, above all, to stop the destruction by carrying out emancipative struggles through many small efforts, by the every day questioning of power and by attacking the powerful institutions. Ever so slowly the defensive attitude will change to allow for the creation of alternatives. And this won't happen in a final fight, but rather as a slow process of resistance, of solidarity and of learning.

**Notes**

1 All interviewees attended the First Encuentro for Humanity and Against Neoliberalism celebrated in July–August 1996 in Chiapas.

2 Massimo de Angelis is a professor in the Department of Economy at the University of London and a founder of the group fHuman, in support of the Zapatista rebellion.

3 I refer to Harry Cleaver, a founder of the group *Red Acción Zapatista* (Acción Zapatista Network) based in Austin, Texas.

4 Friederike Habermann is a German economist and a member of the collective REDaktion and Zapapres.

5 Those who were interviewed were Adelina Bottero and Luciano Salza, who also participated in the Civil Encampments for Peace. The answers are the product of a discussion held by the Collettivo to which they belong.

6 Ulrich Brand is a researcher at the University of Frankfurt/Main working on issues involving the democratizing role of non-governmental organizations in environmental global politics. He is a member of the editorial board of the Socialist magazine, *Links*

(leftist); and a member of the internationalist group Penumbra that was formed after the invasion of Chiapas by the Mexican army in February, 1995.

[7] Marc Tomsin is a member of the Comité de Solidarité avec les Peuples du Chiapas en Lutte (Committee of Solidarity with the People of Chiapas in Struggle) of Paris. He actively participated in the movement of May, 1968 in Paris, and is currently a proofreader and syndicalist.

# 7

# PEOPLES' GLOBAL ACTION: DREAMING UP AN OLD GHOST

OLIVIER DE MARCELLUS

PEOPLES' GLOBAL ACTION (PGA) against WTO and "free" trade is a rallying point for those:

- Who reject "free" trade, not for its "excesses," but for what it is: the latest form of imperialism and capitalist domination.
- Who are skeptical of any kind of "global governance"; and
- Who propose another paradigm, based on self-sufficiency, diversity, autonomy and popular sovereignty at the most local level possible.

PGA is also the very improbable idea of a "non-organization" capable of action at a global level.

In just a bit more than two years, PGA has organized four large international mobilizations, raised great hopes, scared some bourgeois, and held two international conferences. At the same time, it remains a highly improbable beast, a non-organization attempting to organize huge events, living by hook and by crook — and usually on the brink of implosion.

PGA is an offshoot of the international Zapatista movement, founded in a meeting that prolonged the Second Encuentro in southern Spain, and drawing a lot of its European support from people who also support the Zapatistas. There is also a certain ideological and organizational resemblance, both being rather unorthodox, eclectic networks attempting to stimulate radical opposition worldwide. The principal difference is that PGA aims beyond debate and exchange to propose action campaigns against neoliberalism, worldwide.

What follows are extracts from a PGA text, written for the second PGA Conference in Bangalore, India, August 1999, and from *PGA Bulletin* No.4, accompanied by my personal comments and explanations.

**1. What is Peoples' Global Action (PGA)?**

"From the 23rd to the 25th of February 1998, peoples' movements from all continents met in Geneva, Switzerland, and launched a worldwide coordination of resistance against the global market, a new alliance of struggle and mutual support called the Peoples' Global Action against 'Free' Trade and the World Trade Organization (PGA). This new platform intends to serve as a global instrument for communication and coordination for all those fighting against the destruction of humanity and the planet by the global market, building up local alternatives and peoples' power.

"The hallmarks [principles] of the alliance are:

"1. A very clear rejection of the WTO and other trade liberalization agreements (like APEC [Asian–Pacific Economic Council], the EU [European Union], NAFTA [North American Free Trade Agreement], etc.) as active promoters of a socially and environmentally destructive globalisation;

"2. A confrontational attitude, since we do not think that lobbying can have a major impact in such biased and undemocratic organizations, in which transnational capital is the only real policy-maker;

"3. A call to non-violent civil disobedience and the construction of local alternatives by local people, as answers to the action of governments and corporations;

"4. An organizational philosophy based on decentralisation and autonomy." [1]

At the second PGA conference in Bangalore (August 1999), the basic principles were completed and radicalised:

"After a day of discussion in small groups, the plenary took the collective challenge of broadening the function of PGA: it was agreed by consensus that the network should in the future work as a tool for communication and coordination *for all the struggles against the effects of the global capitalist regime, not only against the institutions and agreements that regulate it*. This means that the efforts of communication and coordination will in the future be extended to all the topics related to capitalist exploitation, as well as its relation with patriarchy, racism, violence, environmental destruction, and the different forms of struggle to eliminate these forms of oppression. The expectation is that the PGA as a process will eventually reach a stage in which it is able to articulate grassroots resistance at global level, working as a global movement, rooted in the basis of peoples' movements all over the planet, and playing a direct political role from below (despite not being constituted as organization).

"This change in the definition of PGA was a continuation of a general wish that was already evident at the first conference (Geneva, February 1998), when the first draft of the manifesto, consisting of one and a half pages focused on the WTO and other trade and investment agreements, grew through a participatory process to an eight-page text on the impacts of capitalism on different social groups, the environment, etc. This wish also was apparent in the projects supported by PGA. For instance, the global day of action on June 18th [1999] was a carnival against capitalism, and the Inter-Continental Caravan for Solidarity and Resistance had among its five main topics of struggle issues such as biotechnology and the nuclear industry. Another important decision taken by consensus was to include the following text as a new PGA hallmark, one of the basic points of consensus which will not be discussed since they are the fundaments on which the network is built: '*We reject all forms and systems of domination and discrimination including, but not limited to, patriarchy, racism and religious fundamentalism of all creeds. We embrace the full dignity of all human beings.*' [This has become the second PGA hallmark, and previous hallmarks 2, 3 and 4 now become hallmarks 3, 4 and 5 respectively.] This hallmark was introduced due to the fact that the denunciation of 'free' trade without an analysis of patriarchy, racism and processes of homogenisation is a basic element of the discourse of the (extreme) right, and perfectly compatible with simplistic explanations of complex realities and with the personification of the effects of capitalism (such as conspiracy theories, anti-Semitism, etc.) that inevitably lead to fascism, witch-hunting and oppressive chauvinist traditionalism. With this new hallmark, PGA repudiates all reactionary forms of resistance to capitalism.[2]

"The PGA is an instrument for coordination, not an organization. Its objectives are inspiring the greatest possible number of persons and organizations to act against 'free' trade through non-violent civil disobedience and people-oriented constructive actions, offering an instrument for co-ordination and mutual support at the planetary level for those fighting 'free' trade and giving more international projection to the struggles against 'free' trade and the WTO. The political analysis and call for action of the PGA are reflected in its manifesto, a living document that will be revised at every PGA conference.

"The PGA has no membership, and it does not and will not have a juridical personality. No organization or person represents the PGA, nor does the PGA represent any organization or person. The PGA will only facilitate coordination and information flow with the help of conferences and information tools.

"The conferences of the PGA are convened by a committee conformed by organizations and movements from all continents representing different sectors of society (plus the local organizers of the conference). This committee determines the program of the conference, takes decisions about participation in the conference and use of resources, decides which publications can be printed under the name of the PGA, and checks the content of the information tools of the PGA.

"The committee cannot speak in the name of the PGA."

## 2. A brief history of Peoples' Global Action

From the 18th to the 20th of May 1998, heads of state and ministers from all over the world met in Geneva for the 2nd Ministerial Conference of the World Trade Organization (WTO), and to celebrate the 50th anniversary of the multilateral trade system (GATT and WTO), the main instrument of transnational capital for organizing and enforcing global economic governance. This event was aimed, in the words of its organizers, to 'celebrate the past while preparing the way for the future' of trade liberalization — i.e., of the destruction of rural societies, dignity in labor, the environment, cultural diversity and self-determination.

"Around 50 representatives of peoples' organizations from the South and the North met to prepare the resistance against this event in El Indiano (Spain) in August 1997, right after the 2nd Inter-Continental Encuentro (Gathering) for Humanity and against Neoliberalism. The objective of the meeting was developing common plans against the commemoration of the GATT and the WTO and developing lasting instruments of communication and coordination in the struggle against the WTO and other 'free'-trade agreements. The organizations represented included mass-based farmers' movements from India (KRRS), Philippines (KMP), Indonesia (KAP), Brazil (MST), Peru (CCP) and Bolivia (FCB), indigenous peoples' organizations from Nigeria (MOSOP) and Mexico (CNI and Assemblea de la

Resistencia Civil from Chiapas), trade unions from Nicaragua (CST) and diverse organizations from the North.

"One of the decisions taken at that meeting was launching a network for maintaining the communication and coordination after the days of action against the Ministerial Conference in May 1998. The original idea was to use the network that was to be constructed in the Second Intercontinental Encuentro for this purpose, but it was felt by most of the participants that the articulation and decision-making procedures of this network were not sufficiently clear in order to take such a decision in a legitimate way. It was hence decided to convene an international conference in Geneva in February 1998 to establish such a network and to discuss the plans of action against the Ministerial Conference of the WTO. It was decided to call the new network *Peoples' Global Action against 'Free' Trade and the WTO,* in short Peoples' Global Action (PGA).

"More than 300 delegates of people's movements from 71 countries of all continents gathered in Geneva from the 23rd to the 25th of February for the *founding conference of the PGA*. Teachers hunger-striking against privatization in Argentina met women organizing against quasi-slavery in the 'Maquila' factories of Mexico, Bangladesh, Salvador, and Nicaragua; women's rights activists; farmers struggling against globalization in India, Philippines, Brazil, Estonia, Norway, Honduras, France, Spain, Switzerland, Bangladesh, Senegal, Mozambique, Togo, Peru, Bolivia, Columbia and many other countries; Ogoni, Maori, Maya, Aymara, U'wa and other indigenous peoples fighting for their cultural rights and physical survival; students struggling against nuclear power or the repression of striking workers in Ukraine and South Korea; postal workers from Canada resisting privatisation, militants against 'un-free' trade from the United States, environmentalists, unemployed, fisherfolk, anti-racists, peace mobilisers, animal rights activists...

"Such a world-wide meeting of women and men of grassroots movements was an extraordinary experience, bringing new vision, hope and determination to us all. Despite the huge material differences, struggles in privileged and under-privileged parts of the world could witness that they have more and more in common, setting the stage for a new and stronger sort of solidarity. The conference itself, largely housed in squatted halls and houses, depending entirely on the freely offered work of the Genevan "alternative" sector, was an example of this.

"The *first worldwide co-ordination of local actions against 'free' trade* took place during the WTO ministerial conference and was a huge success: many different demonstrations, actions and Global Street Parties took place all over the world from the 16th to the 20th of May, in a total of 29 countries.[3]

"During the days of action and the following months, a wave of repressive measures took place against activists associated with the PGA network. The police arrested and mistreated hundreds of protestors in Geneva and other cities where major actions were taking place, and in the following months some of the key organizations and activists were arrested and their flats and offices searched by the police. A seminar organized by people associated with the PGA was raided by the police, who arrested all the participants for debating and discussing the globalization of the economy.

"However, the *planning of* actions continued: the second conference was prepared to take place before the Third Ministerial Conference of the WTO in Seattle (USA), and the conveners of the PGA endorsed two major projects for the first half of 1999: the Inter-Continental Caravan for Solidarity and Resistance from the 22nd of May to the 20th of June and the Global Day of Action against Financial Centers on June 18th.[4]

"The *Inter-Continental Caravan for Solidarity and Resistance* brought together around 450 representatives of peoples' movements from the South and the East with a diverse network of European grassroots groups for a full programme of actions, meetings and demonstrations. The groups preparing the caravan in Europe ranged from organizations of the unemployed to groups working against genetic engineering, from squatted social centres to feminist organizations, who invited the participants of the caravan to a total of 10 countries[5] in a route that culminated in the protests against the heads of state of the most industrialised countries of the world, who met in Cologne [Germany] for the World Economic Summit, also known as G8 Summit.

"Although the largest chunk of the caravan participants represented Indian peoples' movements (which were the ones that proposed the project in mid–97), there were also representatives of the landless farmers' movement in Brazil, supporters of the Zapatistas from Chiapas [Mexico], the organization of landless labourers from Bangladesh, the indigenous peoples of Chile, the Afro-American Network, human rights organizations from Nepal, an environmental organization from Ukraine, an anti-nuclear organization from Pakistan, etc. Among the Indian participants, the majority represented farmers' organizations, but also other social sectors such as the fisherfolk, the Adivasi (i.e. indigenous peoples), and movements against big dams.

"The actions taken by the caravan included demonstrations in front of the headquarters of multinational corporations such as Novartis, Monsanto, Cargill, Nestle and others, at institutions such as the World Trade Organization (WTO), the NATO, the Food and Agriculture Organization (FAO) and the European Central Bank, and at events such as the summit of the European Union. Some direct actions, such as the destruction of two fields of genetically modified crops and one biotechnology laboratory in collaboration with the French Peasants' Confederation, or the painting of Novartis' building in Barcelona along with a wide range of social and ecological organizations, were also in the programme of the caravan.

"In Cologne, the organizations represented in the caravan raised their voice against the plans of the industrial nations to continue pushing for trade and investment treaties that are designed to benefit transnational capital at the expense of people and nature. They specifically opposed the attempts to start a new round of negotiations within the World Trade Organization, a plan proposed by the European Union and endorsed by the USA and Japan. They also rejected and opposed the very concept of Third World debt, called for a ban on the use of genetically modified organisms in agriculture and denounced militarism and the nuclear industry in the North and the South. Unfortunately, their protest was repressed by a totally disproportionate and aggressive police force. Fifteen thousand policemen and policewomen from all over the country were brought to Cologne to make sure that any confrontational opposition would be crushed before starting. The media played their usual role to silence the mass arrests and the brutality of the police force.

"The day when the World Economic Summit (G7) started, one day after the caravan reached Cologne, decentralised actions were taking place all over the planet on the *Global Day of Action against Financial Centres* on June 18th. Movements ranging from the Chikoko Movement in Nigeria to the Pakistani trade unions, from the Argentinean churches to the squatters of London, took the financial centres of their cities to manifest their rejection to the rule of the G8. Such co-ordinated resistance in a total of 41 countries[6] showed that the process of convergence of resistances is gaining strength and speed."[7]

For the *third WTO Summit in Seattle*, another call went out, sent also in the name of the Industrial Workers of the World (IWW) and the Direct Action Network (DAN) on the west coast of the USA. First reports indicate that at least 74 cities around the world organized events, large or small: 18 cities in India (including New Delhi,

Bangalore and the Narmada Valley), 14 in Canada, 9 in Germany, at least 8 in the United States, 7 in Great Britain (including an important confrontation in London) and as many in Italy, plus Geneva (5000 persons), Buenos Aires, Mexico City, Prague, Brisbane, Amsterdam... There were demonstrations in cities of Pakistan (8000 persons), Sri Lanka, Turkey, Israel, Ireland, Iceland, etc.[8] (There were also demonstrations in Korea, the Philippines and Greece apparently without links to the call to action. In France, people responded massively to a separate call of the ATTAC movement, which reports 75,000 participants in 80 cities.)

But of course, the divine surprise was in Seattle itself, where the Direct Action Network (DAN) actually stopped the WTO summit from opening on November 30!

The DAN is a network of committees formed at the beginning of the summer in eight west coast cities ranging from Vancouver, Canada to Los Angeles. Citing the 4 PGA "hallmarks" (see above), inspired by the Indian farmers "cremation" of genetically modified crops, the uprising in Chiapas and the takeover of London's financial district by Reclaim the Streets during the June 18th Global Day of Action, this network (which seems to mostly regroup students and young radicals) not only co-sponsored the call to global action on November 30th, but organized for Seattle in an incredibly serious, creative and efficient manner. A twenty page action packet detailed exactly how they planned to form clusters of affinity groups technically and politically prepared to block all the approaches to the Seattle convention center by creative, non-violent actions, tripods, lockdowns, how to pursue resistance in jail in case of mass arrest, how to deal with media, first aid. They dared a prophesy:

"Envision...

"Thousands of people theatrically processing through Seattle with giant images and puppets graphically showing the economic and ecological devastation left in the wake of global capital. Mass nonviolent direct actions and blockades shutting down roads and arteries leading to the ministerial of the WTO... breaking down corporate globalisation and showing glimpses of the world as it could be — global liberation... life, creativity and resistance hurled in the face of thousands of deadening bureaucrats, business people and politicians at the WTO ministerial... The cacophony against capital will be deafening when nine days of large scale street theater preparations culminate in the largest festival of resistance the world has ever seen. We will make revolution irresistible."

Today, Clinton must be wanting to know why the police didn't take this challenge more seriously. It is true that it was difficult to imagine that there would be thousands of people on hand (in the rain, at 7 in the morning on a weekday!) to carry out this daft plan! I myself could only believe it as I saw it happen — sections of the two converging marches (one led by a group of progressive steel workers, the other by the PGA North American Caravan) breaking off to block the 13 approaches to the convention center, the people so determined that the police had soon exhausted its stock of gases without succeeding in breaking the siege. By the time the much larger march of the unions and NGOs approached, the day was won, and a large proportion of the marchers abandoned the official (legal) trajectory to fraternise with the DAN in a huge cross-city festival that ended only at nightfall in a last shower of gas and concussion grenades.

During the four succeeding days, the spirit of the demonstrations was as beautiful. I will never forget how, after the brutal repression and hundreds of arrests of Wednesday, we literally danced back into the "No demonstration zone" ("No Constitution zone") the next day, with passing motorists, bus drivers and workers on the construction sites cheering us on. Throughout the city, in the jail and around the jail (besieged by the protestors for three days), the air was alive with the awareness that this was a rare moment, probably the birth of a new popular movement in the USA.

Seattle sent back to Europe a huge wave of enthusiasm. Here in Geneva we were solicited by all kinds of organizations from surrounding countries itching to come and demonstrate against WTO. Unfortunately, there was nothing very spectacular going on at WTO! So people fell back on the anti-Davos (World Economic Forum) demo, organized every year by the Swiss PGA groups. Last year we were 200. This year about 1500, with people (including Mr. Bové) riding buses for 40 hours from as far as Rome, Bordeaux and Paris just for a whiff of tear gas and the pleasure of delaying Bill's motorcade. In Italy, our friends of the "antagonist" movement (particularly the squatted social centers) took a tip from Seattle with a spectacular non-violent disobedience demo of 20,000 people that penetrated and apparently obtained the closure of a scandalous illegal immigrants detention center. The ball is still rolling!

### 3. What next for PGA?

PGA has aroused amazing enthusiasm in very diverse quarters around the world, no doubt because (following the lead of the

Zapatistas) it attracted many who had been waiting for such an inclusive but radical anti-capitalist appeal. Co-ordinating neither parties nor NGOs, but autonomous, grass roots movements, PGA has opened a new political space that could give an international projection and a larger political significance to the struggles of these movements. There has been a real "circulation of struggles": the Indians inspiring the Genevans or Britons, who in turn inspire young Americans to do even better... a process of mutual discovery that started with the second Zapatista-inspired Encuentro in Spain, when Reclaim the Streets and activists of continental Europe, for example, discovered each other.

Judged by the actions that it has inspired or co-ordinated, it has been an incredible success, and (at least in some countries) has definitely contributed to making "free" trade issues and WTO known, and to giving them a bad reputation.

Like the Encuentros, it has linked North and South in a more reciprocal kind of solidarity. WTO and the neo-liberal offensive in the North has made it more evident that we do indeed all have a common enemy.

The groups most actively involved in the North have in general been relatively small and composed of young people from the "alternative" and "autonomous" political scenes. This limitation was no doubt unavoidable, given the political recuperation of most mainstream organizations, and unions. On the other hand, for many of these groups PGA has been the first chance to break out of more particular struggles (squats or anti-fascism, for example) to attack neoliberal capitalism more generally. The movements from the South lent authority to a discourse that broke with social-democratic and NGO "development" conceptions. This was particularly evident with the InterContinental Caravan, organized in the name of southern mass movements by small, active radical groups, but supported politically and financially by unions, NGOs, and foundations, who finally admitted the legitimacy of much that the Caravan had to say and do. The most promising development was the real involvement of farmers' organizations in France, Switzerland, Poland and Germany: city and country, farmers and young city activists actually working together. Getting the confidence of the Swiss farmers, for example, is a long and delicate process! For Seattle we finally demonstrated together (although not exactly on the same positions).

Thus, somewhat paradoxically, PGA's strong cards are in the South, but it has actually been much more productive in the North, where a profusion of "street parties" and other actions have made a significant impact in places like Geneva, London or Prague, and now in North America. On the other hand, the Southern movements (with notable exceptions) have been less involved than anticipated. They have very difficult conditions and their own very full agendas. These don't necessarily put WTO in first place, since in most regions the IMF programs have already imposed *de facto* what WTO wants to perpetuate as international law. A big movement in Nigeria, for example, may be willing to participate in co-ordinated demonstrations if it also coincides with local deadlines, but it generally won't organize a major demonstration just for a far away summit. The very idea of committing themselves to some kind of international action and political responsibility can be new and difficult. Political realities and subjectivity are still strongly bound to the national level. Organizations are accustomed to sending a delegate to conferences for information and solidarity, but not to keeping in regular contact and committing themselves to action. Some representatives even agreed to be convenors for PGA and then went home and apparently forgot about it, provoking unfortunate misunderstandings.

The weakest point of PGA is its organization. This is not really surprising since it is not supposed to be one. Sometimes this contradiction seems almost fatal. The conveners' committees have generally worked badly. This is no doubt due partly to the low priority necessarily given to this task by organizations that are often engaged in literally life and death struggles. This problem is compounded when organizations with huge mass bases prove to have extremely few resources and cadre at the top. The original idea, that the secretariat, would be assured by the organizations present in the conveners committee, has not worked out. The work has actually been done by a "support group" whose existence was only formally recognized this August [1999] at the Bangalore conference. This group was mostly composed of young European activists, with time and energy to put into the bulletin, web page, fund-raising, etc. While vital to the success of PGA, it gave rise to some fear that an informal hierarchy could take hold. At Bangalore some people of Asia and Latin America agreed to join the support group, which now has a clear mandate from the PGA assembly.

Despite this shaky organizational situation, PGA has undertaken half a dozen very large projects in very short succession. One of the results of this hyper-activism was that the Bangalore conference, following hard upon the Caravan, was not well prepared at all. Our contacts, particularly with Latin America, have suffered as a result of this. Is it really possible to organize such ambitious projects without being an "organization"? Without finances? Will the informal power structures, that necessarily emerge in such a situation, get out of control? So far, PGA has survived all these problems by the sheer, contagious power of the idea that it proposes.

PGA has always had the ambition of being also a space for international exchange on alternatives and of political reflection, things which over-engaged activists always tend to put off. The problem is compounded by the fact that PGA still works essentially through e-mail, which is often only very partially available in the South (for example, in the form of a Hotmail account in a shop 20 miles away!). For the long term, it is the richness of the political debate that we manage to start between continents and political traditions (Gandhians, Latin American movements, autonomous Marxists, anarchists) that will be decisive. The success of the resistances to WTO in Seattle will quickly provoke a counterattack. This will probably take the form of social and environmental "clauses" in WTO, which will divide the northern reformists, big union leadership, from the radicals and the southern States. (Already it is interesting to see how the "Bové-mania" is often used in the media to defend the big European farmers export subsidies — exactly the contrary of what Bové and the small farmers' organizations are proposing!) We should be losing no time to push our advantage, to attack the underlying principles of WTO, "free" trade and the capitalist "paradigm" in general. This is an open appeal for the participation of all of you to the debates that we hope to develop on our PGA web page! Your responses to this paper could be a beginning.

In terms of future actions, PGA has called for actions and initiatives around the world on the 1st of May to re-affirm our collective will to build an alternative to capitalism.

**Notes**

1 Leaflet for Bangalore Conference.

2 *PGA Bulletin* No. 4. Bulletins and other texts on the PGA are on the PGA Web page at http://www.agp.org.

3 PGA Bulletin No.4.

4 Web pages http://stad.dsl.nl/~caravan and http://www.greennet.org.uk/june18/ respectively.

5 The countries visited were Austria, Belgium, France, Germany, Italy, the Netherlands, Norway, Spain, Switzerland and the United Kingdom. There were visits arranged in the Czech Republic,

Denmark, Finland and Poland, but these could not take place due to delays in the processing of the visas.

6 Argentina, Australia, Austria, Bangladesh, Basque Country, Belarus, Brasil, Canada, Catalonia, Chile, Colombia, Czech Republic, Finland, France, Germany, Greece, India, Indonesia, Israel, Italy, Malaysia, Malta, Mexico, Netherlands, Nepal, Nigeria, Pakistan, Poland, Portugal, Romania, Senegal, South Africa, South Korea, Spain, Sweden, Switzerland, Thailand, United Kingdom, Uruguay, United States and Zimbabwe.

7 Leaflet for Bangalore Conference.

8 For more details, see the PGA web page at <www.agp.org>, or the Direct Action Network at <www.agitprop.org/artandrevolution>.

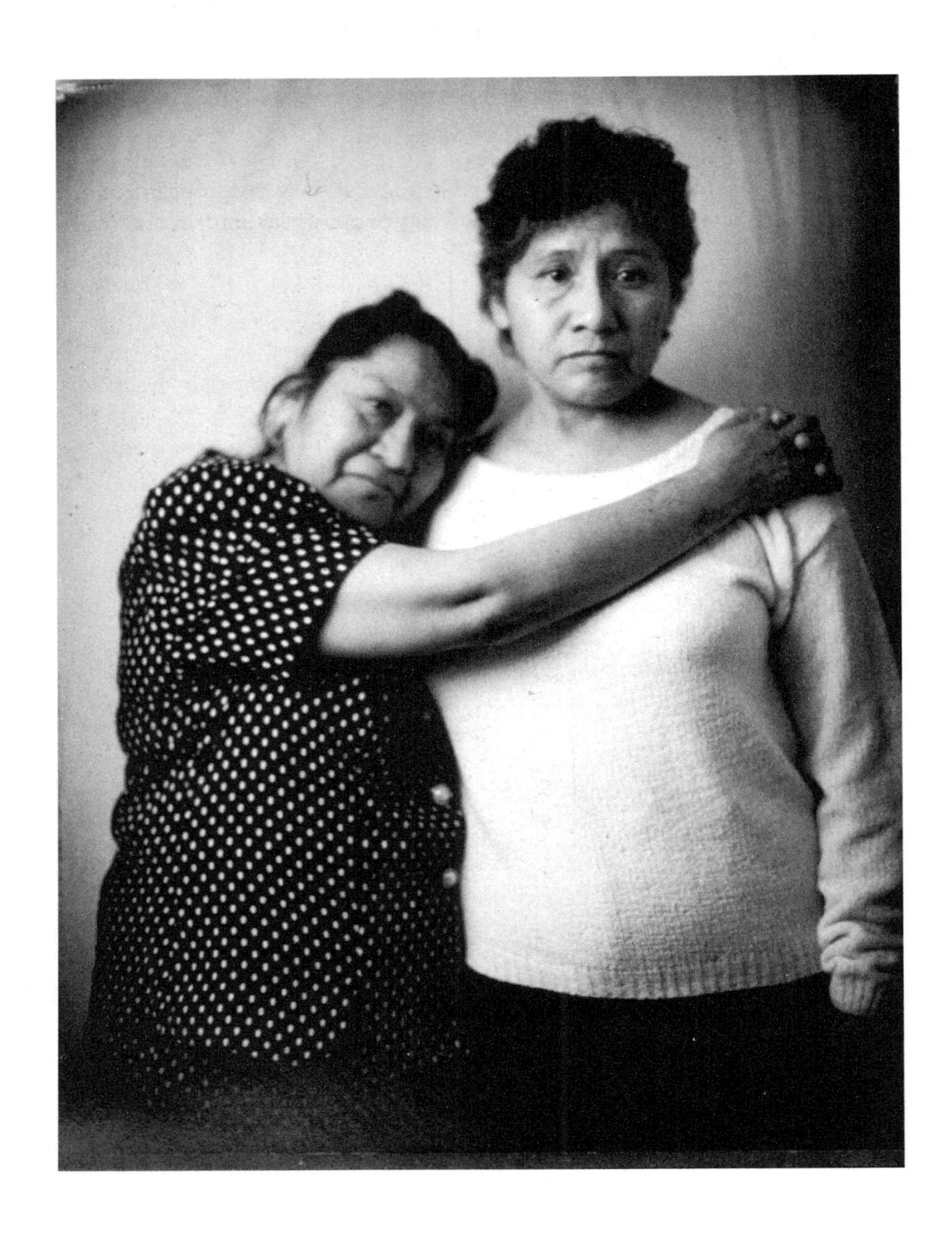

# 8
# RETHINKING CLASS COMPOSITION ANALYSIS IN LIGHT OF THE ZAPATISTAS

MONTY NEILL[1]

HOW CAN THE planetary working class stop the capitalist machine? As capital enters its sixth century of increasing world domination, this should be the central question. If those who work in the realms of theory and analysis are to make a useful contribution toward an answer, they must understand not merely capital, but more importantly, the nature and shape of the working class, in order to overcome capital and create new societies.

My contribution to answering this question has relied in part on a body of work which emerged primarily in Italy in the 1960s and '70s. A theory of "class composition" was a significant element of that work.[2] In this piece, I revisit this theory in order to criticize and extend it in light of my understanding of the Zapatistas, in particular, and in general of anti-capitalist struggles not directly or entirely derived from the European factory-based proletarian movements of the past two centuries.

To me, the Zapatistas represent not only a powerful moment against capital, but also a challenge to many of those who have not been able to understand the nature of their struggle. Ironically, among them are many who have intellectual roots in the same theories of class composition as I have.

A quick summary of class composition analysis as it emerged in Italy is as follows: the working class strategies of the twentieth century typically had at their core, as leading subject, a particular class sector. In the struggles of the post-WWI period, the "mass worker" of the industrial factory acted as the "vanguard" of the class.[3] These workers put capitalist planning into crisis by blocking an accumulation process that was largely based on their work. A class vanguard gathers the rest of the class around it as a focus of demands and struggles, because other social sectors, such as schools and medical care, are modeled on the factory. That is, the power of the industrial workers resides simultaneously in their strategic position in production and in their role as the model for general social reproduction.[4]

By the late 1960s, the class struggles against the various basic "deals" around the planet were simultaneously putting those deals into crisis and forming a cycle of struggles.[5] However, the roles played by the apparent vanguards were not what they appeared. For example, even within the Keynesian-Fordist "deals" and social-productive structures which dominated western Europe and the U.S., a focus on the mass factory workers ignores the struggles of black people against apartheid, and the struggles of women against the unpaid labor of reproducing the work force for capital and their subordination to men (Dalla Costa and James, 1975). The concept of a class vanguard is therefore problematic.

Vanguardism ignores the divisions within the class or attempts to overcome those divisions by asserting the primacy of some sectors. The conception of the vanguard is that these key sectors can impose a unity on other sectors of the class through a resistance to capital that promises to benefit the non-vanguard sectors. However, this unity papers over contradictions that actually prevent the unity from withstanding capital's counterattacks.[6]

Ignoring the multiple forms of working class power within the complexity of the division of labor induces an overestimation of the structural power of the apparent vanguard sector, not so much of its ability to provoke a crisis of capital, but more importantly of its ability to resolve the crisis in favor of the working class and of its capacity to initiate successfully a post-capitalist society. The capitalist division of labor fragments the class, producing within each sector a partiality that renders the sector inadequate as a basis for constructing a new society. Because capital modeled society on the factory (hence, the "social factory"; see note 2), this vanguardism proposes a unified post-capitalist society, but such a society may owe more to capitalism than to anti-capitalism, precisely because its model is the capitalist factory.

The Zapatista experience critiques vanguardism and provides a strategy to begin reconstructing society out of the fragments of the division of labor. It refuses the vanguardism not only of the party but also of any class sectors. It takes the position that everyone is a vanguard when they struggle against capital and for a new, non-exploitative society. It does not, in this coming together of oppositions, presume a homogenous post-capitalist society or "one" society.[7]

Class composition analysis developed in an effort to theoretically locate the potential or actual class vanguard. If we reject the conception of the vanguard, then why should we return to a discussion of class composition? If analysis and theory are to play a useful role in overcoming capitalism, theorists need to describe the dynamically changing class composition on a world scale as well as in its many particulars, looking for the material and social bases of anti-capitalism and post-capitalism; that is, they must conduct an analysis of class composition not in order to locate a new vanguard, but to help the many class sectors come together against capital. This assumes that a richer understanding and self-reflection will help the struggle.

My position is that there is one planetary working class, but it remains divided in the ways in which it is internally organized and also externally confronts capital. There is no single vanguard class sector; many sectors form their own vanguards where they are fighting capitalism. In any particular struggle, there may be a leading sector around which the struggle coalesces. Class composition remains a useful tool for analyzing situations and struggles, but it must be freed of its too-narrow beginnings.

### *Alquati on Class Composition*

Romano Alquati's *The Network of Struggles in Italy* (circa the late 1960s) will serve to focus this critique of class-composition analysis. He argued that working class struggles comprise a network, not just regionally or nationally, but even on the international level. A network is the unity of struggles in both their *vertical* and *horizontal* articulations. The vertical articulation locates the point within the capitalist circuit of production/reproduction at which the struggle occurs; the horizontal articulation describes the spatial distribution and linkages. This combined vertical-horizontal articulation of struggles pivots around decisive points of interconnection: *nodal points*.

Nodes, points of connection within the network, may be strategically hierarchized, including internationally. They will represent the points of advanced mass struggles. However, there is no simple (mechanical) correspondence on the vertical plane alone: that is, there is no direct equivalence between the level of capitalist production and the avant garde of mass struggles of the class.

For Alquati, the *political* composition of the class cannot be deduced from its *technical* composition (the kinds of work done with various kinds of technology in various specific productive relations). Rather, technical composition reflects previous political compositions (struggles and deals shaping the development of capitalism, locally and on a world scale); and political recomposition of the working class must both use and subvert the technical composition of capital, that is, move within and attack all the circuits of capital.

As with 1968, cycles of struggles transform the network of struggles, both vertically and horizontally, thereby recomposing the class (see also *Zerowork*, 1975). Thus, class *recomposition* is the dynamic development of the class through struggle in given or changing conditions of capitalist deployment of labor power. Recomposition is not a mechanical reflection of the current capitalist articulation of labor power. Even if the recomposition makes political use of the objective articulation (the value composition and productive structures of capital), the class' recomposition dynamically transcends the static and objective differences between the technological levels and the levels of exploitation of living labor within the working class, e.g., the ratio of workers in different branches of industry and agriculture. It transcends the hierarchies of capitalist work and wages embodied in the working class.

The network of struggles may be conceptualized as the dynamic process of *circulation* (communication) *of struggles*, in which struggles are homogenized within the broad zones of capitalist production of given types of labor power (e.g., European zone). The late '60s was a period of international recomposition, both vertically and horizontally, of the working class (c.f., *Zerowork*, 1975). That is, the working class politically recomposed itself through the process of struggle (see also, Caffentzis, this volume).

The factory workers working in the centers of power and command of international capital, Alquati argued, were the apex of the international struggle. At the lowest level were the mass struggles of the proletariat in zones still struggling to attain the introduction of specifically capitalist forms of production and accumulation. International nodes, points of the maximum accumulation of information concerning struggles, are generally the points of maximum massification and greatest direct combination of different moments of the anti-capitalist struggle. This generally occurs at the points of greatest physical concentration of different massified masses of labor-power, as in European or U.S. leading productive centers (now, we might conclude, expanded to other locales as well, such as South Korea). But of no less strategic importance to the working class is the utilization of the integration of the capitalist circuit, as the accumulation of information is very dense within the international network of the large international capitalist groups. At these points of massification will be found the propelling forces of working class struggles.

*Decomposition* of the working class occurs when capital defeats the working class and imposes its own recomposition (c.f., *Zerowork,* 1975). Technology is often central to this, as has been known since at least Marx (1967), but so are law, military/police action, and state economic policies such as wage policies or economic supports for the unwaged or low-waged. During successful capitalist offensives, capital turns struggles into modes of accumulation, decomposes working class organization or anti-capitalism, creates new technologies in its image, and expands its spheres of domination both geographically and socially.[8]

### *A Critique of Alquati*

We critique this decades-old piece from an important comrade in order to make a few points about class-composition analysis. First, the analysis must transcend the "workerism" from which it sprang, as in fact it has in understanding the capitalist productivity of "women's work" and in understanding the essential roles played in the accumulation process by the working class, (starting with women) in so-called "underdeveloped" areas (Dalla Costa and James, 1975; Caffentzis, 1990; Mies, Bennholdt-Thomsen & Werlhof, 1988). Still, class composition discussions often appear to be limited to the founding conceptualizations, and thus limited to their founding workerism.[9]

Second, the tie to capitalist technical composition — to workers in key industries, be they auto or computer or "service" — poses a complex problem. As Alquati says, such workers occupy pivotal places in major locales of capitalist production, and as such can wreak havoc on capitalist planning and accumulation. Yet, as he notes, there is no simple mechanical relationship between the technical composition of capital and the political power of the workers employed by capital of any given technical composition. As we know, workers working at the lowest levels of technical composition of capital have historically been among the most powerful protagonists of working-class struggle against capital.

Affirming the power of the Zapatistas, Holloway (1998b) asks, "Anyway, which does more 'damage to capital' — a prolonged strike by industrial workers or a rebellion in the jungles of Mexico which stirs up again the idea of revolution and the dream of a different type of society?" In short, we do not agree with Alquati's concept, clearly still held by many descendants of Italian autonomist theorists (e.g., Wildcat, 1997), that the lowest level of anti-capitalist struggle is found in the zones struggling to obtain specifically capitalist forms of production. Alquati's formulation is faulty both as to the level of power found in such relatively less-capitalistically-organized spaces and as to whether the struggles in those spaces must lead to capitalist development — even in order to gain power against capital. This simultaneously critiques a conception of capitalist accumulation and a conception of class struggle.

Third, Alquati's piece seems to focus on the vertical articulation and gives less attention to the horizontal. By "spatial distribution and linkages," it would appear he means such things as connections across sectors of production or across nations or continents. Thus, for example, a struggle gains power as either or both kinds of connections are strengthened, forming the horizontal axis of networks of struggle.

Fourth, even taken together, the vertical and horizontal articulations do not allow a sufficient understanding of the powerful "social sector" struggles that emerged in the 1960s and '70s: the struggles of women, people of color, immigrants, and the national-liberation struggles of the "Third World." These struggles, for Alquati (at least in the late 1960s) as for many others to this day, would appear to come from outside of working-class struggles.

For us, however, the working class includes diverse and complexly interacting sectors. "Social struggles" are in the main working class struggles, but as happens with unions and political parties of the industrial working class as well, they often are also struggles for arranging a deal within capital and thus often take an accommodationist, even capitalist form. (Just to note, women, people of color, etc., are often involved powerfully in struggles at their paid workplaces as well as in the "social" spheres.)

In terms of the goals of struggle, a class composition analysis that does not take account of social struggles is an analysis of clearly limited usefulness for a class that reorganizes not only its relationships to work but all its social relationships. In terms of a more empirical assessment of class power and struggles, the vertical and horizontal articulations of the working class as defined by Alquati cannot sufficiently capture the potential power of the class either against capital or for itself. Even while it negates the Leninist separation of politics from economics, Alquati's formulation continues to separate and to one-sidedly prize the "economic" over the "social," implicitly perpetuating the mechanistic "base" — "superstructure" concept Marx (1970) briefly propagated with historically unfortunate results.[10]

Let me be clear: I do not argue that the "factory" and the "mass worker" are not relevant. I argue that to see other struggles solely through the prism of the factory and the factory struggles is to fail to see the power of these other struggles, which are not just adjuncts to the factory. The factory is fundamental to capital, not only as a locale for intense extraction of surplus value, but also as a model for other structures and institutions of capital: the school, the office, the prison, in some ways even the family (though the patriarchal family is itself a model for some manifestations of the capitalist factory). Thus, not only do struggles in the factory attack often-critical points of accumulation, understanding the struggle against the factory in the factory is one basic element for understanding struggles against the factory in the school, office and home.[11]

The problem is seeing the factory as the only fundamental node of capitalist accumulation and of anti-capitalism. Women's struggles have revealed the home and the sphere of reproduction to be also fundamental to capitalist accumulation. A multiplicity of struggles over decades has revealed how powerful are struggles in what has variously been labeled the "periphery" or the "Third World" — and how central to capital is this "periphery." In both cases, the organization of exploitation and the resistance to it cannot be understood in terms of or reduced to the factory model. Put in other terms, the factory in its various manifestations is essential and indispensable to understanding capital and the struggle against capital, but it is not the only thing that is essential and indispensable. Thus, those who seek anti-capitalist revolution must not wear blinkers that hinder their seeing how capitalism functions on a planetary level and how revolution against capital emerges in different forms and places.

### *Learning from the Zapatistas*

There is no purity in the Zapatistas' methods, and thus methodological purists are appalled. They appear as a mix of social democracy, Leninism, anarchism, Central American and Mexican revolutionary traditions (including some nationalism), what remains of indigenous communalism centuries after the Spanish conquest (and before that the Mayan states), and the long history of Mayan struggles against Mexico and against world capitalism. Just as capital uses all its history in reorganizing its structures to keep the working class divided, off balance and "decomposed," the EZLN method proposes an evolving mix to bring the class together in progressively higher levels of struggle against capital.

It would be a mistake, however, to suppose that there are no principles behind the methodological mix. The EZLN has asserted foremost a radical participatory democracy.[12] Thus, when an agreement was negotiated with the Mexican state in 1994, the agreement was submitted to the Zapatista communities for ratification and was rejected. It may be that the EZLN itself pushed for rejection of the deal it negotiated, but even so it seems clear that there was a widespread consultation. The EZLN has said it was not a decision of the military leadership to launch the January 1, 1994, assault, but a decision of the people. (Having seen Zapatista villages in Chiapas, it is readily clear that anyone who wishes to rejoin the state-PRI side can easily do so, and will likely be well-paid, albeit only briefly, for doing so.)

The meaning of this democracy shows up in several ways. First, the EZLN has chosen not to become a political party to contest for state power by elections or to proclaim themselves a vanguard looking to seize the state. While they have created alliances with political parties, particularly with the social democratic PRD, it is probably most useful to understand these alliances in the context of attempting to construct a strategy that simultaneously increases the likelihood of survival of the EZLN, and more importantly the people and communities, and hastens the unity of 'civil society' against neoliberalism. (See Esteva, 1999 for a discussion of "civil society" in the Mexican context, which is not the same use of the term as emerged in Eastern Europe or the U.S.)

The radical democratic solution can be seen also in the words of a letter from Marcos to the EPR, the People's Revolutionary Army, a guerrilla group which has a focoist conception of sparking revolution through its own military action. Said Marcos, "What we seek, what we need, is that all those people without a party and organization make agreements about what they want and do not want in order to become organized to achieve it (preferably through civil and peaceful means), not to take power, but to exercise it." Whether, as Marcos has put it, Mexican "civil society" can in fact initiate the revolution which leads to the revolution, as the Zapatistas hope and struggle to create, remains to be seen, but it is a pluralistic, diverse and democratic approach to revolution.[13]

The Zapatistas do have a strategy of revolution: that different sectors will reach agreements and act on them, initiating a chain of events which proceeds through the collapse of the hegemony of the PRI, the ruling party, which is the "revolution to initiate the revolution," and thence on to the construction of a new society. It also seems clear that the EZLN does not yet know how to do this, they too are learning as they walk, but Zapatistas know that the old methods have failed and that new ones must be developed.[14]

We read Marcos as saying that contrary to the long-established conception of the goal of the left as seizing state power in order to build "socialism" (and ultimately communism), the EZLN is proposing that people organize themselves to exercise power, that is, to live "socialism/communism" at least in political terms and, in time, economically. In doing so, we can conceive the "withering away" of the state as a process of class struggle through the self-organization of the working class, including the overcoming of its internal contradictions (such as wage hierarchy, race, and gender). It is, perhaps, that "civil society" can withdraw from the state, leaving a useless shell which will collapse. Here it is worth recalling that this conception of civil society emerged after the Mexico City earthquake when "society" took care of itself because the state was simply an impediment to rebuilding (see Midnight Notes, 1988 and Esteva 1999). Rather than the free association of the producers being an end state, it is a current political activity of the working class against capital. The famous ends and means dichotomy is overcome because the means are the ends. "From the people [through the party] to the people," the Maoist line, ceases to have an intermediary party that is actually the state in embryo.

In a sense then, the fusion of Mexican Marxism and indigenous communism leads to a proposal to move directly to post-capitalist communism. This idea has been proposed before, for example by Amilcar Cabral (1969), who found that the most resolute anti-colonialist groups in Guinea-Bissau were those whose social structures and relations were the most communist and had the least hierarchy and lacked a state or state-in-embryo. The idea of an African road to socialism that built on communal land ownership and indigenous pre-capitalist social organizations was widely discussed in the 1960s and '70s. The sway of state socialism, however, was then too dominant for this road to be widely pursued in practice; now capital is working extremely hard to eliminate the possibility of Africans turning to that previously missed road.

The question of Mayan "original communism" has begun to spark debate about the extent of such communism and its meaning. Anti-colonial and anti-capitalist struggles in Chiapas and among indigenous people in Mexico have a history of half a millennium. These struggles cannot be reduced to the categories derived from the struggles of the European working class, including those that have developed further in Africa, Asia and Latin America. From outside, we can note the incorporation of that history, its categories and language, in the words of Marcos and the Zapatista commandantes. But to those outside, this history is mostly unwritten and substantially invisible, though this is beginning to change (c.f., Burgos-Debray, 1984; *Abya Yala News*). Bringing together two substantially distinct histories of anti-capitalism opens ground for new theory and practice, making the potential struggle richer, but simultaneously posing new problems and complexities.

After the fall of the Paris Commune, Marx turned his attention to a variety of issues concerning pre-capitalist social structures, including issues of gender. His writings on these themes were collected as *The Ethnographic Notebooks* (Rosemont, n.d.; Shanin, 1983). Our point here is that Marx was considering ideas that appear to contradict the "Marxist" postulate according to which capitalism is "progressive," that people around the world will have to undergo proletarianization in order to subsequently overcome capitalism, and that the working class created by capitalism is the sole source of positive anti-capitalism. He was exploring other means of understanding and attacking capitalism, thus undermining his own Eurocentrism.

This discussion poses a clear challenge to "workerism," including the original class composition analysis, which in its own way appears to reproduce the Stalinist "stages of history" argument, as it assumes in effect that capitalism is the *necessary* precursor to communism (under Stalinism, of course, "socialism" as the development of the productive forces prepares for communism). This line of thinking connects to Marx, who argued that freedom necessarily requires the productive capacity to free humans from onerous and time-consuming manual labor, and that such productive capacity necessarily must exist in order for communism to be established. It is precisely this conception that Marx himself began to challenge and which comes again to us at the end of the twentieth century from a variety of struggles, including quite prominently that of the Zapatistas.

In its critique of Holloway, Wildcat (1997) cites Marx's (1959) famous discussion of the "realm of freedom," which "begins only where labour which is determined by necessity and mundane considerations ceases, thus in the very nature of things it lies beyond the sphere of actual material production... Freedom in this field can only consist in socialized man, the associated producers, rationally regulating their interchange with Nature, bringing it under their common control." By now, this conversation should be informed powerfully by the ecological and indigenous movements' challenge to "bringing nature under control." Some feminisms also challenge this version of the reduction of "work" as it ignores the reproduction of humans and implies (at the least) that people cannot find freedom in this realm of human activity. I suggest a rethinking that looks both at freedom beyond onerous labor and at freedom in recognizing necessity (reproduction and nature) and changing one's relations with other humans and with nature.

If the direct leap from pre-capitalist communism to post-capitalist communism may not be possible for most of humanity, living in conditions far removed from the presence of indigenous people's original communism, it is still true that more than half of humanity lives quite directly on the land or has access to the land — mostly in Africa, Asia and Latin America, but also substantially even in Russia and other former Soviet states. If one is to think of different roads to communism, many such roads must start from the land (Mies & Shiva, 1993; Esteva, "Indigenous Autonomy," this volume).

The issue of the form or extent of pre-capitalist communism is, unlike for the EZLN, a far less immediately practical issue for those of us living in urbanized metropoli — we *apparently* have no such social relations which could be a source of anti-capitalist power and of developing communism. But it would be a mistake to view the issues posed as therefore not relevant.

### *The Nature of Anti-capitalism*

We might envision capital as a power grid overlaid on a vast nebula, with the working class as that nebula.[15] Workers are captured by and in some ways defined by the grid, the multifold structures and processes of accumulation. That is the sphere of exploitation. However, the nebula is life: capital must draw on it and cannot survive without it, but the workers have life and can survive without the grid. This is the sphere of everyday life, however corrupted and influenced by capital which seeks to control it and tap its energy and creativity. But no matter how controlling, capital cannot *be* everyday life, which thus remains a great reservoir of energy against capital. This is in some ways more visible when, as with the Zapatistas, everyday life incorporates social structures and relations that pre-date capital and have visible anti-capitalist potential. But such potential is everywhere — though being everywhere is no guarantee it will be mobilized against capital.

Let me put this just a bit more formally (c.f., Caffentzis, 1997). Capital creates identity via work and commodities. Wage workers sell their labor power and purchase consumer products, thereby creating identities as workers and consumers. Refusal and resistance move in all these circuits. It is only because workers can resist and refuse that they have the ability to negotiate to sell their labor power. If they have no autonomous space, if they are fully capital, they cannot negotiate and therefore cannot sell their labor power.

This is another way of saying that capital depends on the life energy of the working class — but that life energy cannot be reduced to capital nor be fully possessed by capital.[16] As capital attempts to control all aspects of life, the logical end of capitalist success would be a pure machine — as science fiction writers often suggest — including a bio-engineered machine assembled largely out of human genes.

It is the space outside of capital, the space of human life not defined by capital even if substantially controlled by capital, that is the fundamental source of power against capital as well as the basic source of capital itself. That is, working class struggles necessarily come also from outside the working class' existence as actual or latent labor power and move not only within the circuits of capital but also extend or create spaces outside of capitalist circuits.

This point increasingly is being explored. On the one side, the analysis of the creation of the capitalist body and mind has long been developed. Arguably, this capitalist tendency to control, define and produce the human body has intensified over the centuries, and the computer is being used to intensify it still further (c.f., Midnight Notes, 1982; Neill, 1995), as is biotechnology. In this, the human is fragmented, decomposed, constructed as labor power, and denied humanity.

John Holloway (1998a) suggests that the fundamental contribution of the Zapatistas is to recompose the human through the assertion of "dignity." They claim that revolution starts not from capitalism, but from "dignity." He also insists on the emphasis of revolution as process, not product, arguing that "communism is not something we move towards, but something that we struggle to invent... The struggle, as [the Zapatistas] put it, is the struggle to convert 'dignity and rebellion into freedom and dignity': dignity is the means, dignity the end, there is no distinction" (internet communication, Feb. 2, 1997).

Laura Fiocco, in a similar vein, says that democratic behavior becomes communist when its central purpose is to "produce the collective subject (where we can feel the power and love of being together). If we start from here, to enlarge the field of solidarity means to enlarge the collective subject. But this process is not just a quantitative enlargement, it is a relocation of the field of struggle to a higher level. The new subject — constituted in this process — produces its own goals which *can't* be thought before its constitution" (internet communication, Jan. 29, 1997).

These arguments do run the risk of discarding entirely an understanding of structures. One can analyze structures and recognize that the structures of social relations must be revolutionized without being a "structuralist," and I suggest it is inadequate to only consider fluid subjectivities developing their being collectively. The abandonment of considering social structures (which I see in Holloway, 1998a) also runs the risk of not thinking about such things as relations of production or ownership, that is, of class as materially constituted: everything becomes collapsed into "dignity." (In this, the critique of Holloway by Wildcat, 1997, has some cogency.) Clearly, however, exploring these aspects continues to be correct in response to "structure-only" variants of Marxism, as well as to the "workerist" variants.

I suggest that while the communist movement must create its future through its struggles, including the creation of new social structures, it is also true that glimmerings and ideas of the future, of what is desirable and could be made, continuously infuse struggles and provide some sense of a goal. If life is anti-capitalist (if only because capital must seek to control and confine life, and thus to immiserate and alienate it and very potentially to exterminate it, in order to ensure accumulation), then social struggles asserting life have anti-capitalist energy, aspects and possibilities. (As always, however, capital seeks to channel the energy into its productivity. Thus, for example, the struggle against housework as the production and reproduction of labor power can become work in restaurants and day care centers precisely to (re)produce labor power while undermining the power of the refusal of housework.)

In sum, since the class struggle to cease to be proletarian necessarily and fundamentally rests on resistance to capital, which imposed proletarianization on humans, the analytical framework developed by Alquati and his comrades is valuable because it helps us understand some very important aspects of the struggle. But it needs both correction and radical expansion, and the two are related: Correction in understanding better the planetary composition of capitalist accumulation and thus of the working class as a whole (i.e., not limited to the "factory"); and expansion, to understand the capitalist machine as a vampiric and parasitic structure growing out of life, but not itself living, while the working class has life based on its being outside of work as well as being "living labor," and that this life and its growth, not only in its immediate resistance to capitalist particulars, is the basis of revolution.

### *Building Post-capitalist Society within Capitalism*

The working class cannot beat capital only with resistance and opposition. One should keep in mind Marx' observation that the new society emerges from the womb of the old and try to protect and hasten the development of the embryo — though we should not assume a single world society.

Elements of post-capitalism exist in many places. Most will be isolated or absorbed, sometimes crushed, but mostly used as fuel for accumulation. This does not mean we should simply dismiss them: their limitations speak to the limitations of the overall class struggle, which needs to incorporate and build on these struggles.

Struggles reveal not only opposition to capital and weaknesses of capital, but elements of post-capitalism. As is well-known, strikes and other working class battles often reveal much of possible post-capitalist relations, revealed through solidarity, the joys of having time away from work, and new relations among women and men, workplace and community (c.f., Riker, 1990). Yet having been thrown up so quickly, albeit necessarily rooted in various actual experiences of the class preceding the moments of struggle, they seem ephemeral. Rather than being based on regular daily life, they demand exceptional moments to survive; thus, unless the exceptional moment lasts and becomes daily life, the social relations of post-capitalism that are based on those moments are soon submerged in the reassertion of capitalist existence.

An alternate strategy to expecting the working class to throw up its post-capitalist possibilities in the heat of anti-capitalist battle is the rather deliberate constructing of alternative institutions or relationships within the larger current society, sometimes in the hope of living outside of capital, sometimes in the hope of creating better social arrangements within capital. The materialist critique of such efforts is usually that they are "utopian," rooted in the desires of a limited class sector and not generalizable; that is, not having an adequate material basis or not adequately reflecting needs and desires of enough of the class. Many efforts quickly cease to be anti-capitalist and become simply small deals within capital or spurs to new schemes of capitalist development — as anti-capitalism, they too are ephemeral.

If struggles against capital are in themselves insufficient for creating something new, attempting to create the new while ignoring the world capitalist system will merely produce new commodities or pools of labor for capital. That is, the working class must simultaneously attack capital and create its own society/societies. (P. M., 1985, coined the term "substruction" to indicate the need to simultaneously subvert the old and construct the new.)

Within the strategies of wage-based anti-capitalism of the 1960s and 70s, there was an understanding that gaining a sufficient wage enabled not only an expanded resistance to waged work, but also the possibility of constructing different social relations within the time and space provided by this wage (Neill, *et al.*, 1997). Thus, for example, from wages for housework to wages *against* housework, in which it was understood that a further development of struggle presumed the development of social relations among women that could occur within the relatively liberated time and space of the higher wage (Federici, 1975). This is analogous to the idea of the liberated zone in which new social relationships can develop (c.f., Hinton, 1966). The Zapatistas also argue for such zones, the Zapatista communities, in which new relations are being developed, relations which can form the basis for further struggle against capital and a further deepening and widening of the new society.

### *Towards the New Commons*

This critique of class composition analysis is directed at what it leaves out, not at what it includes — though as a result, what is included becomes problematic for *how* it is included.[17] In effect, it argues there is but one road to revolution, and it lies through capitalist development. Thus, intentionally or nor, it argues that capital is progressive. Others now argue that capital not only is not progressive, it is the destruction of humanity.

Those who seek the end of capitalism seem now to face some polarities. First, revolution emerging from the ongoing struggles of workers, especially in factories, creating new social relations in and through their struggles; or revolution consciously and deliberately created as new social and productive relations built to be outside of capitalism. Second, revolution as seizing and using the means of production, which implies capitalism as the precondition of communism; revolution as a negation of most of those means of production as necessarily destructive to human and other life, which implies capitalism as an historical dead end that cannot presage communism because of how it conditions human relations and relations with nature. Can the working class resolve these polarities, overcome them into a new synthesis — suggesting they are inter-penetrating, intertwined aspects of a complex common and uncommon shared existence as a working class on a planet with finite material resources?

To the second: It seems increasingly clear not only that capitalist development cannot sustain human life and even endangers our species existence, but also that the eradication of capitalism cannot be based on a more rational use of the existing means of production or even minor adjustments of the productive apparatus, as has been claimed in most variants of Marxism. The role of technology and the use of energy resources, for example, must be re-thought in light of the growing knowledge of their impact on the planet's ecology (c.f., Sarkar, 1999). But that is beyond the scope of this piece. Here, we focus on the first of the polarities.

Capital cannot be defeated without both opposition and creation. Both can take many forms, depending on the particular circumstances in which people find themselves. For example, if there are places where it is more likely that people are able to use their control over land to create non-capitalist social spaces, that strength inevitably limits capitalism and increases the likelihood of a profits squeeze, pushing capital to exploit more intensely those whom it can control. Clearly, as the case of Africa shows, capital is not eager to allow any sizeable spaces to escape control, and thus will always mobilize to prevent such escapes. This scenario suggests traditional "support movement" activity in, for example, the U.S. and western Europe, although it should not be sneezed at, is inadequate and inevitably fails to see the commonality of both problem and solution. To see different possibilities and particularities in struggle, to grasp the complex diversity of the class in its composition and political recomposition is not to treat different particularities as being inside or outside of the class struggle against capital.

The EZLN enables a revisiting of history. As capital now uses all its history to continuously "decompose" the working class, so the visible experience of the EZLN demonstrates that we need to reconsider the history of struggles around the planet over a long time span. The EZLN looks in part to the pre-capitalist communalism of the indigenous people — but not that alone. In fact, the composition of the EZLN communities is quite complex, involving not only indigenous people who have few experiences beyond their communities, but indigenous workers who work on large farms, or building dams, in rural and urban areas. Thus, the mixing of the traditions of struggle includes not only the Mexican Marxists from Mexico City who moved to Chiapas in the 1980s and the rural indigenous anti-capitalism of half a millennium, but also the experiences with more modern local capitalism. As Collier (1994) shows, the participants in the EZLN are often themselves relatively recent migrants within Chiapas (see also King and Villanueva, 1998; and Lorenzano, 1998).

The point is not to duplicate what the Zapatistas have done (which anyway cannot be done) or to select one historical strategy and argue for it, but to learn to create new proletarian combinations. While not all sectors of the world's working class look directly to a living continuation of the social structures of original communism, all sectors can find their non-capitalist spaces and build further on them.

The essence of capitalism is creating a working class (the accumulation of living labor), producing workers and social relations conducive to work for capital. The struggle against work is clearly a struggle against surplus value as the alienated product of exploited labor used to support the expansion of capitalist social relations. It is also a struggle against the unnecessary expenditure of human labor in the production of use-values, against the production of use-values that are of use only within the social construct of capital. It is also about the reorganization of time so that "work" is not reduced to inhuman efficiency but is defined by human needs. And it is about changing the relations and values that dominate society. Thus, the fundamental questions of the economy are social and political, not "economic." This is true both within capitalism and after capitalism, as the working class creates multiple new commons fitting varying circumstances and desires.

Capital has from its start sought to enclose all commons. From colonization to slavery, from factory work to housework, from any activity to the deepest thoughts and feelings, the history of capital is its extension into the human commons. In fighting what has been called the "new enclosures" (Midnight Notes, 1990), the working class is not seeking only to defend what human commons remains from the past or what commons workers' struggles created under variants of twentieth-century "socialism," but also to reassert, redefine, and extend the commons, to create a multiplicity of mutually supportive new commons (see Midnight Notes, 1997).

Under capital, work, be it waged in the factory or office, unwaged in home or school or prison, indirectly waged in small farming and selling, is the antithesis of the commons, however much capital fosters cooperation to spur production. Human relations remain within and outside these circuits, but capital deforms and channels them.

From these observations, I can draw several conclusions. First, the struggle against capital and for humanity exists in all social relations and circuits. Thus a strategy must consider the relationships among all the circuits and how to strengthen them against capital. Second, since the essence of capital is the creation of work, the struggle against work must be understood as central. This struggle is centuries, even millennia old. It predates capital and continues throughout capitalism. The defeat of working class strategies that sought to overcome the socialist deals of the twentieth century through the struggle against work does not signal the end of the struggle against work. Rather, it signals that the working class must rethink itself and recreate itself through struggles. (This means, as discussed above, clear thinking about "work" and what should be meant by that term, both as social relations and as material/immaterial production.) The struggle against work, and thus against all forms of exploitative hierarchies within the class, circulates through all the circuits of life in and outside of capital, resisting capital and creating new social forms within capital. It is the struggle for the commons.

A new working class strategy will develop through multiple aspects of struggle and practice. If theory is to be an element of struggle, it must live in the interplay between analyzing struggles and analyzing capital. We are arguing for a deliberate impurity of method in theory and practice, for simultaneous analyses postulating either no vanguard or multiple vanguards, for listening to the particulars of struggles to hear both the anti-capitalism and the post-capitalism (commons-ism or communism) that might exist, for pushing to make all kinds of new circuits of struggle.

To move ahead, I suggest some basic work. I recognize some of it is now being done, perhaps much of it, as networks of communication slowly develop.

1. Exchanging knowledge (not just "information") about how new class political recompositions are emerging or trying to emerge in particular struggles.

2. Proposing strategies as to how such emerging recompositions can deepen or can interact with other class forces in mutually reinforcing ways. This involves listening to and watching the struggles, but also participating in them.

3. Analyzing how such recompositions or suggested strategies might level existing class hierarchies or capitalist relations within the working class, keeping in mind the limitations we necessarily have as products of a capitalist world division of labor.

4. Using the analysis of capital's strategies and development to learn to avoid capitalist traps.

5. Strengthening an analysis of capital that actually helps identify capital's weaknesses and how best to resist capitalism.

6. Analyzing anti-capitalist struggles from ecological and feminist perspectives.

7. Identifying forms of immediate political organization that do not reproduce the capitalist division of labor. Since it seems highly evident that no one person can keep up even in a cursory manner with all the aspects of struggle, sharing that work though political organizations is necessary, as is developing supportive and cooperative relations among many organizations.

8. Translating as well as developing a new political language, so we can communicate more clearly.

This work does not create struggles or bring class sectors into mutual support. However, there is a use for a revised and expanded class-composition analysis for people engaged in struggle.

This work needs to be done in light of the Zapatistas. To me, this means a few essential things. The EZLN has brought to light, or created, new things about the world struggle against capitalism. To do the same in other places requires patience and humility. Anti-capitalist activists cannot easily come to conclusions; the world situation is too complex, with too many new factors; we must not quickly dismiss that which may have an appearance that does not fit a preconception of what is "revolutionary." Those of us in the U.S. and Europe (and perhaps elsewhere) must be wary of the "Eurocentrism" of reducing all struggles to the models derived from the struggles of the European working class.

Class composition suggests that the working class composes itself, makes itself and transcends itself, through struggle. We conclude that the Zapatistas, with whatever limitations and however uncertain their own immediate future, have furthered our hope that this process is in the making; they have given us some wisdom and have sparked new energy and creativity. We thus have a better possibility of navigating across and out of the desert of capitalism and into the time and space of the new commons.

## Notes

1 This article is revised from Part V of *Towards a New Commons*, by Monty Neill with George Caffentzis and Johnny Machete (1997), prepared for the second Intercontinental Encuentro against Neoliberalism and for Humanity, 1997. The entire original is posted on the Midnight Notes website: http://www.midnightnotes.org. Part I introduces the Zapatistas. Part II outlines a conception of working class strategies and "deals" of the second half of the twentieth century. Part III reflects on the Zapatista's strategies (some of which is incorporated into this piece). Part IV touches on three issues raised by the Zapatista struggle and the first Intercontinental Encuentro: localism, homogeneity, and networks.

2 C.f., Baldi, 1972; Tronti, 1972; Bologna, 1972; *Zerowork*, 1975; Semiotext(e), 1980, for some of the key shorter works available in English.

3 "Vanguard" here indicates who, within the working class, is most effective against the capitalists. It does not equate to "vanguard party," nor to "class consciousness." The vanguard is not simply the undifferentiated mass worker, but is analyzed as a sector within the mass worker, as I show in the discussion of Alquati, below. In searching analytically for the vanguard, one is also looking for the core revolutionary subject.

4 See note 2.

5 On class "deals," struggles putting capital into crisis, and cycles of struggles, c.f., Midnight Notes (1992), Neill, *et al.* (1997), *Zerowork* (1975), p.m. (1985).

6 See Neill, *et al.* (1997), part II, "Strategies and Deals."

7 See Esteva, "An Encounter of Discovery," in this volume. This social-cultural plurality was also proposed by p.m. (1985, 1995).

8 Caffentzis (this volume) describes the "decomposition" of the U.S. working class under capital's response to the working-class offensives initiated in the '60s. For an example specific to the shipping industry, see Carlsson (1998).

9 In their critique of Holloway's (1998a) then-in-draft chapter, "Dignity's Revolt," Wildcat (1997) refers to the importance of Alquati in particular for informing their thinking. Wildcat does not overcome the limitations of workerism.

10 We might, however, think of the horizontal articulation as including the "space" of race, gender, etc.; c.f., Midnight Notes Collective (1981). Or, we might conceptualize three, not two dimensions, with the 'social' struggles as a third articulation interacting with the horizontal and the vertical. But we think both these approaches will not adequately describe class composition. Alquati's vertical and horizontal articulations must be relocated within a different conceptualization of the structure of capital and of class struggle.

11 Here we include the computerized factory and social factory as falling within the trajectory of the factory in capitalism, though with many particular differences. This altered factory relationship is in turn becoming a model for schools and other social areas.

12 In addition to Zapatista documents (1994), see Esteva (1999) and Holloway and Pelaez, eds. (1998).

13 A reminder: the EZLN has not proposed themselves even as a model for Mexico, never mind the rest of the world. In the first Encuentro they called and hosted in Chiapas, they did not tell the participants what to do. Indeed, the Zapatistas only rarely participated in the actual discussions. Rather, they provided a space for dialogue and thought (see Neill, "Encounters," this issue). They sent, therefore, a message: think for yourselves, but let us also work together. The value of studying the Zapatista struggle is not to construct a "Zapatology," but to enable us to understand how they have developed a revolutionary project.

14 From conversations in Mexico, it has become clear that there are criticisms of how the Zapatistas have realized this conception of revolution. It has been argued that they have allied too strongly with some sectors rather than others, especially the urban barrios and working poor. Even if accurate, this may be more a matter of the circumstances in which they find themselves than a matter of Zapatista preference. In any event, the critique itself operates within the concept of revolution proposed by the Zapatistas, and there seems to be little doubt concerning the enormous support

for and authority of the Zapatistas within these urban sectors.

15 On the cover to *Computer State Notes* (*Midnight Notes* #5, 1982), we portrayed such a grid over a nebula.

16 In *Towards the New Commons*, part IV (Neill, *et al.*, 1997), we note that capital must have access to diversity, but must reduce that diversity to a usable homogeneity to control it, while maintaining the diversity in a capitalist, hierarchical form in order to have productive energy (as discussed in Caffentzis, 1990). Workers, however, must develop a homogeneity with respect to capital that denies capital access to the energy found in difference (a unity of resistance), all the while recognizing diversity toward each other, much as biological diversity is a requisite for a healthy environment. Sarkar (1999), however, argues against this biological diversity metaphor.

17 Alquati's piece is in fact titled *The Network of Struggles in **Italy*** (emphasis added). We have critiqued his work because his analysis of capital and class leads it toward a flawed perspective of struggles that are not occurring within the vanguard sphere as he conceives it. Nonetheless, it is potentially valuable to analyze the composition of the class involved in specific struggles — the dockers of Liverpool, teachers in Detroit, factory workers in Korea, the Zapatistas, etc., in order to better learn from those struggles and to support them. That is, our critique of Alquati is not that he helped develop a class-composition analysis to further particular kinds of struggles, but that he understood and located those struggles in a way that helped to perpetuate a narrow workerism.

## Bibliography

*Abya Yala News*. Journal of the South and Meso American Indian Rights Center. (1994). Oakland, CA. Vol. 8, Nos. 1 & 2

Alquati, Romano. (n.d., late 1960s). *The Network of Struggles in Italy*. Typescript in English of notes summarizing the piece (unknown note-taker). Much of the stating of Alquati's position is taken verbatim from these notes.

Baldi, Guido. (1972, May–June). "Theses on Mass Worker and Social Capital." *Radical America*, (6) 1, 3–21.

Bologna, Sergio. (1972, Fall). "Class Composition and the Theory of the Party." In *Telos*, #13.

Burgos-Debray, Elisabeth. (1984). *I, Rigoberta Menchu*. London, Verso.

Cabral, Amilcar. (1969). *Revolution in Guinea: Selected Texts*. New York: Monthly Review Press.

Caffentzis, George. (1997). "Why Machines Cannot Create Value: Marx's Theory of Machines." In Davis, Jim; Herschel, Thomas; & Stack, Michael (Eds.), *Cutting Edge: Technology, Information Capitalism and Social Revolution*. London: Verso.

Caffentzis, George. (1990). "On Africa and Self-Reproducing Automata." In *Midnight Notes* # 10 (1990).

Carlsson, Chris. (1998). "The Progress Club: 1934 and Class Memory." In James Brook, Chris Carlsson, and Nancy J. Peters, *Reclaiming San Francisco: History, Politics, Culture*. San Francisco: City Lights.

Collier, George. (1994). *Basta! Land and the Zapatista Rebellion in Chiapas*. Oakland. Institute for Food and Development Policy.

Dalla Costa, Mariarosa, and Dalla Costa, Giovanna F., editors (1995). *Paying the Price: Women and the Politics of International Economic Strategy*. London: Zed Books.

Dalla Costa, Mariarosa, and Dalla Costa, Giovanna F., editors (1999). *Women, Development and Labor of Reproduction: Struggles and Movements*. Trenton, New Jersey: Africa World Press.

Dalla Costa, Mariarosa, and Selma James. (1975, 1972). *The Power of Women and the Subversion of the Community*. Bristol: Falling Wall Press.

Esteva, Gustavo. (1999). "The Zapatistas and People's Power." *Capital & Class*, 68, Summer, pp.153–182.

Federici, Silvia. (1975). *Wages Against Housework*. Bristol: Falling Wall Press.

Federici, Silvia. (1999). "Reproduction and Feminist Struggle in the New International Division of Labor," in Dalla Costa, Mariarosa, and Dalla Costa, Giovanna F., editors (1999).

Hinton, William. (1966). *Fanshen*. New York: Vintage.

Holloway, John.(1998a). "Dignity's Revolt." In Holloway and Pelaez (eds.).

Holloway, John. (1998b). "Open Reply to an Open Letter." *Wildcat-Zircular*, No. 45, June. English translation in *Common Sense* 24, 1999.

Holloway, John, and Pelaez, Eloina, eds. (1998). *Zapatista! Reinventing Revolution in Mexico*. London: Pluto Press.

James, Selma. (1975). "Wageless of the World." In Wendy Edmond and Suzie Fleming, eds., *All Work and No Pay*. Bristol: Falling Wall.

King and Villanueva. (1998). In Holloway & Pelaez.

Lorenzano. (1998). In Holloway & Pelaez.

Marx, Karl. (1970). *A Contribution to the Critique of Political Economy*. New York: International Publishers.

Marx, Karl. (1967). *Capital*, Vol. I (esp. Ch. 27, p. 530). New York: International Publishers.

Marx, Karl. (1959). *Capital*, Vol. III. London: Lawrence and Wishart, p. 820, cited in Wildcat, 1997.

Midnight Notes. (1997). *One No, Many Yeses*. (*Midnight Notes* #12.)

Midnight Notes (1992). *Midnight Oil: Work, Energy, War, 1973–1992*. Brooklyn: Autonomedia (*Midnight Notes* #11).

Midnight Notes. (1990). *The New Enclosures*. (*Midnight Notes* #10).

Midnight Notes Collective. (1990). "Introduction to The New Enclosures." *The New Enclosures* (*Midnight Notes* #10); reprinted in Midnight Notes (1992).

Midnight Notes Collective. (1982). "Mormons in Space," in *Midnight Notes* #5 (*Computer State Notes*).

Midnight Notes Collective. (1981). "Race Space: High and Low," in *Midnight Notes* #4 (*Space Notes*).

Mies, Maria, and Vandanna Shiva. (1993). *Ecofeminism*. London & New Jersey: Zed.

Mies, Maria, Veroika Bennholdt-Thomsen, and Claudia von Werlhof. (1988). *Women: The Last Colony*. London, Zed.

Neill, Monty. (1995). "Computers, Thinking, and Schools in the 'New World Economic Order.'" In James Brook and Iain A. Boal, eds., *Resisting the Virtual Life*. San Francisco: City Lights.

Neill, Monty, with George Caffentzis and Johnny Machete. (1997). *Towards the New Commons*. http://www.midnightnotes.org

P.M.. (1985, 1995). *bolo'bolo*. Brooklyn: Semiotext(e), Foreign Agents Series.

Riker, David. (1992). "The Struggle Against Enclosure in Jay, Maine," in Midnight Notes (1990), 42–53.

Rosemont, Franklin. (n.d.) *Karl Marx & the Iroquois*. Brooklyn, NY: Red Balloon Collective Pamphlet (c/o M. Cohen, 2652 Cropsey Ave., #7H, 11214). Rreprinted from *Arsenal*.

Sarkar, Saral. (1999). *Eco-Socialism or Eco-Capitalism? A Critical Analysis of Humanity's Fundamental Choices*. London: Zed.

Semiotext(e). (1980). *Autonomia*. *Semiotext(e)*, III(3).

Shanin, Teodor. (1983.) *Late Marx and the Russian Road*. London: Routledge & Kegan Paul.

Tronti, Mario. (1972, Winter). "Workers and Capital," in *Telos*, 14, 25–62.

Wildcat. (1997). "Open Letter to John Holloway." *Wildcat-Zircular*, No. 39, September. English translation in *Common Sense* 24, 1999.

*Zapatistas! Documents of the New Mexican Revolution.* (1994). Brooklyn: Autonomedia.

*Zerowork: Political Materials* 1. (1975). Some of the articles that are particularly relevant to this paper have been reprinted in Midnight Notes (1992).

# 9
# QUESTIONS FOR RAMONA: ZAPATISMO AND FEMINISM

CLAUDIA VON WERLHOF

WHEN IN JANUARY 1994 1 heard for the first time about the rebellion of a so-called "Zapatista-movement" in the Mexican state of Chiapas, and when I saw the pictures of armed men with masks, I thought: "No, please not again!" After having experienced the politics of armed men in the sixties and seventies in Latin America, especially in El Salvador, I belong to those who react allergically to all forms of violence (see Werlhof, 1975; Topitas, 1994). Didn't the guerilla, the "armed struggle," and generally the intent to overcome the system by using its own means, fail everywhere, and didn't it only double the existing violence (see Debray, 1975)? However, Veronika Bennholdt-Thomsen, who had done research on Chiapas for years, told me that the case was different this time, the rebellion being an indigenous upheaval "from below," and not politics "from above," like the guerilla activities initiated by urban intellectuals. In addition, I noted that the rebels included many women, about 30% (see Gorman, 1995).

Is the Zapatista rebellion, which already has been described as the "first insurrection of the 21st century" (see Topitas, 1994, p. 14), the "social quake" after the earthquake of Mexico City in 1985 (see Werlhof, 1986b)? And why did it start in the countryside, where already

---

*Claudia von Werlhof teaches at the Institute of Political Science, Department of Social and Economical Sciences, University of Innsbruck, Austria.*

the first insurrection of the 20th century, the Mexican Revolution, had started too? And what does it mean that both upheavals are connected with Emiliano Zapata, the leader of the Mexican Revolution, who still seems to be alive in the minds of the people, at least in the South East of Mexico today? (Zapata, the "campesino" wanted Mexico to be a free country of free peasants without private property and without a central state power.) And wasn't the Ejido-system a success of the Mexican Revolution, being at least a guarantee for the peasants' access to the land in many parts of Mexico since that time? In Chiapas this reform has not yet occurred; indeed, here one would still need a Zapata. The actual reform of Article 27 of the Mexican Constitution has cancelled the old agrarian reform resulting from the revolution. "By law we are not supposed to have access to the land anymore," the peasants say (see Gonzales Esponda and Polito Barrios, 1994, p. 240). This is due to the fact that the Mexican land is left to the new "partners" of the North: it is Mexico's present to the United States and Canada, who are now accepting Mexico as a member of the "First World," inserting it into the North American Free Trade Agreement (NAFTA). Thus, the insurrection of the Zapatistas started on the same day that the Mexican government capitulated to the North. On the first of January 1994, the day that was heralded to the Mexican people as the day of their biggest triumph, was the moment that the rebels cried out "Now it's enough!" ("Ya basta!"). It is, indeed, the first rebellion against "neoliberal" politics and its globalization, a politics that is doing away with the last remains of the sovereignty of the single nation-states (see Bennholdt-Thomsen, 1994, p. 260).

**Questions to Ramona**

In 1995 I went to Mexico and Chiapas to better understand the Zapatista movement. I visited many people, men and women, from and around the movement, and discussed with them the questions treated in this article. I am formulating them as "questions to Ramona." Ramona is one of the leading heads of the Zapatista movement and is representing the "Women's Committee" of the indigenous communities. My questions to Ramona are rhetorical questions about the "word," the language used by the Zapatistas, their concepts and pictures. I want to know how she is understanding the situation and what it means for the women, for the indigenous communities of today, for the indigenous patriarchy and possibly also matriarchy (the "deep" Mexico) and, last but not least, for our situation in the West.

**Autonomy**

"Autonomy" is one of the words you like most (see "Peasant Communities," 1994, p. 245). But in your language "autonomy" means something totally different than in our language. In our language "autonomy" means independence from others as an individual who strives for living without any bonds with other individuals or groups. Such an "ego-logics" presumably is completely alien to you (see Keller, 1986; Ernst, 1996). It is an autonomy that stems from the machine-model of a society, in which the individual is just an interchangeable spare part (see Bamme et al., 1983). Whereas we understand by autonomy individual independence from nature and society, you mean by autonomy the economic independence of communities from the central state, as self-suppliers, and political self-determination (see Bennholdt-Thomsen, 1994, pp. 264–265). This means that you are organizing your economy in the way of a subsistence agriculture, or you would need the latter as a basis at least. But you do not speak about that. And the question for me is, who would provide the economic basis for an autonomy in your sense? Would this be done by all the members of the community together, or would it rest upon the women again and as always, without even being recognized (Bennholdt-Thomsen, 1994, pp. 267268)? If you are denying the meaningfulness and "fertility" of women's work, taking it automatically for granted, your "autonomy" then would be built again on the patriarchal sexual division of labor of the "white man." Thus, where you are trying to get rid of all forms of colonialism, you would, paradoxically, keep its "internal basis." If the women remain "the last colony" (see Mies, Bennholdt-Thomsen, and Werlhof, 1988), you would retain a sort of "Trojan-horse," being a permanent threat to your autonomy and the rest of your further achievements.

Do you agree with me? I know that the discussion about the autonomy of the indigenous communities in the meanwhile has been extended to all parts of Mexico (see Esteva, 1994a). This shows how far the decay of the Mexican political system and its institutions has already gone. But nowhere have I read of a discussion about the basis of your "autonomy."

**Law and Rights**

In the negotiations with the government you are concentrating on carrying through your own legal system. You think of a local legal system, which does not necessarily have much to do with the universal, abstract law system of the West. In contrast to this you want to reintroduce and exercise your own local indigenous rights. Indeed, rights are not just an invention of the West or modem times. Indigenous ideas about rights that presuppose neither abstract legal norms, nor the formal "posing" of positive rights (see Ernst, 1993; Goettner-Abendroth, 1988), are also discussed in the West (see Lauderdale, 1993, 1996). Like the concept of a matriarchal society, your legal system does not know imprisonment and it needs no legal apparatus and especially no police or military force. Gustavo Esteva told me that a man who would kill another man would in your community not be put in jail, but would have to take care of the family of the killed person for the rest of his life-the idea being that the perpetrator would be made responsible for the consequences of his act, and thus one would no longer need a criminal law.

But there are many people who feel that the concrete legal practice within the communities could eventually lead to violations of so-called "human rights" (see Esteva, 1995). And indeed, in many indigenous communities patriarchal social relations under certain conditions allow the men, for example, to rape women of the community, to marry them against their will, to keep them in economic dependence, and to exploit them as a labor force. Therefore you have formulated the "revolutionary women's rights" from 1993 that have been called the "first upheaval" before the "general upheaval" (see Topitas, 1994, pp. 82, 93, 103). Now, the question is, does this proposal contradict the men's concept of law and rights?

On the other hand, it has to be asked whether something like equality, emancipation and "human rights for women" are enough, or can help at all. We women from the West can tell you that this needs to be doubted. Violence against women occurs despite the formal acceptance of so-called human rights that expressly include women. Never have the law or rights protected women effectively against violence. This is because the so-called human or "natural" rights are fundamentally perceived as men's rights over women and nature (see Bloch, 1991; Gerhard, *et al.*, 1990). So the claim for the Western human rights will be a disappointing experience for women, if not a boomerang. Therefore, I think the solution of the problem has to be found within the communities themselves. Violence against women can never be legitimate, if you think about democracy, power, and politics, the way you do. From your point of view there can be no justification of the violence against women, be it in indigenous law or be it in Western law.

Law and rights have had too much to do with patriarchy since its first inception (see Werlhof, 1996, pp. 27–60). Therefore one has to dig deeper into the question. One would have to recognize women's rights and especially mother-rights the way they are in societies without patriarchal social relations of domination (see Werlhof, Schweighofer, and Ernst, 1996). So, especially with respect to the question of law and rights, you would have to profoundly criticize your own indigenous understanding of them. If not, it is likely that you would simply reintroduce a new structure of domination in the communities, or confirm the old one. In any case, the right of women to have access to the land (see Topitas, 1994, p. 95) is an appropriate and very important one to start with, because in patriarchy it has typically been denied to them (see Mies, Bennholdt-Thomsen, and Werlhof, 1988).

**Justice**

"Democracy! Freedom! Justice!" These are your central and often-repeated political concepts. Justice has, of course, much to do with law and rights. By justice you understand veracity, credibility and honesty. Bishop Samuel Ruiz, who loves you so much, expressed it in the following way: "There is no justice between poverty and wealth... There is a world of domination and of subjection, and ... the one doesn't exist without the other ... As long as we thought that we would have to treat equal spheres, we thought that we had to help on one side. . . . But, since we found out, that it is a question of justice, we have to take a decision. One cannot be with the people who are below, without telling the dominant people very clearly, that they have to come down... . The mighty have to get down from their throne, and the powerless have to raise themselves" (see Ruiz, 1994, p. 192). This shows that "your" Bishop does not think about justice anymore the way the West is doing it. Since Roman law, the West defines justice as "suum cuique," which essentially means to give the rich what belongs to them, and the poor what belongs to them (namely nothing). In this concept of justice, the equality or comparability of social relations is presupposed, as if they were independent from one another. Justice under these conditions starts from a status quo of relations of domination, and confirms what from your point of view is injustice. If I understand you well, you finally want to stop the injustice of equality between the dominating and the dominated by revealing the fact of domination itself as untruthful, unworthy of belief, and dishonest, so that it will have to disappear before something like a real justice could come into being.

I like this very much, but I think the same has to be applied to the relationship of dominance of men over women. Justice as equality of men and women does not help as long as women are dominated. If there is to be justice for women, then men have to step down from their throne of power over women, and the women have to rise up — not on the throne, but simply to (be) themselves.

**The Land**

"Land and freedom!" This is what you wanted all the time, since colonialism (see Bennholdt-Thomsen, 1994, p. 264). Indigenous people belong to the land, and the land belongs to them. It is their basis. You will get what you need for your "autonomy" by producing yourself what you need. Some feminist colleagues and I call this subsistence production (see Mies, 1991; Werlhof, 1985e). Therefore, the land is nothing external to you, but it is the place that you are rooted, the depth from which you have emerged. You call the land "your mother." It is the mother of all human beings, animals and plants. She has birthed them. She is nursing them; she is body, spirit and soul in one. From this point of view the privatization of land, especially now in the neoliberal economical system (see Topitas, 1994, p. 241), can never be accepted by you. How can your mother be divided, sold, and transformed into private property of people who are not even there (see Deloria, 1973)? Therefore you are proposing that land is not a commodity, but it is a "communality," communally owned by all the indigenous peoples and peasants in general.

"Land or death!" This is again the question for you, in contrast to us in the West, who believe that this question will never be important for us again. How silly we are! We too knew the communal land, the "Allmende" as we called it or the "commons" (see Illich, 1982; Boehme, 1988). To remember this tradition may be seen as the only possibility, to return to a situation where the land is not destroyed anymore. Only when you depend on the land on which you live would you bother about its well-being and an "ecological" way of life, in which a subsistence production and a politics of "regionalization " as an alternative to the globalized capitalistic economy are viable (see Bennholdt-Thomsen, 1994). How could "autonomous" self-supplied communities remain subjugated in the long run? Freedom through the land is an inexpressible taboo for those interested in domination. Land doesn't need domination; to the contrary, it dissolves it. But we in the West think that there is no life in freedom without dominating the land (including the peasants, the women, and the colonies worldwide). What a long way we in the West still have to go to get to our roots.

**Community**

You say that where there is community, there is the "good life." No good life without community. Community means living together, respecting one another, sharing things, not having to be sad because of loneliness and living without real troubles, because there is always someone who would help in case of necessity. "Community" is the heart and the soul. It is even a "cosmic" community where the relationship with nature is reappearing as human culture (see Klingler-Clavigo, 1995). This is a community of the "deep" Mexico, as Guillermo Bonfil Batalla is describing it.

Of course, we know that the indigenous communities of today have been reorganized by the Catholic Church in colonial times and after, and that they, do not represent this lovely picture anymore. The subjection of women especially has been responsible for this decay of the community. But you still know, at least, what you mean by community. In the West this is not the case anymore. In the meantime, we have destroyed practically all forms of community, and in the end we are dissolving the nuclear family, too. Whereas we have been forced to live as individuals and "egos," you have maintained a concept of "the indigenous" as "communal man" (and woman?), who lives in a community and not in a general competition of each against each (see Illich, 1982). In comparison with you, we have lost our roots and our community and do no longer know what a life of dignity and truth would feel like. And many people don't even want to know this anymore. But soon we will again need the community more than any other thing in the world. And this is when our individualistic model of life will have come to an end. (It is already becoming too expensive.)

Your concept of community is, again, very female. Wouldn't it have to be central to every community to care about the next generation-and this means to look from the perspective of the women and children in the community, and not from the perspective of a male public sphere that is defined independently from the "private" one? So the question remains how to build a community that would not be based on the subjugation of women and children, but would, in contrast, be centered (positively) around them.

**The Army**

For Marcos the Zapatista Liberation Army is "the heart of the movement" (see Esteva, 1995, p. 208). I don't know any other army that would call itself a "heart." "To follow one's heart" means, as you say, to find one's own dignity. So is your army the first in the world that wants to lead the people to their dignity? Or are you an army at all? "We are the product of 500 years of struggle.... We are the heirs of the real founders of our nation, we, the ones without possessions... invite all of you to join this call as the only way not to starve in the face of the insatiable thirst for power of a dictatorship which lasts more than 70 years...of sellers of the fatherland... who are taking away from us everything, absolutely everything... " (see General Command of the Zapatista Liberation Army 1994, p. 20). And again Marcos, who has set up this army with years of work: "The question is, that they want to kill us... On the First of January we did not march out for a war to kill or to be killed. We left, instead, to be heard... It was neither suicide nor adventure" (Marcos, 1994, p. 27). And: "We believe that our war can serve those... who suffer like we do..." (Topitas, 1994, p. 156). The army as guardian and servant: It wants to serve, like "politics" as you understand it?

The paradox of this "army" can only be understood if one knows from where it stems, and the circumstances under which it came into being. "It was the people themselves who said: Let's start now! We don't want to wait any longer, because we are all starving. .. . So the struggle started" (Topitas, 1994, p. 159). The whole people had been asked before and the communities themselves proposed the insurrection. The army is well accepted in the civil population. They know that the rulers fear the union between the armed and the civil population. The armed people say: "We are peaceful people. We have a lot of patience. If not, we would have started with our rebellion a long time ago" (see Topitas, 1994, p. 156). Behind this you find the indigenous concept of "Ñk `op" again. In this case it means that you cannot decide to start an insurrection and not realize it afterwards. This would be "illogical" (p. 183). And you saw "that it is bad to die without having fought" (p. 36). It was the last alternative; everything else had already been tried.

Is there anything like a "symbolic" army, an army that is expressing the wish and the will for resistance, but that is not "really" an army in the sense of the military concept? If you equate "army" and "war" with struggle, only then are you able to explain the paradox of "an armed liberation army which has invented a resistance which is strictly free from violence and has eliminated the traditional guerilla with its violent concept of power from the project" (see Dietrich, 1994, p. 137). Today our problem is that after such a long militaristic history full of wars we think that struggle is always the same as war, violence, and militarism. We don't know a struggle anymore that would not contain militaristic forms of conflict. And this means that we have left to the state and to the military the responsibility to deal with conflicts, and we behave as if in this way we have been liberated from conflicts altogether. We behave as if the (so-called "legal") violence that the state/military uses would be justified and "necessary" on the one hand, and as if we, on the other hand, would have nothing to do with it. This way we fancy to be peaceful, because we have left violence to others.

Maybe it makes sense to characterize your army this way. It wants to bother about something that can neither be delegated nor displaced. We could distinguish between the institutionalized army of the state (which, as we see every day, can also be directed against the proper people-that is to say an abstract apparatus that does not stem from below but from above) on one hand, and the "guerilla" that wants to seize power, on the other hand, and finally the so-called "popular resistance" as a third possibility (see Virilio and Lothringer, 1984, pp. 110–111). Distinguishing between the regular army and the guerilla, including terrorist groups, on one side and popular resistance on the other side, the Liberation Army would undoubtedly belong to the tradition of popular resistance (compare Virilio and Lothringer, 1984). It doesn't omit the question of death, it stems from its own milieu, and it is using no special means besides several guns, which is not very special if one thinks about the norms of modern military equipment. Furthermore it has to do more with civil disobedience and peaceful resistance than with a so-called "armed struggle" (see Ebert, 1983). Its members are not socially atomized and "deterritorialized" urban individuals, but "are able to do something" independent from "technocratic situations" where only terror is possible. You do not use terrorist strategies. You try to avoid situations of violence, but you have arms in order to show that you are going to defend yourself. Marcos is repeating, again and again, that it is his aim to make the army superfluous and to abolish it when the threat has ceased to exist. This struggle would never be won through gunshots. Nevertheless, an ambivalence remains. It is so difficult to avoid a further "patriarchalization," especially in the case of crisis, and every fighting party is in a crisis. Where there are arms, "male bonding" is to be expected, which has the tendency to become independent and to produce the legitimation for its continuation (see Voelger and Welck, 1990). This has been the case in indigenous movements, too (see Muentzel, 1978).

The participation of women in armed conflicts is a special problem. Indeed, it belongs to the oldest traditions of humankind, that women are actively defending their communities, especially the life of their children, without hesitating. They have even been feared because of this attitude (see Eisler, 1987; Aliti, 1993; Loraux, 1992). But under the conditions of today one has always to take into account that the "equality" of women in the army, from which Marcos is speaking, could in the end also be a step in the opposite direction. Does the struggle-experience of the women contribute to a new, modernized form of patriarchalization? Or does it improve the conditions for the re-invention of even matriarchal relationships in the community as would be more likely in the case of a people's resistance? Isn't it that nearly all popular upheavals in history, including the ones that lead to the big revolutions, have been started and in their beginning even guided by women (see Mies and Reddock, 1978)? Will the experience of women in the Zapatista Liberation Army result in greater awareness, so that women could begin to concern themselves about the huge problems in the community more actively and without any fear of conflicts? Or will they only have learned in a new way to subject themselves and to obey, even if they may have commanded in the army, too? Could the popular resistance in the end be transformed into a new model of domination, and will it then only have contributed to its training (see Topitas, 1994, pp. 47, 163)? On the other hand, what was the alternative?

### The Question of Matriarchy and the West: What Is a "Civilization"?

My last two major questions have, to my knowledge, not been discussed much in Mexico yet. One question refers to a so-called "matriarchy" in Mexico, and the other to the issue of "Western civilization." The question of matriarchy is the question of the character of the Central American "civilization," which in the form of the "deep Mexico" seems to have become a social vision again. Has this civilization or culture been an essentially female" or nonpatriarchal one? Guillermo Bonfil did not pose this question, he didn't even realize it. So should the "beautiful indigenous cause" only end up in a local "post"-capitalistic neopatriarchy? Does one want to miss the chance to overcome relationships of dominance and violence at the "lowest" level, too? To avoid this, these relationships have to be discussed (see Bennholdt-Thomsen, 1994). Or has even the "deep" Mexico been organized in a patriarchal way, and were even the Mayas no longer matriarchal at the time when the West knew their societies (compare Popol Vuh, 1993)? Would a "matriarchal" society in Central America still have to be "discovered"?

In your language, Ramona, your thinking and acting, I could not find a patriarchal tradition. Your pictures and concepts seem to me much more "matriarchal": they do not claim domination of any kind. Your language remains bound to concrete experience and thus is not abstract. It speaks of "general" problems and conflicts in life, but it is never "universalist." It is a language that could be valid for the world in its totality, without being "totalitarian" at all. It remains rooted in the "depth" and from there it directs itself against the ruling and the mighty, without wanting to replace them, and it points in the direction of a (worldwide possible) culture, free from domination. Your language is friendly, positively related to life and nature, it is erotic and tender, motherly and very near to the earth, full of love and soul, and last but not least, supported by a tremendous spiritual freedom. This language does not stem from the darkness of historical patriarchies, including the modern capitalistic ones. But patriarchy — besides capitalism — is the reality today, in your indigenous communities as well (see Bennholdt-Thomsen, 1988; Gunn Allen, 1986). And might not a new "deep" but patriarchal Mexico finally attract everything you have wanted to do away with since colonial times?

Guillermo Bonfil spoke of the existence of two different civilizations, the Western and the Central American, as if they could be analyzed independently from one another. He said that the latter had been subjugated by the former. But what if the subjugated (part of a) civilization is really going to liberate itself from the subjugating one? What kind of civilization will be the result? And what will then happen to the subjugating civilization? If (part of a) civilization is able to exist independently from the other one, then the question arises, whether the subjugating (part of the) civilization would be capable of independence from the subjugated one or not. Why did it subjugate another civilization? If it did it because it could not develop on its own, it is not deserving the name "civilization" as such. How can something that is not (or does not want to be) self-sufficient, namely the subjugating civilization, carry the same name as something that has always been self-sufficient, namely the subjugated civilization?

In case your indigenous civilization should again emerge as an independent one in Mexico, the actual situation would suddenly be completely per- (or better) re-verted: The indigenous civilization would be recognizable as the independent, the Western as the dependent one. It was the West that needed colonialism — cheap raw materials, labor power and international markets — to become a "Western civilization" (see Mies, Bennholdt-Thomsen and Werlhof, 1988). What will happen to "Western civilization" if the colonial situation that it is based upon broke down not only in Mexico but elsewhere too? Does Western civilization break down when there are no colonies anymore? Does "Western civilization" mean to have colonies? Is "Western civilization" defined by the fact that it has subjugated other civilizations and is nourishing itself from them? Or would the West become a real civilization only if there are no colonies anymore? And would this civilization then still be a "Western" one? What we define as "Western civilization" is a product of modern times and colonialism. By "Western civilization" we do not refer to the Middle Ages or an old, European-type civilization that no longer exists (see Gimbutas, 1982). Whereas you will be able to relate to your own traditions, we in the West are standing emptyhanded. We invented so many heights, but have lost our "depth". Where are our own roots and forces, the heritage of our culture and former civilizations that might not have been parasitic and maybe not patriarchal (nor capitalistic, of course) either?

The decay of Western power in Mexico (the end of the "fictitious" Mexico, as G. Bonfil says) also means the decay of power and civilization in the West. Therefore, we in the West have to ask the same questions as you. The difference is that we do not know how to do this without subjugating others. But whereas we are not even really asking these questions, you are already preoccupied with the answers.

With your upheaval — which is not only an insurrection — and with the perspectives it has in relation to the global economic crisis and neoliberalism as a form to globalize this crisis, the relations suddenly appear to be turned upside down. Now it is the West that is weak. Does it destroy non-Western (or your) civilization completely, is it going to decay because it is losing its basis? Does it let the non-Western civilization be independent, to also decay? There is only one solution: The reconstruction of a non-Western civilization in the West and all over the planet. And this cannot mean replacing the external colony by an "internal" one (or maintaining it). When women remain to be treated as "the last colony," it would only repeat internally what had just perished externally.

**Notes**

1 This is a revision and translation of a part of "Fragen an Ramona: Die Zapatisten, die Indianische Zivilisation, die Matriarchatsfrage und der Western," in Werlhof (1996), pp. 189–224.

2 All quotations are translations by the author.

**Bibliography**


Aliti, Angelika (1993) *Die wilde Frau. Rueckkehr zu den Quellen weiblicher Macht und Energie*. Hamburg: Hoffmann & Campe.

Bamme, Arno, Renate Genthe, Guenther Kempin, and Guenter Feuerstein 1983. *Maschinen-Menschen, Mensch-Maschinen*. Reinbek: Rowohlt.

Bennholdt-Thomsen, Veronika 1994."Die Zapatistas und Wir," pp. 257–268 in: *Ya Basta! Der Aufstand der Zapatistas*, edited by Topitas. Hamburg: Verlag Libertaere Assoziation.

Boehme, Hartmut 1988. *Natur und Subjekt*. Frankfurt: Suhrkamp.

Bloch, Ernst 1991. *Naturrecht und menschliche Wuerde*. Frankfurt: Suhrkamp.

Bonfil Batalla, Guillermo 1989. *Mexico Profundo: Una Civilizacion Negada*. Mexico: Grijalbo.

Bonfil Batalla, Guillermo 1994. "Geschichten, die noch nicht Geschichte sind," pp. 169–174 in: *Ya Basta! Der Aufstand der Zapatistas*, edited by Topitas. Hamburg: Verlag Libertaere Assoziation.

Debray, Regis 1975. *Kritik der Waffen. Wohin geht die Revolution in Lateinamerika?* Reinbek: Rowohlt.

Deloria, Vine, Jr. 1973. *God Is Red*. New York: Gosset and Dunlop.

Dietrich, Wolfgang 1994. "Die wuetende Erde Mexikos," pp. 125–143 in: *Ya Basta! Der Aufstand der Zapatistas*, edited by Topitas. Hamburg: Verlag Libertare Assoziation.

Ebert, Theodor 1983. *Gewaltfreier Aufstand*. Frankfurt: Waldkircher Verlagsgesellschaft.

Eisler, Riane 1987. *The Chalice and the Blade*. San Francisco: Harper and Row.

Ernst, Werner 1993. "Formale Form als Rechtsgewalt." in: *Ethica: Wissenschaft und Verantwortung* 1 (2): 163.

Ernst, Werner 1996. "Metapsychologie und egologisches Subjekt," pp. 80–110 in *Herren-los: Herrschaft-Erkenntis-Lebensform*, edited by Claudia von Werlhof, Annemarie Schweighofer, and Werner

Ernst. Frankfurt, Paris, New York: Peter Lang.

Esteva, Gustavo 1994a. "Basta!," pp. 65–78 in *Ya Basta! Der Aufstand der Zapatistas*, editedby Topitas. Hamburg: Verlag Libertaere Assoziation.

Esteva, Gustavo 1994b. *Cronica del Fin de Una Era*. Mexico: Editorial Posada.

Esteva, Gustavo 1995. *Fiesta: Jenseits von Entwicklung, Hilfe und Politik*. 2d ed.Frankfurt/Wien: Suedwind.

General Command of the Zapatista Liberation Army 1994. "Erklaerung aus der Selva Lacandona," pp. 20–22 in *Ya Basta! Der Aufstand der Zapatistas*, edited by Topitas. Hamburg: Verlag Libertaere Assoziation.

Gerhard, Ute, Mechtild Jansen, Andrea Maihoffer, Pia Schmid, and Irmgard Schultz, eds. 1990. *Differenz und Gleichheit: Menschenrechte haben (k)ein Geschlecht*. Frankfurt: Ulrike Helmer Verlag.

Gimbutas, Marija 1982. *The Goddesses and Gods of Old Europe*. Berkeley: University of California Press.

Gonzales Esponda, Juan, and Elizabeth Polito Barrios 1994. "Bauernbewegungen in Chiapas," pp. 230–244 in: *Ya Basta! Der Aufstand der Zapatistas*, edited by Topitas. Hamburg: Verlag Libertare Assoziation.

Gorman, John 1995: "Understanding the Uprising: Two on Chiapas." *Native Americas* (Fall): 62–63.

Goettner-Abendroth, Heide 1988. *Das Matriarchat 1: Geschichte seiner Erforschung*. Stuttgart, Berlin, Koeln: Kohlhammer.

Gunn Allen, Paula 1986. *The Sacred Hoop. Recovering the Feminine in American Indian Tradition*. Boston: Beacon.

Illich, Ivan 1978. *Fortschrittsmythen*. Reinbek: Rowohlt.

Illich, Ivan 1982. *Vom Recht auf Gemeinheit*. Reinbek: Rowohlt.

Keller, Catherine 1986. *From a Broken Web: Separation, Sexism, and Self*. Boston: Beacon Press.

Klingler-Clavigo, Margit 1995. *Kosmovision in Konflikt. Interview, 22 November*. Frankfurt: Hessischer Rundfunk.

Lauderdale, Pat 1996. "Indigene Nordamerikanische Alternativen zur Vorstellung von Recht und Strafe in der Moderne: Was die Natur uns lehrt," pp. 133–156 in: *Herren-los: Herrschaft-Erkenntnis-Lebensform*, edited by Claudia von Werlhof, Annemarie Schweighofer, and Werner Ernst. Frankfurt, Paris, New York: Peter Lang.

Loraux, Nicole 1992. *Die Trauer der Muetter: Weibliche Leidenschaft und die Gesetze der Politik*. Frankfurt: Campus.

Marcos, Subcommandante 1994. "Marcos zur 'Moderneë,' " pp. 27–38 in *Ya Basta! Der Aufstand der Zapatistas*, edited by Topitas. Hamburg: Verlag Libertaere Assoziation.

Mies, Maria 1991. *Patriarchy and Accumulation on a World Scale: Women in the International Division of Labor*. 4th ed. London: Zed Books.

Mies, Maria, Veronika Bennholdt-Thomsen, and Claudia von Werlhof 1988. *Women, the Last Colony*. London, New Delhi: Zed Books.

Mies, Maria, and Rhoda Reddock, eds. 1978. *National Liberation and Women's Liberation*. The Hague: Institute of Social Studies.

Muentzel, Mark 1978. *Die Indianische Verweigerung. Lateinamerikas Ureinwohner zwischen Ausrottung und Selbstbestimmung*. Reinbek: Rowohlt.

"Peasant Communities of the Selva Lacandona," 1994, pp. 245–250 in *Ya Basta! Der Aufstand der Zapatistas*, edited by Topitas. Hamburg: Verlag Libertare Assoziation.

Popol Vuh 1993. *Das Buch des Rates*. Muechen: Eugen Diederichs.

Ruiz, Samuel 1994. "Interview mit Bischof Samuel Ruiz," pp. 187–192 in *Ya Basta! Der Aufstand der Zapatistas*, edited by Topitas. Hamburg: Verlag Libertaere Assoziation.

Topitas (Angela Habersetzer, Annette Massman, Beate Zimmermann, Danuta Sacher, Gaby Schulten, Herby Sachs, Theo Bruns, and Ulrich Mercker, eds.) 1994. *Ya Basta! Der Aufstand der Zapatistas*. Hamburg: Verlag Libertaere Assoziation.

Virilio, Paul, and Sylvere Lothringer 1984. *Der reine Krieg*. Berlin: Merve.

Voelger, Gisela, and Karin von Welck, eds. 1990. *Maennerbande, Maennerbuende. Zur Rolle des Mannes im Kulturvergleich*, 2 vols. Koeln: Rautenstrauch-Joest-Museum.

Werlhof, Claudia von 1975. *Prozesse der Unterentwicklung in El Salvador und Costa Rica*. Saarbruecken: Breitenbach.

Werlhof, Claudia von 1985e. *Wenn die Bauern wieder kommen: Frauen, Arbeit und Agrobusiness in Venezuela*. Bremen: Peripheria-Verlag/Edition CON.

Werlhof, Claudia von 1986b: "La Burla del Progreso." *El Gallo Ilustrado* (22 June): 34.

Werlhof, Claudia von 1996. *Mutter-Los: Frauen im Patriarchat zwischen Angleichung und Dissidenz*. Muenchen: Frauenoffensive.

Werlhof, Claudia von, Annemarie Schweighofer, and Werner Ernst, eds. 1996. *Herren-los: Herrschaft-Erkenntnis-Lebensform*. Frankfurt, Paris, New York: Peter Lang.

# 10
# MAKING *LA CIUDAD*

## DAVID RIKER ON POLITICS AND FILMMAKING

DAVID RIKER, a long-time member of the Midnight Notes Collective, is the director of the highly-acclaimed film *La Ciudad,* which depicts the lives and struggles of Latino immigrants in New York City. Filmed between 1992 and 1997, it is David Riker's first feature film and it has attracted so much attention that he has been interviewed many times concerning the film and its making.

*La Ciudad* is another aurora of the Zapatistas, since it is made in the spirit of directness and inclusiveness and as a political project intended to cross many boundaries within the working class. The actors of the film, almost all non-professionals, are men and women who have been uprooted from every corner of the Americas during the decade of the 1990's. As you will read, the making of the film was (itself) a continuous encuentro.

The film is told in four separate stories, bridged by scenes at a neighborhood photo studio where newly arrived immigrants have their portraits made. In the first story, "Bricks," a young day laborer, scavenging for bricks from a demolished building, is killed when a wall collapses. In "Home," two Mexican teenagers from the same village meet by chance and fall in love, only to lose each other in a vast housing project. "The Puppeteer" tells of a homeless father's dreams and difficulties in enrolling his young daughter in school. The final story, "Seamstress," concerns a sweatshop worker who has not been paid the back wages she is owed and who desperately needs money to send back home to her sick daughter.

We introduce David Riker's thoughts on the making of *La Ciudad* in the form of a digest of (five) interviews made in *Filmmaker* (Interview with Stephen Garrett in the February–April 1999 issue), *Cineaste* (Interview with Robert Sklar in the Vol. XXIV, Nos. 2–3 issue), *Release Print* (Interview by Julia Segrove Jaurigui in the December/January 1999–2000 issue), *Revolutionary Worker* (March 26, 2000), and for the Aella Conference on Latina and Latin American Women (New York, May 2000). It is accompanied by a photo essay on *La Cuidad* made up of stills from the film as well as other related photos by David Riker and Victor Sira.

**1. Political Perspective**

I look at what has happened since 1973 as a process of enclosure very similar to the enclosures at the birth of capitalism five hundred years ago in Europe. It shows that it's essential for capitalism to develop to actually produce this uprooted proletariat or working class. What we've seen since the mid 1970s, on a global level, are new enclosures, which are as important in their consequences as the original enclosures...

So now, in the year 2000, we find ourselves in a world in which a huge percentage of workers are actually at an immense distance from their place of origin, from their home, and the immigrant has become the central subject of our time. The uprooted worker is now at the core, at the center of the global economic system. And whether those uprooted immigrants are from Latin America, working in New York, Chicago, Los Angeles, or in some of the rural parts of the U.S.; whether they're in Europe; or whether in fact they're just part of smaller migrations within Latin America, from the country to the city, from one country to another, from Nicaragua looking for work in Mexico or Costa Rica; they are key to understanding what is happening today on the planet. (RW)

Every immigrant community is going through a process of change, of establishing new roots or creating a new identity, and *La Ciudad* is an attempt to portray a community in formation. Immigrants arrive and their first experience is one of greatest weakness, that is they are isolated, they are individuals, they are alone, and they find themselves coming into a very powerful system of relationships. And they are exploited, and they are abused, and they die, and they are deported. And inevitably, the result of that conflict is for the new immigrants to contruct new relationships. I saw that there was an incredibly dynamic Latin American culture developing in New York. So the combination of wanting to make a film about what it feels like to be an immigrant and seeing the Latin American culture in New York led me to make a film that combined them. (AELLA)

**2. The Filmmaking Process**

Throughout the process of making *La Ciudad*, Riker's goal was to make a film that reflects what the Latin American immigrant community looks like and what it is feeling at the end of the century. He chose to cast non-actors in almost every role. In order (to prepare) the Latino immigrants for their roles, Riker created a dramatic workshop and used a combination of improvisational techniques and acting exercises to prepare the cast. "The dramatic workshop," explains Riker, "is like an incubation space, where the stories develop and relations between the non-actors emerge. One of the goals of the workshop is to take a person who starts off saying, 'You're crazy to have me play the lead role,' to the point where she says, 'There is no one who can tell my story better than me.'" (RP)

How do you get non-actors to act real? You've got to get beyond anything that's going to make them self-conscious. I'm using methodologies that are common in community organizing. The idea is that communities can be transformed only when people identify what their problems are in their own words.

If you draw a picture of your mother, you start with a blank sheet. Where are you going to put her? And what is she going to be doing? When you do it, all these things are going to be kicked up. From that you start to talk about stories. For instance, I'll ask [the actors] to remember the moment that they left home, the last moment they saw their children. If a guy starts saying that he got on a bus to leave home, I'll say "Let's form a bus," and we organize the chairs into a bus. So he starts acting it out. And all these other people witness it, and their emotions get caught up. Who else knows that pain. A lot of people. And then we say, "Does that pain have a place in our film?" Yeah, it does, and we need to tap into it in the film. These workshops lasted generally two to three months and increased in intensity and frequency right up until we shot." (FM)

You have to picture a group of very strong construction workers. One of them was a Sandinista guerrilla from Nicaragua who — when we were doing an exercise one day of remembering a painful experience — told us how all of his friends were with him in the Sandinista

JUKI

331 2162

movement and how one morning they were attacked by the Contras and only two survived. And all of his friends were killed. And, as this guy was telling the story, he was really bawling, he was crying like a baby. And the electrical worker from Peru, the former National Guard from Honduras, and the construction worker from the Dominican Republic — all men who didn't know each other well — were sitting in that sacred circle listening to this man from Nicaragua, and their own feeling(s) and their own experiences were coming up. So it's important that anyone who attempts to construct a dramatic workshop like this is prepared — because there is a responsibility. When these emotions come out you have to then make sure there is no damage done. Which means that, before everyone goes home at the end of the day, the men individually and as a group are strong again. Not strong again but are really at another level of strength. And you forget about your film. You can't just be thinking about making your film, you see. What you are doing is creating a place in which true emotion and true personal memory is being expressed. (RW)

The only time that new Latin American immigrants are dealing with white people in a city like New York is in a subservient or hostile or dominant group relationship. You're the INS, you're a boss, you're a policeofficer, a social worker and you've got a beef with them. I had to overcome that not once, but with every person. It's part of why it took a long time to make the film. You cannot make a film like this without the complete trust of the people who are in it. Not only do they have to accept you enough to cook dinner and have you go to their children's baptism, but then they have to go beyond another fault line — to get in front of a camera. A very big part of my experience directing the film was to understand what that meant. For sweatshop workers to come out of the sweatshop and into the light and stand in front of a camera required them to cross many, many lines. I don't think anyone would make a film like that unless they feel a strong desire to do it. In addition to the normal struggles of filmmaking — of getting funding, of getting supported making it through, getting the film in the can — here the obstacles are in every street, every home, every person you meet. (C)

Writers have a political responsibility to recognize that their work is going to have consequences. And I wanted feedback from the people whose lives were going to be most affected by the story, so I would present the stories to them in outline form. The garment workers all felt that [the seamstress in the story] would turn to God for help, so I accepted it; I may not pray, but they all would. So I interviewed men and women about their prayers and where they pray — on the subway, in the elevators, waiting for buses. And in the film, the woman prays on the subway. This kind of collaboration has been the driving force for each of the stories. (FM)

And I really want to reject the idea of the director as this iconic figure that sits in a chair and tells everyone what to do, 'cause it isn't true, and it's damaging to have that image. Most of the work you do is just hard work and draining and you carry a heavy burden because the consequences of your work are going to be great, and you have to be open to changing and to discovering you're wrong. (RW)

### 3. The People of *La Ciudad*

For every immigrant that participated in this film, the decision to be involved was very, very complex. They had to put aside the fear that is extremely prevalent in undocumented communities and say, "I'm going to do it. I'm going to stand in front of the camera, whatever the consequences." The motivation was so deep that the question of the wage was just a practical issue. But the idea that dominates the immigrant experience in this (country is that you) will be invisible. You leave your home, you make this incredibly long journey, you come to a border, and when you cross that border you leave one life behind. You become undocumented. You have no identity. You come to the big cities or go to the ranches or work in the back of the hotels in Las Vegas. You will remain invisible." That's the unwritten rule of the immigration story today. And the making of *La Ciudad* was premised on, "You'll be visible. You'll stand in front of the camara with a light on your face and tell us exactly what you're going through and what you're feeling."

So how did we reach an agreement about salary? I told the person organizing the day laborers. "You decide what is aceptable and you tell me. And it's my problem to go and find it. But remember, I'm not a Hollywood studio — at that point I only had a small grant — and the money I pay I am going to earn by working nights on Wall Street. Also, this film is to express to the outside world what you're going through. In other words, it's a committment you're making, it's not just a job for hire. That's all I ask you to consider."

They came back with a rate of $75 a day for the leads, a little bit better than the best rate they get on the street. Supporting actors would be given a hot meal. That is what we had with "Bricks." By the time we got to "Seamstress," the daily rate, I think, was $100 a day

for the leads and the extras worked for free. If it was Sunday, all we did was provide subway tokens. If it was Saturday and they were losing a day's work, they were given $30. In other words, it was political discussion about what was required to make the participation of the workers possible. And at no time did I encounter a person who wanted to get rich. (RP) (slightly re-ordered)

And the risks that they took...I never felt that I was putting them in risk to be in the film. But from their point of view, it is different. Many of them were only in the United States for a few years by the time I started working with them — some even less. The very act of stepping outside of their day-to-day routine and talking to me and meeting with us in the churches or the theaters where we were and slowly workshopping to the point where they were the center of attention for a camera crew of 40 or 50 people represented huge potential risk. And why then did they do it? The only explanation is that the film is very, very important to them. (RW)

Every person actively involved in making the film was profoundly empowered. It didn't change the fact that they were still working on the streets or in the garment shops and that their status was still undocumented. What did change was their sense of who they were in this country. I say this because they testified over and over again that to break the stranglehold of fear and particpate in the film, to directly talk about things they kept inside themselves, was very empowering. (RP)

The metaphor we used when we made "Bricks," was that without mortar, bricks have no value, they have no purpose, you can do nothing with them. You need cement in order to build things. And the same is true of people, and in this case of the immigrants arriving in New York City. They have left their cement behind. When you leave your village and you come to New York City and you find yourself on a street corner with people from eleven different countries, where is the cement that you had? You have to find or create new mortar. Without it, there will be no future.

The men at the beginning of *La Ciudad* are not able to find that mortar, and the idea at the end of the film, in the final story, "Seamstress," is that the women begin to. They take the very first step. When they stop working, it's a kind of mortar. And the same story that we're talking about regarding the Latino community is behind the idea of a white culture and a white community... Everyone that has European roots has a history of warfare — the Scots, the Irish, the English, the Dutch, the French, the Italians. How is it that we're all now supposed to be somehow the same? I know among Mexican filmmakers there's often talk about telling the story of what if the roles were completely reversed between the U.S. and Mexico, and making the details very, very accurate to make it believable. So like the *Grapes of Wrath*, American families are all having to pack up their belongings and trying to get to Mexico to find work, and having to cross the river at night. So a New Yorker finds himself on a street corner in Cuernavaca, Mexico standing beside a guy from Wisconsin, half a dozen people from Washington State, some out of work auto workers from Arizona, and a couple of guys from Long Island. And they have nothing in common and may even want to kill each other, but they're treated exactly the same way. It's a really interesting premise.

The term "community" and the notion of "community" is a difficult one and a problematic one everywhere and always. Because from the outside, a community has one appearance, and from the inside, it has a different one. Within the Latin American story, it's particularly difficult to talk about a Latino community, because it's changing so rapidly. The population of Latin Americans in New York is growing exponentially, and new communities are arriving that have no historical relationship with those that are already here. That is, there's no reason to assume that Peruvians or indigenous communities from Ecuador have a relationship with the Dominican community that's already in New York, or any connection with the Puerto Ricans in New York, or any reason to be involved with the Mexicans from Puebla. Each group of new arrivals finds themselves living beside and working beside people from other parts of Latin America that they have very little in common with historically. They've never spoken before, never met before, but in the eyes of New York City, in the eyes of the bosses for whom they work, in the eyes of anyone driving by them on the street, they are considerd to be of a kind. But as soon as you begin to talk with them, you find out that on one corner you have Mexicans, on another corner you have Guatemalans, on another corner you have Ecuadorans, and they in fact are keeping to themselves. They keep to themselves until the truck pulls up, and then they all run and push and shove and what happens is that the contractor chooses a few men from each group, and so these men who would just as soon have kept to themselves find that they have to deal with each other and they have to work together. So capital brings together and helps to form this Latino community. (AELLA)

# OTHER ESSAYS

*A March of the Chhattisgarh Mukti Morcha*

# INTRODUCTION TO "VICTORY OVER A LIFE OF LIVING DEATH"

JOHN ROOSA

IN TERMS of industrial production, the region of Chhattisgarh is vital to India. It has one of the country's largest steel plants, a hundred smaller scale steel-related factories, six massive cement factories, a paper mill, and an aluminum plant. Its extensive coal mines yield a sizable share of India's total coal production. If one wants to understand the relationship between the working class and capital in India, Chhattisgarh, near the middle of India in the state of Madhya Pradesh, is a good place to look. Whatever the concrete, precise meanings to the Indian government's new economic strategies of 'globalization' and 'liberalization,' one should be able to locate them in Chhattisgarh.[1]

Despite its centrality to the Indian economy, the region is not well known in the rest of India. To the extent that it is known, it is usually perceived as a remote hinterland, a backward, primitive land of tribal people that has contributed nothing of significance to the great cultural traditions of India. There are no famous temples to which pilgrims flock and there are few scenic sites to be rendered into icons for the tourism industry. One would search in vain through the standard history textbooks of India for reference to Chhattisgarh. The nationalist movement and all its anti-colonial upheavals — the Non-Cooperation movement, the Civil Disobedience movement, the Quit India movement — appear to have bypassed Chhattisgarh. For Indians living in the megacities of Delhi, Bombay, and Calcutta, Chhattisgarh might as well be off the map. It is marginalized and occluded as a region fit only for the anthropological study of picturesque and primitive tribals even as those tribals produce the steel and coal on which the cities depend.[2]

Chhattisgarh is in what is known as the "tribal belt" across the middle of India, extending from Gujarat in the west to the Bengal region in the east, through portions of Madhya Pradesh, southern Bihar and Orissa and extending southward into Andhra Pradesh.[3] Most of India's tribals live in this swath of land. The term "tribe" is still widely used in India to refer, without pejorative connotations, to those societies that remain outside the brahminical religion and caste structure. Many tribes speak Austro-Asiatic languages that are neither within the Indo-European family (like the north Indian languages) nor the Dravidian family (like the South Indian languages).[4] The caste society that existed in the plains districts of Chhattisgarh was more open and unorthodox than elsewhere in India. From the early nineteenth century, many of the Chamars, an untouchable group who constituted about twenty percent of Chhattisgarh's population according to the first census in 1866, were followers of the Satnami religious sect that rejected caste hierarchy and the worship of Hindu deities.[5]

The colonial state, having installed a civil bureaucracy in Chhattisgarh in the early nineteenth century, did not exploit its mineral resources. Prior to 1947, the district possessed one cloth mill and one jute mill, both of modest size, and only a few roads. For revenue, the state taxed the villages. It taxed everything it could. It collected a tax on the cultivated land and introduced new taxes on the use of grazing lands and forests. To control shifting cultivators and nomadic pastoralists, officials strove to settle them onto permanent plots of land where they could be more easily taxed. The excise department tried to monopolize liquor production and impose a hefty tax on liquor sales. Seeing new opportunities for profit, moneylenders, merchants, and land grabbers began migrating into the region. Throughout the tribal belt, there was an increasing intervention of the state into the agrarian economy over the nineteenth to early twentieth centuries and tribal revolts marked every step of the way: the Kol rebellion of 1832, the Santhal rebellion of 1855, Birsa Munda's revolt of 1898, Aluri Sita Ramaraju's revolt of 1922–24, and so on. In Chhattisgarh itself, an uprising occurred in 1910. There is barely a district in this tribal belt that does not have a revolt against the colonial state in its history.

The British anthropologist Verrier Elwin, who lived in the tribal regions of Madhya Pradesh in the 1930s–40s (then called the Central Provinces), wrote enthusiastically and compassionately of the tribes there. Placing no overriding importance on technological progress, he saw in the settlements of the Maria, the Baiga and the Gond tribes a refinement in the science of human relationships. The sight of their destitution and ill-health, he wrote in 1934, were certain to keep one awake for many nights "haunted by the scenes of suffering." Living among them at a time when the depredations of the police, forest officials, and merchants were already well-established, he recognized that poverty and disease were their "fundamental problems." But he wished to write about the beauty of their culture: the way they raised children, the way youths first experienced sexuality, the way they danced, painted, and told stories. As he later reflected, "I wanted to save what was beautiful and free." His romanticism of the tribes as 'noble savages' was perhaps overdone, but it cannot be easily dismissed as the fanciful wish-fulfillment of yet another Westerner disillusioned with modernity; it was based upon a careful, clear-headed study of tribal society and an intimate engagement with living reality.[6]

After national independence in 1947, the Indian state continued some of the colonial state's parasitical exactions — the excise and forestry departments remain notorious for their authoritarian character to this day — and discontinued the neglect of industrial investment. The Indian state introduced industrial projects of unprecedented size. With Soviet financial and technical aid, the state constructed a public sector steel plant in the city of Bhilai in the 1950s. The plant quickly became the center of a burgeoning network of mines and factories. As workers and managers arrived from outside, the indigenous tribal population went from being a majority to a minority. At present, with a population of about 11 million people, spread over some 20,000 villages and several large cities, Chhattisgarh has a tribal population that constitutes only 35 percent of the total. The cities are entirely dominated by non-Chhattisgarhis.

From Delhi, the dramatic transformation of Chhattisgarh over the last 40 years appears as a success story of economic development. The picture is not so rosy in Chhattisgarh itself. In exchange for supplying the steel and coal that the rest of India consumes, the people of Chhattisgarh have had their land expropriated and polluted. Outsiders have occupied the better paying jobs in the factories and mines while the tribal Chhattisgarhis have been left with the most back-breaking and lowest-paying jobs, especially as coal miners, digging into the ground with thin shovels and filling up baskets of earth to be dropped into waiting dump trucks. The combination of a high amount of industrial development with a large rural and tribal population whose livelihoods have steadily become more desperate, has created an explosive situation. Chhattisgarh can be considered as India's Chiapas or its Ogoniland.

The text below conveys much of the existing situation in Chhattisgarh — the concentration of landholdings, the arbitrary power of the factory owners and the police, the desperation and fatalism of the poor, the ecological degradation — but it also conveys the very creative strategy of a movement that struggles against these conditions. All manner of left organizations have been working in Chhattisgarh over the past 40 years: Gandhians, socialists, Maoists, Soviet-aligned communist parties. Yet one organization has been very successful in building a unity among the victims of development and offering a powerful vision for a new society: the Chhattisgarh Mukti Morcha (Chhattisgarh Liberation Front). The CMM's success has been unique because of its ability to combine trade union politics with concern for the general problems of the society: those relating to agriculture, ecology, technology, gender relations, alcoholism, education, housing, health and the maintenance of regional and tribal cultures. The CMM's strategy, what has been called "social unionism" in other contexts, has been to make the union itself into a social movement. The CMM was able to bring various sectors of the society together, educate them about the issues, and afford them chances to discuss common problems and cooperate in a concrete struggle. With a novel organization transcending the traditional dichotomy between the trade union and the political party, the CMM has become an important model for political activism in India.

The CMM grew out of the Chhattisgarh Mines Shramik Sangh (CMSS), a trade union begun in 1977 by the coal miners in the Delli-Rajhara area. Working under contractors for the Bhilai plant, these miners were among the region's lowest paid and least organized workers. There was no permanency to their employment, no guarantees, and no safety. The trade unions of the political parties (Congress, Janata Dal, Communist Party of India) were based in the urban proletariat and uninterested in organizing contract laborers. This division between permanent waged workers and limited term, contract, seasonal, workers is common to many Indian industries, and trade unions usually neglect to organize the latter. The CMSS soon grew to encompass other miners in the limestone and dolomite mines and began to address a large range of issues facing the miners. The CMM was formed in 1978–79 as an umbrella organization to coordinate the new trade unions and their social activities.

Shankar Guha Niyogi was the leader and main inspiration behind the CMSS and the CMM. Niyogi could become such a leader because his own life nearly embodied Chhattisgarh itself. He experienced every type of labor in Chhattisgarh after moving there from his native Bengal in the early 1960s at the age of about twenty. He first worked as an apprentice and a skilled worker in the Bhilai steel plant. His involvement in a union of the blast furnace workers and in Maoist politics cost him the job in 1967. He soon left for the forests where the Maoists, organized into the new Communist Party of India Marxist-Leninist (CPI-ML), were beginning to wage guerrilla warfare. In the early 1970s, he left the party and traveled throughout Chhattisgarh, picking up odd jobs on the way, whether in the fields or forests, catching fish or shepherding goats. Wherever he went, he joined the local struggles over water and land. By the mid-1970s, he was working and organizing in the quartzite mines. During India's Emergency of 1975–77, Niyogi spent 13 months in jail. This was Indira Gandhi's period of dictatorship when all civil liberties were suspended and many political activists rounded up and thrown in jail as threats to "internal security." Over the course of his 48-year life, he spent a little over three years in jail on eleven different occasions.

By the start of the CMSS in 1977, Niyogi had, in his fifteen years in Chhattisgarh, experienced a wide range of labors. He had come to intimately know the lives of factory workers, miners, peasants, forest tribes, pastoralists, and prisoners. He was also a veteran of the various political movements in India and their strategic debates. In formulating a program for the CMM he broke with every existing political formation in India and yet combined something from each. His basic perspective was Marxist; his aim was to build a working class movement that could challenge capitalism. To this he added a feminist perspective. In starting the CMSS and the CMM, Niyogi was committed to making women full participants in the movement. Women formed half the labor force in the contracted mine work, often working with their husbands as a two-person team. Niyogi also adopted an ecological perspective. For the CMM, ecology was not just a matter of industrial pollution in the cities, it was a matter of the vitality of the peasant holdings in the villages: the status of the irrigation facilities, the crops grown, the seeds used. Given the rural origins of contract workers, the conditions in the villages were directly determining their dependence on the labor market. The unity of Marxism and ecological concerns was captured in the movement's flag: one red stripe above one green stripe. The CMM's various unions became known as the "red and green unions."

The CMM, under Niyogi's leadership, became a center for the cultural and educational life of the workers. From 1979 onwards, it organized an annual festival in honor of a peasant leader of the 1857 revolt in Chhattisgarh. With its folk dances, music performances and poetry readings, the annual Vir Narayan Singh Day became one of the region's cultural high points. Many of Niyogi's writings on Chhattisgarh express the same enthusiasm as Verrier Elwin's for tribal culture, the same rational enchantment and the same desire to preserve what was "beautiful and free."

The CMM devoted its funds towards building schools, houses, even a hospital. The union office itself was designed to represent its vision of a new Chhattisgarh: folk crafts were used and displayed; a mini-forest was nurtured in the back with all types of trees found in the region; a monument was erected on which were engraved the names of the movement's martyrs of the 1977 massacre, and stones, with the red and green flag flying above, marked the death of other union martyrs. International news was spread through the union ranks and the story of Nelson Mandela became commonly known. The CMM had a grand vision and one that many people in Chhattisgarh came to share. The movement's slogan became "A New Chhattisgarh for a New India."

In the interests of decentralizing power in India, Niyogi, along with India's socialist party, advocated the breakup of the existing 22 states into smaller units and the redrawing of the states' boundaries. The idea was and is reasonable enough. Chhattisgarh, now just one district within the state of Madhya Pradesh, is larger than some European countries. The Madhya Pradesh state government administers a territory slightly larger than Iraq. It stands to reason that smaller states would allow for more efficient and democratically controlled administrations. Niyogi recognized that making Chhattisgarh its own state would not automatically cure all of the region's problems but would make their resolutions easier.[7]

One of the most novel aspects to Niyogi's political strategy concerned the question of technology. Following the old law of capitalist development — when faced with a worker's struggle, get rid of the workers — Bhilai introduced mechanization into the surface coal mines in the late 1970s. Instead of distributing the workers out like ants across a site, to dig with hand tools and carry the soil in baskets upon their heads, the company planned on bringing in huge earth movers. The CMSS resisted this in 1980 by striking and offering an alternative proposal for increasing productivity without retrenchment. The struggle for an alternative labor process was by and large successful and the union was able to prevent most of Bhilai's plans for mechanization. Here, the CMSS and Niyogi broke new ground for the Indian left which has tended to simply accept whatever mechanization was implemented in the name of increasing the productive forces — the only caveat the left ever raised was on whether the technology was foreign or indigenous. Niyogi was an opponent of a mechanization that would force workers to lose their jobs, yet he was not opposed to technological progress itself. He spoke in terms of alternative paths to technological change, different types of technology. The same thinking has been behind CMM's work on irrigation. While the government has been building huge dams with loans from the World Bank and Japan, and expropriating hundreds of thousands of people in the process, the CMM (among other groups in India) has been promoting small-scale irrigation systems. Niyogi addresses the question of technology in a section of the speech below.

While the miners' union movement was emerging and their wages rising, the coal contractors and steel plant owners expanded liquor sales to the workers. The political economy of alcohol in India is extremely important. The cheaper forms of liquor (toddy, arrack) where legal, are a monopoly of the state governments, which then awards contracts for their sale. These liquor contractors are powerful political bosses in many states. In the first five years of the CMSS, the consumption of liquor nearly doubled among the miners. The CMSS union leaders, unlike many others in India, had the wisdom to take steps to combat drinking. They organized a public campaign against alcohol consumption and by 1981, in the city of Rajhara with 100,000 people, only one liquor shop remained in business. Niyogi did not demand prohibition by the government nor did he forcibly drive out the liquor contractors (which CPI-ML groups have done elsewhere). He promoted a public campaign, encouraged women's participation and relied on the people to overcome the drinking habit on their own. Moreover, the dynamism of the union, its work on schools and houses for example, gave the people a hope for a better life and a sense of being able to make a positive contribution to society. The great theme of the CMM was self-dignity and it has done much to make the Chhattisgarhi workers confident and politically educated.[8]

The following speech was given on August 18, 1990, to a meeting of young activists who had come from a variety of organizations in Chhattisgarh. This was the first time they had assembled to work out a common program under a united front. The CMM's struggle was intensifying over the course of 1990 as many workers were out on strike to demand minimum wages, work safety, abolition of contract labor, and union recognition. The CMM had achieved a number of victories and was expanding into the cement factories, the small scale steel units, and the chemical factories. The major industrialists of Chhattisgarh, determined to put a stop to the CMM, refused to recognize the new unions and bargain with the CMM. A key element of Niyogi's battle plan was to hold a mass rally in Bhilai of people from every part of Chhattisgarh. The August 18 meeting was part of the preparations for this rally which was held six weeks later on October 2. The rally clearly demonstrated the CMM's strength and forced the industrialists to choose: either negotiate with the CMM or resort to terrorism. They chose the latter option. Niyogi was aware by April 1991 that the industrialists had put a contract out on his life and that he would soon be murdered. He refused the protection of bodyguards saying, "If Rajiv Gandhi could be assassinated with all of his protection, what chance do I have?" The assassins descended upon Niyogi's house at 4:30 in the morning, September 18, 1991, and fired six bullets into him while he was sleeping.

At the time the hitmen were busy plotting Niyogi's execution, the Indian central government in Delhi was preparing a death sentence on millions of India's poor: an IMF structural adjustment agreement. India promised the IMF in November 1991 that it would implement an economic austerity package as a condition for receiving an immediate $2 billion dollar stand-by loan and some $5–7 billion in later years. Following the customary IMF prescriptions, the Finance Minister, Manmohan Singh, announced sweeping plans for privatizing the public sector, removing import controls, promoting exports, eliminating subsidies on basic commodities such as rice and wheat, slashing health and education budgets, and devaluing the rupee. When considering this New Economic Policy in the context of Chhattisgarh, it is obvious that it was not really new for the workers — it was more of the same old anti-democratic and anti-worker policies. The industrialists of Chhattisgarh were encouraged, in the name of 'international competitiveness,' to suppress worker demands with greater gusto.[9] In July 1992, when thousands of protesting CMM supporters blocked the rail lines into Bhilai, the police once again massacred the workers, killing sixteen.

The Madhya Pradesh state government is now advertising itself to international and domestic capital as a paradise of labor peace. In one two page ad in the Indian equivalent of *Time* magazine, the headline announced: "Madhya Pradesh has the lowest number of man-days lost among major industrial states." The ad explained that "industrial harmony" and a "happy workforce" had helped make the state one of the top four investment destinations in India.[10] Such myths of the contented worker make for good advertising copy but for poor representations of the reality the industrialists know all too well. Their aggressive drive for capital accumulation, heedless of environmental effects and workers' lives, is making the CMM's agenda ever more urgent. In their effort to make India another "economic tiger" in the manner of the East Asian city-states, and to pretend that the country's huge rural population does not exist, Indian businessmen are sowing the dragon's teeth of ever greater social violence and ecological destruction.[11]

This particular speech was chosen because it covers the whole range of topics on which the CMM worked. It reveals much about the CMM, Chhattisgarh, and Niyogi himself. More than conveying a certain sum of information, it allows the reader to easily imagine Niyogi alive, reasoning before a group of people and inspiring them with a determination to transform their society. Unlike a report from an outside observer, Niyogi's speech expresses the particular idiom of radical politics in India through its metaphors, rhetorical strategies, and historical allusions. However, rooted in the specific conditions of Chhattisgarh, it reiterates the same message proclaimed by the Zapatistas in Chiapas: to be courageous in the face of repression, to never be intimidated into submission, and to find an end to a life of living death in a community of resistance.

**Notes**

[1] This introduction draws primarily upon the materials assembled in the book *Sangharsh aur Nirmana: Shankar Guha Niyogi aur unka Naye Bharat ka Sapna* [Struggle and Organization: Shankar Guha Niyogi and his Dream of a New India], edited by Anil Sadgopal and Shyam Bahadur 'Namra,' (Delhi: Rajkamal, 1993). It also draws upon People's Union for Democratic Rights, "Shankar Guha Niyogi and the Chhattisgarh People's Movement" (Delhi, 1991, pamphlet); Jeremy Seabrook, "Death of a Socialist: the Chhattisgarh Liberation Movement," *Race and Class* 35: 2 (1993); Sharat G. Lin, "Shankar Guhar Niyogi: Beyond Conventional Trade Unionism in India," *Bulletin of Concern Asian Scholars* 24: 3 (1992); Anil Nauriya, "What the Chhattisgarh Movement Means," *Economic and Political Weekly* (30 November 1991); People's Union for Civil Liberties, "Bastar: Development and

Democracy," (Hoshangabad, 1989, pamphlet); All India People's Resistance Forum, "Bastar: Pro-Imperialist Development Strategy versus People's Struggle," (Nagpur, 1993).

2 Chhattisgarh figures into Nirmal Verma's Hindi novel *Raat ka Reporter* (1989) in an intriguing way. The main character is a journalist in Delhi who is hounded by the intelligence agencies during the martial law period of the mid-1970s after returning from research in Bastar, a district of Chhattisgarh. Under state surveillance, he begins to imagine all of his personal relationships to be marked by suspicion, dishonesty, and secrecy. His experience in Bastar and the nature of his research are never described. Bastar thus comes to signify a radically alien world where the state has committed unspeakable atrocities against tribal communities whose solidarity lies outside the logic of the mutual indifference of middle class individuals. Verma's novel has been translated by Alok Bhalla as *Dark Dispatches* (Delhi: Harper Collins, 1993). The Bengali writer, Mahasweta Devi has lived and worked among the tribals in southern Bihar and West Bengal. Several of her gutwrenching stories of tribal society under assault by Indian bureaucrats and businessmen are available in translation. G.C. Spivak, trans. and ed., *Imaginary Maps: Three Stories by Mahasweta Devi*, (New York: Routledge, 1995).

3 Chhattisgarh (meaning 'thirty six forts') covers the entire eastern side of Madhya Pradesh state, from 18 to 24 degrees latitude, and comprises seven administrative districts: Raipur, Durg, Bilaspur, Bastar, Sarguja, Raigarh, Rajnandgaon. With an area of 52,650 square miles, it is about the same size as the island of Java. Since the name is not used for administrative purposes, one rarely finds it printed on a map. As is often the case, the place names on a map do not correspond with the terminology of the people living there.

4 The term *adivasi*, meaning original inhabitant, is the favored term today but I will use 'tribe' since it is more familiar to English language readers. A useful reference work on Indian tribes is K.S. Singh, *Tribal Society in India* (New Delhi: Manohar, 1985). A valuable study on the politics and culture of Indian tribes in one region is Dev Nathan and Govind Kelkar, *Gender and Tribe: Women, Land, and Forests in Jharkhand* (New Delhi: Kali for Women, 1991).

5 Saurabh Dube, "Myths, Symbols and Community: Satnampanth of Chhattisgarh," in P. Chatterjee and G. Pandey, eds., *Subaltern Studies VII* (Delhi: Oxford University Press, 1993).

[6] Verrier Elwin, *The Tribal World of Verrier Elwin: An Autobiography* (New York: Oxford University Press, 1964), p. 289. Elwin's writings on Chhattisgarh include *Folk Songs of Chhattisgarh* (1946) and *The Muria and their Ghotul* (1947). Ram Guha, a historian of India's environment, has praised Elwin for his attentiveness to the tribals' struggles against the colonial state's enclosures of the forest: "Prehistory of Indian Environmentalism: Intellectual Traditions," *Economic and Political Weekly* (4–11 January 1992). A more recent anthropological study of Chhattisgarhi society is Joyce B. Flueckiger, *Gender and Genre in the Folklore of Middle India* (Ithaca: Cornell University Press, 1996).

[7] See Shankar Guha Niyogi's essay and the other contributions in the souvenir volume of the National Convention on Smaller States, April 1993, Hyderabad.

[8] On the political economy of alcohol in India, see James Manor, *Power, Poverty and Poison: Disaster and Response in an Indian City* (New Delhi: Sage, 1993). In one of the most unexpected struggles of the early 1990s, the women of Andhra Pradesh state organized mass protests against liquor contractors. Unable to suppress the movement that had spontaneously spread from village to village, the state government responded in 1993 by implementing prohibition — a remarkable step given that the excise tax on liquor was its single most important source of revenue. See K. Balgopal, "Slaying of a Spiritous Demon," *Economic and Political Weekly*, (14 November 1992).

[9] There is a sizable literature on the 1991 IMF agreement and its aftermath. A book especially relevant to Niyogi's work is Mukul, *Against the Stream: India's Economic Crisis and Workers' Alternatives* (Delhi, 1992). The book is dedicated to Niyogi and Safdar Hashmi, a street theatre activist murdered by Congress Party goons in Delhi.

[10] *India Today*, 31 July 1994.

[11] For brutally honest and well-informed reporting on how 'economic development' in India, especially under the post-1991 New Economic Policy period, has created poverty, see P. Sainath, *Everybody Loves a Good Drought* (New York: Penguin, 1996).

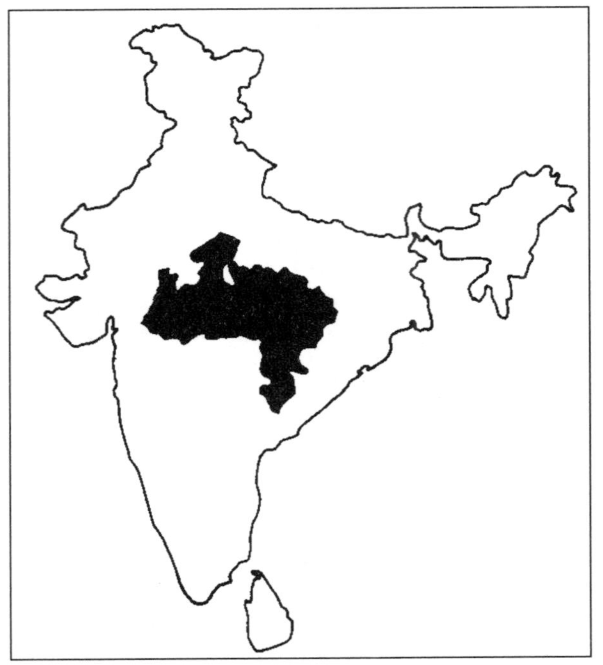

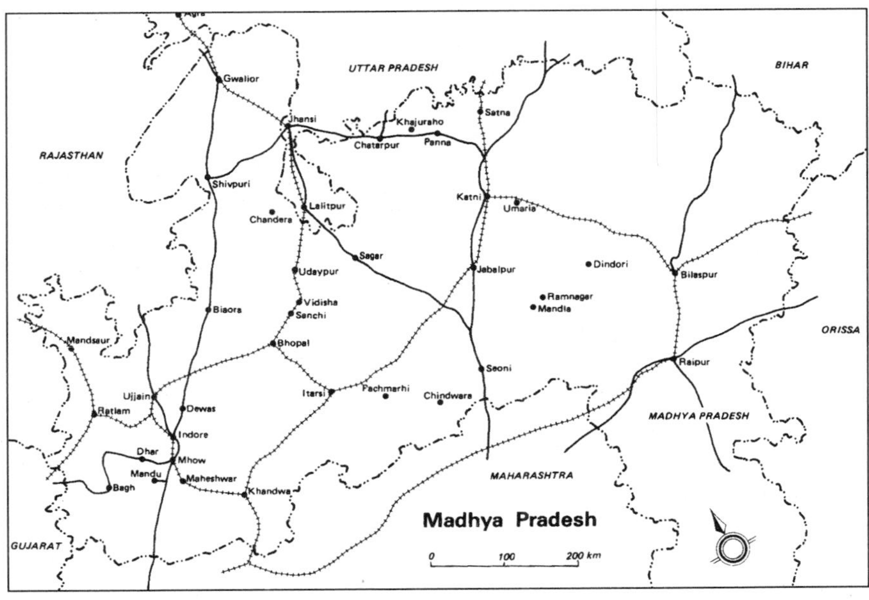


*Location of India's Madhya Pradesh state, top. Chhattisgarh region is in the lower right, below.*

# 11

# VICTORY OVER A LIFE OF LIVING DEATH

## SHANKAR GUHA NIYOGI

So yesterday and today, for two days running, a whole crew of activists have come here and taken part in the discussions.[12] A lot of our friends who didn't take part still carefully listened and thought about the ideas discussed. The thoughts which the activists have so beautifully expressed are related to all the questions of life. They have taken the subjects of today's society — inequality and hatred — and analyzed them carefully, as if opening up the petals of a flower one by one, so that our discussion — our garden — has been made beautiful. Some very nice things have been said and among these, something that everyone said was: "We want a transformation. This system gives us only pain and we want a transformation, we want a revolution." The desire for a qualitative transformation, for a total revolution, is filling everyone's hearts. Now the time for action has come. We're getting older all the time and we don't know whether we'll accomplish the task or not. The work is such that it can't even be completed in a thousand years. For work that can't be completed in a thousand years, what good is it to even waste a moment? Therefore keep going, seize the time, fill it up with work. Don't let the time slip away.

***Illusions, Revolution and Peace***[13]

That dream that you, I, we all have seen of an entirely peaceful society has to be achieved by a revolution. We have understood this and accepted it. But a revolution can occur only when the illusions now current in this country are overcome. As long as they are not overcome there can be no revolution. As long as there is no revolution there will be no peace.

There are a lot of illusions these days. The most important one concerns electoral politics: the Congress Party parades before us and then goes away, the Janata Dal is active here, as is the Jan Morcha, and the BJP [Bharatiya Janata Party] and who knows what else. All these parties give such beautiful assurances and speak in an oily and slippery way: "We're doing this, we're doing that." An illusion emerges from such things. However, there is one more illusion of which we haven't spoken that much. The state wants to create a society in which fear and terror might rule; it wants to prove that fear and terror are omnipotent.

Workers! Do you demand the price of your toil? Peasants! Do you demand water for irrigation? Students! Do you demand a decent school system? Women! Do you demand to be free of your present oppression? All of you should certainly get what you demand, but you haven't gotten it and you can't seem to struggle for it. If you struggle then look what happens: our 'men in uniform' and of course before them, our 'social people' — those whom we call anti-socials, *goondas*, arrive. They send these anti-social men to beat us up and wreck everything and if that doesn't have any effect, they send the police to do some shooting, to create fear and terror. Because of this, the people get demoralized, become doubt-ridden and remain quiet. We should be very clear about this: whatever fear, whatever terror, it can't suppress us, it can't block the path we're on, it can't be an obstacle standing in our way. If it is in the way then we'll remove it, like removing stones from the road, one by one, and proceed ahead.

Friends! This obstacle keeps blocking our path. When it does, we have to be resolute, our thoughts have to be well worked out. If we push on determined and find we still can't move ahead then who knows where we'll go; maybe we'll get lost in a thick fog. Behind us is a very long history — an entire lifetime isn't long enough to recount it. A history of thousands of years, of so many sacrifices! In our country so many people have sacrificed themselves — Chandrashekar Azad, Bhagat Singh, Vir Narayan Singh, Mahatma Gandhi, Ramdhin Gond, the Muriya people of Bastar.[14] Despite gaining this so-called independence, in Rajnandgaon in 1948, workers of the BNC Mill were shot at — that was on the orders of the Congress government. The very first time the BNC Mill workers were fired on was during British rule in 1920; that was the first murder in India's labor movement history. The first shooting in independent India was in 1948 during the

Congress Party's time. Once the Janata Party took over, its first shooting was on Delli Rajhara workers. The BJP's government came to power and they also ordered shootings on the Chhattisgarh people, on the workers of Abhanpur.[15] The Chhattisgarh people have time and again thought out their dreams and tried to bring them into practice and have, in a powerful and united form, raised their voices against the exploiters. But those who want to spread fear and terror, who want to suppress the people, the exploiters, repeatedly suppress the Chhattisgarh people with bullets.

Therefore, you can see that in this country the most dreadful problems are emerging: Punjab, Kashmir, Assam, Bodo, and LTTE.[16] What is the reason behind all this? It is in the nature of the country's unequal development. Egalitarian development can't be found anywhere and so these types of things, in different places, in different forms, on the basis of different problems, are cropping up as results of the same process. At this time too there are visions before the Chhattisgarh people. To realize them our martyrs have sacrificed and now it is up to us to walk along the blood-stained path and fulfill their dreams and design a new Chhattisgarh, a new India. To create this design we need to have a program upon which we can confidently act.

### *Life force and death force*

I started by talking about an illusion. I want to continue talking about illusions with you. In humans, as in all living beings, there are two elements; one is of death, the other of life. These are inside of us. We're alive but a death force is still in us. Upon dying, the body becomes senseless, the life force is spent and the death force overtakes us. The two forces of life and death are engaged in a constant struggle. When the element of life is stronger we can move forward, our dream progresses. When the death force overtakes us then our dream dies. To keep the dream alive, to keep building the road forward, it is necessary that the life force remain dominant over the death force; this is essential. The revolution must remain superior to the illusions; this is also essential. If the revolution cannot win over the power of illusions, then the outcome is certain: our body will be alive but our dream will have died. If that happens, why will life be worth living? There should be some meaning to our lives, the lives of our countrymen, some meaning to this society. Our lives should mean something and to create that meaning we have to keep designing, over and over again, a new future. This is the way it is, not just in Chhattisgarh, but all over India.

But right now I'm not talking about all of India. I want to restrict myself just to Chhattisgarh for the moment. I mentioned before that the Chhattisgarhi people first made sacrifices for the struggle in the time of the British. The people continued to make sacrifices in the time of the Congress government, then during the Janata Dal government, then again during the Congress government, then during the BJP government. My friends, I beg you, remember those sacrifices that our martyrs made in the struggle against the darkness. There is still a darkness today and the light has not yet come. You will have to move ahead with a firmness in your steps and a commitment to a program, nothing will be gained from wasting time.

### Combine the Local and the Universal

In our lives — I'm referring to us activists here, not the general public — there is a problem that I see cropping up again and again. The people always listen to what we have to say but they don't act on it. The result is that even an activist gets affected by this and says, "First of all, man, we have to look after our own family, after that our own neighborhood, our own village. We don't have any energy left for work on the rest of the society. As for the national stuff, well that is big stuff, if we get an opportunity, O.K., we'll work on it." This idea, that you have to begin in the home, begin with the family, is another illusion.

How many activists have gotten trapped in this illusion and can't manage to get out of it. Sometimes a friend will begin working from a false notion of Gandhi, even after reading Gandhi. If one keeps working and working in village development then the work will be limited to the boundaries of the village. As long as we can't find a way to combine the local everyday issues with the more general social ones and we can't establish any relationship between the two, the general issues will go unaddressed.

Let's say there is a river near your village and it floods, then what are you going to do? What will happen when the water enters your village? Won't everyone begin to worry that all the houses will get submerged? But when the water is rising in your village, aren't there other villages which will also be flooded? Won't the water enter those villages and submerge them too? So how are you going to save your own village? Your own house? If there are clouds, clouds everywhere, the rain will fall; if the clouds don't come, the rain won't fall. There won't be any rain in your village, nor in other villages, nor anywhere else in the entire country. What happens in the country also happens in your own locality. This is how the general contains the particular and the particular contains the general. But the limited perspective of making your own village the foundation, or making any other little place or grouping the foundation of your work, is based on illusions. We have to be free of these illusions and put them behind us.

Now let me place before you the biggest illusion here. This is the illusion of fate. In Chhattisgarh they say, "What can we do? Debts incurred in this life have to be repaid in the next life. To pay off the debts of this life, we have to be reborn as a chicken or as an ox. Such is our fate, brother. What can we do?"[17] This is a very powerful illusion. There are two things here: one is fate, the other is the real situation — fate and the real state of our lives — they are in opposition to one another. Our activists in Chhattisgarh are faced with this over and over. Since the question of fate keeps coming up, we should be very clear about it and also about the real conditions. For example, our sisters always say that the men are oppressive and some women, thinking this to be fate, accept it. Fate is connected with the real conditions, but there is no life in it, there is no life force behind it, there is only the death force.

So what then is our situation today, what is the state of our lives? And what will be the situation to follow the present one? And what will be the one after that? How will we move into these future contexts and situations, how will we progress? We need to concentrate on this, to rationally think about it, to devote our hearts and minds to it. As long as we don't sort out our ideas on it, we won't get free of the present situation. Fate means stagnation and death. It's no problem for the person who dies. We'll also die, so what? When I die my corpse will lie right here and man, it will let off such a stink that every one living around here will want to run away. That's how it is for the person who believes in fate, for that person there isn't any problem, but for every one else, there is a very big problem. It is urgent at this time that the element of the life-force contains and checks the death wish. Where there is exploitation, oppression, injustice, there death prevails. Where there is a struggle, where there is a fight, a desire for progress, where there is hope — there is the force of life; it sets off, keeps progressing, keeps moving step by step, and one day it reaches the rendezvous of victory.[18]

## The Land Question

Friends, now, after discussing these illusions, it is time to discuss the problems which are burdening the people of Chhattisgarh. We should have a clear discussion about the ideas which are creating and spreading the illusions. Let us take the land question. Today, I want to talk about the land in this area. The legislative member of Rajnandgaon owns all the land in the city of Durg. The Collector [an administrative officer] of Durg was telling me one day that once Shri Dharmpal Gupta [a wealthy member of the legislature] told him that the Collectorate and its bungalow were on his land. I told the Collector, "Brother, you're a tenant, you better get after the government to pay the rent." There isn't an inch of land left that Dharmpal Gupta doesn't own. He's a big leader in the BJP, used to be in another party and after switching back and forth, he's back in the BJP. All of Durg's land is in his hands. Our Jurdev Saheb, Maharajaji, has so much land — you people from his area [Raigarh district] can talk about it in detail. He's got thousands of acres. And some temple lands, like Nadiya *Math*. He's got a lot of lands like that: Vankhera *Math*, Bhadrachalam *Math*, and these *maths* have a lot of land registered in their names.[19] I've heard that, in order to avoid the land ceiling law, some land is even registered in the names of dogs and cats. Some land is even under the names of children who haven't been born yet.

So the land question is crucial. Consider the good land in this country, especially the land just outside the cities. Durg, Rajnandgaon, Raipur, Bilaspur — wherever you look you see "agricultural farms" on the outskirts of the cities. There you'll find sugarcane planted somewhere, it will be there somewhere. All types of crops are raised there. Out in front you'll even find some small fruit shops. This is the "farm house" phenomenon. If you see the farm house of the biggest power broker around here, Raipur city's Vidyacharanji Shukla, you'll be overjoyed and overwhelmed that such a place even exists. It is quite something just to go around the farm house. The owners of these great estates never touch a plow. They don't know how to plow; there isn't a one of them that knows how. And then there are some neighborhoods of Raipur city where the people living there have their lands in Bemetara, Kavardha, Rajnandgaon, and other places while they all live in Raipur, inside a special enclave. How do these landlords, from every nook and cranny of Chhattisgarh, all living in Raipur, get their income from the villages? No doubt, you all know something about it.

This is the land question that our activists have raised time and again while travelling through the villages. But there is something they haven't paid much attention to yet. There is a sons-of-the-soil slogan that has come up: "Chhattisgarh is for the Chhattisgarhis, Not for Anyone Else." Now who are these Chhattisgarhis, brother? Well, one is our Jurdev Saheb. One is Dharmpal Gupta who has about 2,500 to 3,000 acres. Are they Chhattisgarhis? So what does Chhattisgarh and Chhattisgarhi mean? These guys aren't Chhattisgarhis — they want to create quarrels amongst us. I want to tell you very clearly that we are a family of workers, that we are of one caste (*jat*). We have to speak of ourselves as of the same caste, the same brotherhood (*biradri*). Not just the same caste, but the same lineage (*gotra*). There are two *gotras* in this world, one is of tigers and the other is of men. The tigers are the *gotra* of blood suckers, those who eat the toilers, while the toilers are the human *gotra*, those who earn their bread by labor. Here we are all sitting as one *jat*, as one *gotra*. In order to break us up, to turn us against one another, they have raised this type of slogan. But we have a slogan of our own. We'll get to it later.

**The Trade Unions' Wrong Path**

I want to place before you one more subject. In the industrial areas, like Bhilai, Rajnandgaon, Delli Rajhara, Korba, Hirri, Nandini, Bailadila, Abhanpur, the workers have only one point of discussion: that such and such a demand be fulfilled. Two of our demands are very popular: one, increase the wages and two, hand out a bonus. Long live the revolution. What kind of transformation will come out of this? A qualitative transformation? a *kranti*? an *inquilab*? In Urdu they say "*inqilab*," in Hindi, they say "*kranti*" — meaning a qualitative transformation (*gunatmuk parivartan*). Out of this type of demand, the slogan then becomes "a 10% bonus they will have to give, have to give!" After getting a 10% bonus is there going to be a revolution in our country? Are the workers going to become the rulers? And will the exploiters become paupers? After getting an increase in wages will all our sorrows disappear? Today, trade unions have only two objectives left: increase the wages and increase the bonus. In Chhattisgarh we say "*bhunas*" and if we hear "*bhunas*" our hearts leap with joy. And if we get a half-percent increase then, right on! If we have to give 10 to 20 rupees for union dues then we'll give it right away. "Our leaders are doing great work, they've brought us a one to two percent increase in the bonus. If our bonus increases, so that's it, we've got a revolution."

What else does a trade union do all year? It has only one job, day in and day out: to answer chargesheets. The bosses come and say, you're not working, get out. And they give the worker a chargesheet. The worker then takes the chargesheet to the union leader and says, it's written here that a response has to be filed in 72 hours, or 24 hours. Now, after working on it for however long it is, 24 hours, 72 hours, 3 days, or 7 days, we turn in a response.

What kind of houses do the workers live in? Are they supplied with drinking water? What kind of ideas are the children growing up with? Are they always watching videos, "blue films," imitating Amitabh Bachchan going "*dishum-dishum*" or are they doing something else?[20] Are the trade union leaders thinking about this or not? Many workers are drinking liquor and lying sprawled out in the streets. Our Phaguramji has composed a song.[21] In it he says that even dogs piss in the mouths of drunkards. Who is going to make sure that the workers' leaders are doing their job or not? Where have the workers come from? They've come here from the villages. On becoming landless, they come to the city and become workers, working in the industries, while their relatives continue to live in the villages. In the process, a worker loses his connection with his relatives. Does the trade union concern itself with this or not?

**The Question of Mechanization**

A crucial issue, which affects not just workers but the entire country is what kind of technology will be used in a given line of production? What kind of technology is to be utilized? Is the technology harmful for the country or helpful? Is it beneficial for the country or not? In Bhilai there is a certain machine, an IBM calculating machine. It costs around 250–300 million rupees [about 8–10 million dollars]. You can't even imagine how quickly it can do calculations. It can calculate figures in the millions, in fractions of a second. One day, a certain small part of this machine got damaged. Now if a little part gets ruined in a machine like this, its whole brain goes out. If its brain gets damaged then all of its work gets turned upside down. We know two times two equals four but what did this machine give? It gave eighty. Its brain went haywire like that. So the managers told the American company to repair it. So the Americans said, "This is an old model, spare parts for this aren't even available in our country any more. Why don't you throw out this machine and buy the new model? Its price is 500 million rupees." Now look, brother, for the sake of a little part its whole brain gets ruined and 500 million rupees goes down the drain. 500 million rupees wasted, just like that. Today the management is importing technology like this and betraying the country. I once spoke personally with some leaders of the Janata Dal — now they're ministers — and at that time they said that foreign companies were eating up the country in this way, looting the country. But now after coming to power, they've forgotten all about this.

Nowadays this new industrial policy is in vogue, who knows what kind of industrial policy it is. Rajiv Gandhi's industrial policy was about technology but there wasn't any major change under his policy.[22] The same policy continues today — in a big way. A lot of friends have come from Bastar, they'll no doubt know the place Ravghat in Bastar where iron ore is located. Ravghat's iron ore is about to come to Bhilai. The Environmental Minister, Mrs. Maneka Gandhi, didn't give the permission for this and so the Bhilai management is furious with her.[23] They say that Maneka Gandhi doesn't want this region to develop. They're insisting that the permission be granted immediately. Even though Bastar is so close by, you probably haven't been there. But America, Canada, Australia, Korea and Japan — these five countries — have set up houses in Ravghat. The contract for the area is about to be given by the Internal Ministry. What kind of mechanical process will be introduced there? What kind of technology? Using that kind of technology, the iron ore will be mined and then brought to Bhilai's factories. The whole world knows about this. We are the people of Chhattisgarh and of Bastar but we haven't gone and seen Ravghat. While these Australians, Canadians, Koreans, and Japanese have seen it all. They're preparing a plan. I spoke with one manager. I told him, "Brother, after bringing in machinery the cost of production should go down. You people keep saying this but it's not true and you're cooking up the figures. Actually, that machine's brain went bad and you never take that into account. The depreciation is several times greater than what you're claiming."

In our country, the very best work, technically speaking, is that done by manual labor. The cost of production is lower and its quality is better. Beladila's production has been done by a manual process for the last ten years. The quality of a worker's output there is no different and no less than that of a machine's. We give as good a product as a machine. The proof of this is coal. When the coal mines weren't operated by machines, the quality of the coal wasn't as bad as it is today. Why are these people always talking about technology? They are confusing technology and machinery when they are two separate things.

Technology is something that if you enter into it — like Abhimanyu — you can enter into it but you can't find your way back out. In Abhimanyu's case the end was death.[24] In a similar way, these people are causing countless injuries to this country, they are murdering us, they are murdering our spirit. They are murdering the people's subsistence and creating whole new problems for the country. They are full of death. They wield knives and swords above the life force.

### The Question of Chhattisgarh

Two topics are before you. One is the land question, the second is the machine question. You should be clear about these two things: land and machinery — meaning also industrial policy. You shouldn't have any illusions. You shouldn't have any illusions about these sons-of-the-soil politicians with their slogan of "Chhattisgarh for the Chhattisgarhis." You have to despise this. The other issue is economism: that the trade union should only deal with economic issues. This you also have to despise. These are the two political issues. The CPI and CPI-M activists working in the industrial belt are always organizing on the basis of these two issues; the BJP and the Congress do the same thing. In order to gain a power base, they sow the seeds of political discord; they want to suppress the people's voice, to destroy it, to break up our unity, to spread hatred among the people. You have to despise all these attempts at political disunity.

But what's the alternative? You say, "We'll avoid all that, brother, but what's the alternative?" Now we're ready to give our slogan, in one voice: "Chhattisgarh is ours, not the looters' property."[25] If it is not the property of the looters, of the exploiters, then whose is it? It is ours. It is our Chhattisgarh. The workers', the peasants', the toilers', the honest people's, the patriots', and everyone else's — but it is not theirs.

Tell me sir, you've got a lot of land, how are you a Chhattisgarhi when you exploit the people? You're not a Chhattisgarhi! The Chhattisgarhi people are not exploiters; they don't drink the people's blood. Toilers, patriots, they don't exploit any one else. They are the Chhattisgarhis. When it is their Chhattisgarh, it is not ours. When it is our Chhattisgarh, it is not theirs. The difference between the two is obvious and can be easily seen. Therefore, we will not adopt their slogan, which is one to break up our unity. We are talking about a new Chhattisgarh, "Chhattisgarh is ours, not the looters' property." This is our slogan. Is it right or wrong? This is the slogan we have to adopt. It is not just about economics, it is also about technology.

Our workers from Bhilai are here. I remember when I was a worker in Bhilai. At that time the Simplex company only had two lathe machines. Now I see today that the Simplex company has so much capital, such an abundance of capital, assets of billions of rupees! They are about to build, with no drain on their finances, a sponge iron factory near Beladila on which more than 1.5 billion rupees [$50 million] will be spent. Whoever had only two lathe machines just thirty years ago now has an iron factory and the capability to run a steel factory. One factory is in Bhilai, one in some other place, and one in Ahmedabad. Look at this B.K. Company too. A building contractor in Chandigarh — a B.K. Company; a building contractor in Bangalore — a B.K. Company; a building contractor in Bhopal — a B.K. Company. Building contractors in Bokaro, Durgapur, Raurkela — B.K. Companies all of them. In India there are two big building contractors.[26] One is Jai Prakash — who built the Asiad complex — and the other is your B.K. Company — Bakhtiyar Singh.[27] And what was he before? Fellow workers, you don't know, perhaps you weren't even born at that time. But we know. Before he didn't have anything at all. When he took the contract for sector four [in Bhilai], he didn't have anything at all. His work started out in petty contracting. Now the petty contractor is the country's biggest contractor. Tell me, how much money have the Bhilai people earned?

Now if we're clear about the land question and the industrial question — the industrialists' question — on how the classes exist in both places, on the land and in industry, then we will be liberated from illusions, incorrect lines of thinking, and the death wish. Then the life force will be victorious, the ideas of our martyrs will spread, and the path of freedom will be made stronger. These are the two questions, they are what we have to think about in the process of developing our political program.

### The Beast's Strength and the People's Strength[28]

When it is time to formulate a program, you have to keep these issues in mind. Who has power? Power is of two types. How is that, you'll ask, how can it be of two types? It has to be of only one type. No, there are two types. One type is brute strength. It is brute strength that now runs the state as you can see. The second type is people's strength. Wherever the people's strength is weak, there the death force prevails and the life force wastes away. And wherever the people's strength is dominant, there brute strength and the death force are weak. In Chhattisgarh we say it is a matter of might (*barpeli*). If your *barpeli* prevails then my *barpeli* is useless. If my enemy's *barpeli* prevails, then I'm powerless. If my *barpeli* is inactive, then the death force overtakes me, death gains the upper hand, I become separated from life and hope, the dream dies. Therefore, the problem we face is one of building up people's power, of planning how to build it up.

In Konta, in Kavardha, when our activists staged a hunger strike against the forest officials they were labeled Naxalites and arrested.[29] It's not written anywhere in the constitution that you can just go kill someone or beat them up and throw them in jail. Besides, the Naxalite label isn't even applicable to our activists. I know them personally and know that they're not Naxalites, they're not a part of Naxalite thinking. So why are they called Naxalites and arrested? It is because, in our area, the death force prevails and you can't find the life force anywhere around here. There is no organization, no unity, no solid unity.

Soon it won't be all that easy in Chhattisgarh to call someone a Naxalite and arrest them because the people's strength is emerging here, in Karvadha, in Chauki, in Narayanpur, in Kondagaon, in Kanker, in Surguja. It is coming up in the working class areas of Bhilai and Delli Rajhara, Rajandgaon, and Korba. People's power is being established in all these places and is spreading out. So, S.P. [Superintendent of Police] Mahodaya, there is nothing to worry about if you continue with your ways — do your worst. We'll see who the Naxalites are and what kind of work they do! When all the water in a river rises up, when the water floods, all the rubbish gets swept away and not a trace of dirt is left. When the flood comes you won't have any desire to cry over a past mistake or an activist getting locked up in jail after being called a Naxalite.

But we shouldn't get too happy about hearing this talk about the water rising. Even though the water will become swollen by the rains, it will flow on towards the sea. And then our river will be dried up once more. We have to think about stopping up the water, about damming it and storing it. How can you stop it? You unify the people, take them to the river and dam it. Workers, peasants, intellectuals, patriots — once you build a unity of all these classes, people's power will be able to stop the river. This is work you people are already doing, but you'll have to do it more quickly and forcefully, you'll have to do it with great courage.

None of our martyrs was fearful — from Bhagat Singh to Ramdhin Gond, to Abhanpur's Ramesh Periera. It is from their sacrifices that a people's rule is being established today. In order to destroy people's power, they will create all sorts of disruptions; they will spread terror, use appeals to tradition and caste to break up our unity. We won't let anyone break us up. This is our vow, this is everyone's vow. We won't allow them to sow the seeds of disunity. We will resow the seeds of unity. When we resow the seeds of unity, when we work for the country, there will be an even greater abundance of water. And we'll have to stop this water. Wherever the water is needed then we'll dam it up there. If there is brutality going on in Kavardha, then we'll press the switch in Raipur. The people's strength will arrive in Karvardha and say: "Look out! We've come here in the thousands and we're going to challenge the beast's strength. Who is the beast here? Come on, take us on, try to stand up to us."

You know, a scarecrow is put in the middle of the field, right? When the peasant sticks a scarecrow in the field, all the birds think, "Hey, this must be some man." The poor birds get scared and leave the field. But what happens when some daring bird comes along? Nothing happens to the bird, the scarecrow just stands there. The bird eats its fill and leaves. These men in uniform, all these gangsters who spread terror and fear, are like scarecrows in the field. When I was going to go sit on a hunger strike, just recently in front of A.C.C., there were some men there to kill me.[30] So the Collector said, "Niyogi, don't go there, your life is in danger." Some friends had heard before this that some goondas had gone there with sticks and had already thrashed our Ghoshal Dada and some other friends. So I said, O.K., let them kill me. Who in this world lives forever? If I have to die tomorrow or even today, it's O.K., I've lived long enough, I've already lived for close to the average life span of my countrymen. There shouldn't be any greed about living. Some friends have sacrificed to do great work for the country, to establish people's rule. I haven't been able to give even that much. I have only one dream, that I will be able to live like those friends and martyrs who have taken up the path of sacrifice, who have left singing the song of this country's freedom. If I could have a life like theirs, what greater gift could there be? One couldn't get a gift greater than dying as a martyr even by going to Badrinath and Kedarnath.[31]

So I said, whatever they want to do, let them do it. I'm going to go sit there on a hunger strike. Brute strength did show up but people's power was there too. The workers of A.C.C., the workers of other areas, weren't ready to return home even when it got to be around three o'clock in the morning. They stood there on guard with huge sticks. I told them it wasn't necessary and that they could return home. Injustice has no power, justice has the power. I said, look, nothing will happen to me. I had great difficulty in getting my sisters and brothers to leave. And nothing happened, see, nothing happened.

The beast's strength is like a scarecrow waving in the wind, like a scarecrow to frighten birds. When you get there you'll see, the goondas don't have any power. Why mention the goondas, even the police don't have any power. There isn't any power in this world that can stand up to people's power. So there is no reason to be afraid. Move ahead without worry. That day when we flip the switch in Raipur, it won't matter whether we go to Kavardha or Narayanpur, people's power will prevail everywhere. The death force will be wiped out and buried in the ground. And the life force will stand there tall and proud. It will happen like that, just like that. That is the hope, the desire, your dream and my dream. So go take this to the villages. That power of capital, where is that power of capital in Chhattisgarh? Whose power? The power of the beast. Where is the beast's fort? You'll say its in Raipur.[32] There's nothing in Raipur, those people living in Raipur, whether they're in some party or another, they're just touts for Bhilai's capitalists. So those touts reside there and claim to be the leaders of Chhattisgarh. But the real power is with the Bhilai people, they have it, they have the capital. Those Bhilai capitalists are really in control here. They are showing their power now. So my young friends of Chhattisgarh, my activist friends of Chhattisgarh, you will have to take this message to the villages.

I can't resist from telling you about a great speech Jayprakash Narayanji gave in Patna once a long time ago.[33] He said the seat of dictatorship was in Patna and so the people of Bihar would have to get up and come to Patna — from every village, from every city, from every district. They would all come to Patna and start a sit-in. It was like a trumpet blast, calling people to the movement. A new consciousness was created in the people. Today, I'm telling you friends, I've come with that speech to your home here. The root of Chhattisgarh's capitalism is right there in the Bhilai steel plant. The owners living there and the management, together with the investors, run Chhattisgarh's system of exploitation from that plant; they organize and lead it.

All of you from every one of Chhattisgarh's villages, from Narayanpur, from Ambikapur, from Surguja, from the Mainpat area, from Bilaspur, friends from all the areas will have to come, proudly and confidently, to Bhilai's steel plant. The decision for this will come one day and on that day, all the youth will come from their separate villages, groups of twenty from 4,000 villages, there'll be 80,000 people coming, and 80,000 friends in Bhilai will be sitting there to welcome all of you.

In this way the power of hundreds of thousands will form, people's power will be born, a power that no one will be able to challenge. The power of the beast will have to bow down before this people's power, it will have to prostrate itself. We have to decide when that day will come. When will people's power rise up? What day will it be? What glorious day? We will have to decide. But for right now, we have to spread the message in all directions, to all the villages, come, bring 10 people from your village, bring 20, bring 30. And they will come. Why will our youth come? How much unemployment is there in Chhattisgarh today? So many people unemployed, in each and every village. These CPI people, these Communist Party people, are saying to the villagers, "Let's go, the Mongra dam has to be built." Why? Because there you will get work. Maybe 200 villages will get submerged by it. And then the machinery will have to be operated. Why? So that our unemployment problem will be solved? It will be one month of mechanical work and then they'll be driven away. So friends, let's go, today we have the opportunity to build people's power in the Chhattisgarh area. We can't let this opportunity slip away. We have to come to Bhilai in one united force and raise the flag of people's rule high in the air. That's right, isn't it?

**The Roaring of a Great Ocean**

How many tanks, little reservoirs of water, are there in Chhattisgarh?[34] Your village has one, every village has one. If all the tanks of Chhattisgarh were put together, if the rivers of Ib, Arpa, Indravati, Shivnath and Mahanadi, if all the rivers were brought together here, imagine how much water there would be! A lot of water, a great expanse of water! And this water would be like an ocean and waves would begin to form. These waves would pound against the fortress walls of the exploiters. One wave, a second, a third, a fourth — the exploiters won't be able to save their fort from the repeated poundings. The fort will be near collapse because its foundations are weak; it stands on the foundation of injustice. The fort will fall. But we need the water of all the villages' tanks and of all the rivers too and if we get that water we can create a huge ocean. If all the youth come, from every village, every district, every province, an ocean will form. A great roaring will be heard: "Long live the Revolution! *Inqilab Zindabad!*" It will be a call for a real revolution, a total transformation. Then there will be a war between life and death, life will fight against death and death will fight against life. It will be a battle you will have to join.

**The Story of Spartacus**

I'll tell you a story, a short one, about an ancient revolt. Spartacus was the leader — not like any of the leaders today, he wasn't on the take — he was a courageous leader. He sang the song of freedom. Spartacus was a leader who wanted to free the slaves from their chains. He gave his life for the struggle. After he died in battle, the slave masters still weren't certain who Spartacus was. They asked, "Who here is Spartacus?" A lot of prisoners of war were assembled; they all began to shout, "I'm Spartacus!" One would say, "I'm Spartacus!" and then another. The chant went up in one voice, "I'm Spartacus! I'm Spartacus!"[35] In a similar manner, every village will have to stand up, every one working to establish people's power, "I'm from such and such a village. I'm from Dinaka village." And in this way, every village will rise up. The workers of every neighborhood, every street, every house, every shanty town. The city and the village, shoulder to shoulder, will raise the slogan, "We want freedom!" Who wants freedom? The people of Narayanpur want it, Sarguja wants it, Mainpat wants it, the people of Bilaspur want freedom, the people of Raipur's Lendi Tank want freedom. All kinds of people in every place want freedom. The workers of Delli Rajhara, the workers of Chandikongari mines, the workers in the Hirri area all want freedom. The people of every region want freedom. Look, the beast's power, where does it come from? It doesn't have any power. The beast will die.

**DEATH TO A LIFE OF LIVING DEATH!**

**Notes**

12 I would like to thank Keshav Rao Jhadev and Alok Bhalla for their help in clarifying certain passages and Suresh Sharma for translating the Chhattisgarhi sentences. All errors are mine. The text of the speech is published in Anil Sadgopal and Shyam Bahadur 'Namra', eds., *Sangharsh Aur Nirmana*, pp. 282–295.

13 These three words rhyme in Hindi: *bhranti*, *kranti* and *shanti*. Part of Niyogi's effectiveness as a speaker was his ability to leave the listener with certain memorable phrases. Many of the oppositions he makes later, between fate vs. reality, brute strength vs. the people's strength, consist of rhymed words.

14 Chandrashekar Azad and Bhagat Singh were members of the

Hindustan Socialist Republican Army which carried out a series of bombings and assassination attempts against British targets during the period 1928–30. Azad was killed in a shooting in Allahabad and Bhagat Singh was hanged by the British in 1931. Their names are universally known in India. Vir Narayan Singh was the leader of the 1857 revolt in Chhattisgarh against the British. Ramdhin Gond is a tribal hero of the region. The Muriya are a tribe in Bastar.

15 The Indian government, regardless of the party in power, has evidenced a remarkably consistent commitment to the practice of shooting striking workers. Eleven people were shot by the police on June 2–3, 1977 when 10,000 coal miners on contract labor came to Delli Rajhara. Among the eleven killed were a 12-year-old boy and one woman. Niyogi was arrested before the massacre and kept in jail for a little over a month. This incident occurred soon after the lifting of Indira Gandhi's two-year dictatorship when there were high expectations of greater freedom. On September 27, 1980, hundreds of miners surrounded the central government troops sent to suppress the CMSS's strike in Delli Rajhara. They protested a soldier's attempted rape of a 14 year-old tribal girl. The troops killed one man and injured 38 others in the firing. On September 12, 1984, the police fired upon a march of striking cotton mill workers in Rajnandgaon and killed four. On July 1, 1992, almost a year after Niyogi's assassination, 16 people were killed in Bhilai when the police fired upon workers sitting in civil disobedience on a railway line and then later upon crowds in the city. *Sangharsh aur Nirmana*, pp. 465–471.

16 Punjab, Kashmir and Assam are states in which demands for greater autonomy within a federal India were raised in the 1980s. Bodoland is a region in northern Assam where a movement began in 1987 to demand independence. The government dispatched troops to all four regions in the name of suppressing secessionists and terrorists. There has been a vicious cycle in the four regions of government state terrorism and the opposition groups' terrorism. The legitimate, constitutional demands of the people have been derailed and squelched. The LTTE [Liberation Tigers of Tamil Elam] is a guerrilla force that has been waging war against the Sri Lankan state since the early 1980s and now controls much of the northern ethnically Tamil region. The LTTE was based in Madras, in India, throughout the 1980s and received support from the Indian government. When Rajiv

Gandhi, as Prime Minister, withdrew support, introduced Indian troops into Sri Lanka, and began attacking the LTTE, the organization assassinated him in 1991.

17 This quote is in the Chhattisgarhi language. Niyogi breaks into Chhattisgarhi on numerous occasions in the speech, a language very similar to Hindi but not perfectly intelligible to a Hindi speaker.

18 The phrase 'rendezvous of victory' one might recognize from a poem by Aimé Césaire but it is an accurate translation of the phrase *vijaya ki manzil*.

19 A *math* is a center of Hindu religious learning connected with a temple.

20 Blue films are pornographic films. Amitabh Bachchan was the most popular actor of Hindi cinema. His films usually portrayed the lone hero fighting for social justice by single-handedly beating up and killing many hordes of mafiosos, corrupt officials and their henchmen.

21 Phaguramji is known as the 'people's poet' of Chhattisgarh.

22 Rajiv Gandhi, Indira Gandhi's son, was elected prime minister after her assassination. He advertised the slogan of taking India into the 21st century by adopting and developing the latest technologies.

23 Maneka Gandhi is the widow of Indira's other son Sanjay. She has taken up environmentalism and vegetarianism as her pet projects.

24 The story of Abhimanyu is from the Mahabharata. He is a warrior who has been taught how to penetrate a certain enemy formation but not how to get out of it.

25 The slogan is "Chhattisgarh is not the looters' *jagir*." A *jagir* was a pre-capitalist form of property; it entitled one to rights over land revenue collection but the holder could usually claim rights over just about anything else. Therefore, it has the connotation of arbitrary and totalitarian exercise of political authority. *Jagirs*, where they existed, were abolished after Independence.

26 The Simplex and the B.K. companies were among the leaders of the industrialists' anti-CMM drive and their managers were among those named by Niyogi before his death as the men who hired the assassins.

27 New Delhi hosted the Asiad games in 1983. For the preceding years there was a construction boom in the city for the hotels, dorms, sports stadiums, etc. The violations of laws regarding wages and safety were innumerable and went entirely ignored by the government. The Public Union for Civil Liberties (New Delhi) published a pamphlet on the labor conditions at the construction sites.

[28] The Hindi words are *pashushakti* and *janshakti*. I've translated the former variously as 'brute strength,' the 'beast's strength' and as 'the beast.'

[29] Naxalite is a term for a member of the CPI-ML and derives from the name of a village in West Bengal where an armed struggle began in 1968. Today there are many CPI-ML groups that are arrayed in a variety of coordinating bodies. The party does exist, with a central committee, but does not exercise authority over all the various groups termed ML. Some ML groups are still organizing armed struggle such as the People's War Group (PWG) in Andhra Pradesh while others are emphasizing a more parliamentary line, such as the Indian People's Front (IPF). In Niyogi's final statement before his murder, he stated that his thinking was close to the PWG and the IPF but that he disagreed with both. He was opposed to the tendency of the PWG to think that they could "build up an organization just on the basis of guns" and opposed to the leadership of the IPF to think that Gorbachev and perestroika were new models of revolutionary activity. *Sangharsh aur Nirmana*, p. 305.

[30] A.C.C. is a cement factory. In July 1990, the month before this speech, the CMM's two new unions were recognized and fifty chemical and engineering factories came under the Morcha's control. Niyogi's hunger strike was part of that five-month campaign for union recognition.

[31] These are two sacred pilgrimage sites at the source of the Ganges in the Himalayas.

[32] Raipur is the governmental center in Chhattisgarh while Bhilai is the industrial center.

[33] The late Jayprakash Narayan was a socialist leader from the 1930s to 1970s. The speech to which Niyogi refers is probably of October 1974. Patna is the capital city of the state of Bihar.

[34] The tanks (*talab*) to which Niyogi refers drain rain water in a catchment area for use as irrigation water in one or more villages. They have been in use for centuries and are essential in the semi-arid climate of the Deccan plateau to catch the runoff water and replenish the underground water supply.

[35] It appears that Niyogi saw the film about Spartacus starring Kirk Douglas.

*Bridge, Novi Sad*

*Unidentified Woman Victim, Grdelica Railway Bombing*

# 12
# THE WAR IN YUGOSLAVIA: ON WHOM THE BOMBS FALL?

MASSIMO DE ANGELIS AND SILVIA FEDERICI

*AS WE ARE WRITING — June 7, 1999 — in Kumanovo, Macedonia, the diplomats are negotiating the terms of the "agreement" that is supposed to bring peace back to Yugoslavia. For many people this may signify the end of the war. This, however, is not our view. We believe that the war is not over, and the anti-war movement would be mistaken if it now folded up its tents and shifted its attention to a new issue. This is why this article, written at the peak of the bombings, is presented here in its original form. In our view, the analysis it provides, and the issues it raises are as valid today, when the talks seem to be of peace, as they were yesterday, when the bombs openly intended to destroy Yugoslavia were falling. It is an analysis that wants to contribute to the creation of an anti-war movement aware of long-term trends and patterns, and aiming not just to stop wars once they start, but to prevent their occurrence.*

### 1. Prologue at 5,000 Meters

From the cockpit of an F-16 flying at 5,000 meters, you can't see, nor smell, nor be sprayed with the blood of "collateral damage." The sensory reality of war has been detached, cleaned away from the "productive" activity of the warrior, as it has from the language of NATO's reports on the alleged "mistakes." Here we cannot fail to notice the institutional, racist cynicism of NATO, which weighs the lives of Serbian children and other civilians and finds them less important than those of "Western" soldiers; as we are told that "collateral damage" is "a price worth paying" to force Milosevic to concede defeat with a minimum of politically unsustainable allied casualties. This is trading the human rights of some, in this case mostly innocent civilians, for the human rights of others, with NATO as the self-appointed judge of their relative value.

**2. The (In)humanitarian War**

There is now mounting evidence that the justifications and aims given for the war against Yugoslavia are not credible, and far from protecting Kosovar Albanians the bombings have worsened their plight. We know for instance that:

• the Rambouillet Agreements was never meant to be accepted by the Yugoslavian government, as they were phrased in such a way as to ensure their rejection, demanding (among other things) that NATO have unlimited access to any part of Yugoslavia, by sea, air, and land, and be dispensed from any legal accountability (Pilger 1999).

• on the eve of the first bombings, the Yugoslavian Parliament had approved a resolution accepting the restoration of Kosovo's autonomy, and the presence of a UN peace-keeping force to monitor its enforcement.

• far from protecting the Kosovar Albanians the bombings have increased the rate of their expulsions, killed and terrorized many of them, including the large number of those who did remain in Kosovo, or fled from Kosovo into Serbia.

• the health of Yugoslavian people, ethnic Albanians included, will continue for a long time to be damaged because of the devastation and contamination to which the Yugoslavian territory has been subjected, with the release in the air and ground of immense amounts of toxic substances, including depleted uranium (Depleated Uranium Education Project 1997).

Indeed, as many critics have pointed out, if humanitarian reasons were the motive, then this war was a catastrophic failure. Moreover, how can we believe that NATO is fighting for the self-determination of the Albanian population in Kosovo, when it has denied the same right to the Palestinians and the Kurds (among others), and when the U.S. has subverted every democratically elected government in the world whenever it has suited its needs? Or, as Mumia Abu-Jamal puts it, "Isn't it strange that these same powers have, for half a century or more, turned a blind eye to virtual holocausts throughout the charnel houses of Europe? Where were the Western powers when the Kurds were savaged, herded and decimated by the border states of Turkey, Iraq and Iran? The fate of the Basques in the borders between France and Spain is, for all intents and purposes, off the table. National ethnic minorities continue to be treated like the trash of Euro-states; consider the Roma (so-called Gypsies) who are seen, perceived and treated as the "white niggers" of Europe. Even as we see NATO dropping metallic death on Serbia because of their mistreatment of "ethnic minorities," the cities and towns of Europe are doing all that they can to make immigration as difficult as possible for people seeking asylum." (Mumia Abu-Jamal 1999)

Last but not least, not only has the NATO bombings dramatically increased the flood of refugees, now reaching more than one million; the knowledge that this disaster would inevitably happen was well available before the bombing started. Why then has NATO decided to pursue this strategy? In answering these questions, we may find some hints on the reasons for today's war.

### 3. The Inhuman Agenda of NATO (and G8, and WTO, and IMF, and OECD, and ... )

If the justifications given for the war against Yugoslavia are not credible, then what is the real agenda? To answer this question we must place the war in the context of the major developments that have been shaping politics in the Balkans and internationally since the fall of the Berlin Wall, which marked the end of the Cold War. Primary among them are:

The process of "economic globalization," by which international capital has imposed a neoliberal agenda enforcing debt and austerity on every region of the world, and placed much of the former state socialist countries and the Third World under the control of the multinational corporations and the International Monetary Fund (IMF) and the World Bank (Chossudovsky, 1997; Midnight Notes, 1992).

The crisis of state-communism in Central and Eastern Europe (in part activated by the shift to market reforms) and the resultant eastward expansion of NATO [(Granville 1999), (Holbrooke 1995), (Kluger 1996), (*The Economist* 1989)].

The deepening capitalist crisis (reflected in the collapse of the Asian economies, the profit stagnation in Europe, and the increasing social opposition to further liberalization and austerity) which accelerates the rush to commercially exploit new areas of the world, and the effort by corporate capital to find new sources of cheap labor [(Chossudovsky 1997), (Gervasi 1998)].

Viewed in the context of these developments, NATO's attack on Yugoslavia (the last act in the dismemberment of the country) has many objectives:

The battering of Yugoslavia, added to the entry of Poland, Hungary, the Czech Republic into NATO, continues the political transformation of the map of Europe initiated by the reunification of Germany. It serves to create a capitalist block, stretching from the Adriatic to the edges of the former Soviet Union, and is part of the eastward expansion of NATO, decided by the Clinton Administration since at least 1994, and increasingly urgent for the EU and the U.S., in the face of the growing social opposition to neoliberal programs in Central and Eastern Europe and Russia as well.

The war can be used to defeat the resistance of the Yugoslavian working class to neoliberalism, which has forced the state to put a halt to the planned process of privatization, so that (until the bombings started) state-owned industries were still in place, and so were subsidies to farmers and unemployed workers [(Petras and Vieux 1996), (Dyker 1999), (Judah 1999), (Kuzmanic 1994)]. Not surprisingly, the bombings have targeted all of Yugoslavia's productive structures, including the plant that produced the famous Yugo (a cheap car widely used in the country and exported), making sure that people will have no means to resist their forced integration into the global economy. The bombings are also sending a message to other resistant workers in Eastern Europe, as e.g., the coal miners in Romania, who, early this year had to be militarily defeated, because of their strong opposition to the closing of the mines demanded by the International Monetary Fund (*New York Times* 1999b).

The war also lays the groundwork for the encirclement of Russia which, although weakened economically and militarily, is still seen as threat. Here too, political and economic goals go hand in hand.

The U.S. and IMF anxiety about Russia's "commitment to reform" is now obsessive, since Russia has so far failed to complete the "transition" process. It has not privatized land, it has not shut down its subsidized state-industries, it is resisting the importation of grain from the U.S. Worst of all, as of June 2, 1999, it has, for the second time in less than a year, defaulted on its international debt.

Equally worrisome (from the viewpoint of NATO and the U.S.) are reports that the great majority of Russians regard the U.S.-supported Yeltsin regime with unconcealed hatred, and among ordinary people such terms as "market reforms" and "market economy" have now the force of obscenities, because of the collapse in the standard of living the attempted privatization process has caused (Burbach et al. 1997: 123–124). The support given by the U.S. to the Russian reforms has also generated an anti-American mood in the most diverse Russian circles, and strengthened the ties between Russia and other parts of the former Soviet Union, especially Belarus and the Ukraine. Thus, the possibility of a "nostalgic return," or of a new type of communism is real (Dawisha 1996). In this context, the defeat of Yugoslavia could be used to remind the world, and above all wavering leaders of "transition economies," that there is no alternative to free-market capitalism and demonstrate the futility of resistance to it.

The war against Yugoslavia also gives U.S. and European capital control over a region that is rich in mineral resources and is strategically located at the cross-roads between Western Europe, Eastern Europe and the Middle East, thus dominating some of Europe's most important trade routes [(Gambino 1999), (*New York Times* 1999e), (Flounders 1998)].

In particular, the battering and possible subjugation of Yugoslavia plays a role in the planned commercial exploitation of the Caspian Sea (Gervasi 1998), which has oil reserves comparable to those of the Persian Gulf and, accordingly, has been declared to be part of the U.S. sphere of interest [(Levine 1999), (*Financial Times* 1999), (Finardi 1999), Chatterjee 1998), (Shenov 1999), (*New York Times* 1999a)].

As the Clinton Administration has repeatedly stressed, the stakes here are very high, since it is believed that on the control of the Caspian oil depends the fate of the post-communist world, and how much influence the U.S. will have in determining its outcome (Kinzer 1998).

At stake is the ability of the U.S. to attract into its sphere of influence the post-Soviet Central Asian republics of Kazakhstan,

Azerbajian and Turkmenistan, by giving them an independent economic basis, and thereby weakening their ties with Russia and Russia's influence in global affairs.

This the U.S. plans to accomplish by building a pipeline transporting the Caspian oil to Western Europe — a pipeline that, moving through Georgia and Turkey, would by-pass Iran and especially Russia, so that both countries' ability to profit from the Caspian oil bonanza would be severely limited (Shenov et al. 1999). But to succeed Washington must assure the oil companies and the Caspian republics that it is ready to back their investments by military force against any possible Russian interference (Kinzer 1998). The bombings of Yugoslavia seal the deal, as the first test of both the Russian state's resolve in supporting a client state in the face of a NATO attack, and the U.S. determination to use any available means to make its interest prevail.

Last, the war cements the alliance between U.S. and the EU, and confirms U.S. leadership in the alliance, as well as NATO's role as western capital's only credible military force.

As already in the case of Bosnia (and we could add the Gulf War and Desert Storm in Somalia), one of the casualties of this new military intervention is European independence. Trumpeted since the early 1990s with the Maastricht Treaty and the construction of the monetary union, this has been increasingly sacrificed to the need forovercoming Europe's economic stagnation, whose solution is partly entrusted to a process of eastward expansion [(Martin and Ross 1999), (Ash 1999)].

As the growing flow of European capital to Eastern Europe demonstrates, Europe has much to gain from a "colonization" of the Balkans (Clark et al. 1998). This is possible, however, only through the military intervention of the U.S., the only country in the world that has, persistently, for many decades, been committed to, and prepared for world domination. It is on this basis that Germany and France have accepted the humiliation inflicted upon them at Dayton, and suffered their marginalization in the first major European crisis since WWII, and today they are participating in the destruction of Yugoslavia, despite the risks it involves for the future of Europe.

Finally, the refugee crisis and the prospected integration of the Balkan area's battered economies into the global capitalist circuit provide the European ruling class with a new source of cheap labor right at the heart of Europe. They promote further competition in the labor markets throughout the continent, likely to result in downward pressures on workers' wages — a key objective at a time when European capital is much lamenting its slow growth, and striving to convince European workers to accept substantial cuts in social benefits (Singer 1996).

European workers will pay in another ways as well for the war. In addition to facing a stiffer competition on their jobs, they will also have to pay the bill for the reconstruction, for the "clean up," as Clinton put it, in his Memorial Day pronouncement on May 31, 1999 (*New York Times* 1999d).

Thus, the war in Yugoslavia, with its heavy demand on the military budget of the NATO countries, will also serve immediate domestic goals, by helping to complete (in the name of war spending and investment in the reconstruction) the dismantling of the European and U.S. welfare systems (*Wall Street Journal* 1999). Put in other words, (and to paraphrase Martin Luther King Jr.) the bombs falling on Yugoslavia may indeed explode in Western Europe and the U.S., destroying, for instance, their pension and social security system, threatened by the rising cost of militarization.

Whatever the partition of financial responsibility (no matter which working class is destined to pay more for it) the IMF and World Bank are already providing some post-war reconstruction scenarios (IMF and World Bank 1999). It seems that grants will be provided only to support the basic needs of the refugees, while the inevitable gap in the balance of payments for 1999, for the countries of the region, will be largely closed by further debt. In other words: first the economic and financial elites imposed impoverishing neoliberal policies in the region, policies that shattered the social fabric and created the context in which brutal and murderous nationalisms have flourished. Then, they seized the opportunity for military action resulting in further deaths and enviromental devastation (since diplomatic options were left in a dead end, with the insistence, at Rambouillet, that NATO troops be present in the Yugoslav territory and NATO be allowed unchecked movement in any part of Yugoslavia). Soon, they will wear again the banker's hat to "help" in the reconstruction, cashing in new interest payments and, especially, prospecting a more "stable" environment for business, thanks to NATO heavy military presence in the region.

### 4. The World's Panopticon

Projected on a global scenario, the war on Yugoslavia appears as the other side of the process of financial recolonization that has taken place in much of the world over the last decade, and the increasing subjugation of every aspect of life to the rule of money. By this rule, markets have been introduced where previously there were commons, welfare provisions have been cut across the globe, workers' entitlements have been reduced or eliminated, poverty has been imposed worldwide (Chossudovsky 1998). This war that the World Bank, the IMF and other financial elites managing the global economy are waging, ultimately needs missiles and other deadly weapons, to keep people on course, producing for the global economy, at rhythms and retributions favorable to capital accumulation. In other words, globalization is not possible without the presence a military force capable of breaking the resistance to it worldwide, a resistance often expressed in confused and contradictory forms. Today, only the U.S. has the military capability to pursue "flexible" punishing raids across the globe — hence the European subordination to it. However, the war on Yugoslavia has accelerated the urgency for Europe to match and complement the military strength the U.S., especially in those technologies that make prompt and flexible intervention possible (Nicoll 1999).

Today, war and conquest are not the outer manifestation of inter-capitalist rivalry, as the early twentieth century critics of imperialism like Hobson and Lenin claimed (Lenin 1967). In the late twentieth century inter-capitalist rivalry occurs within an alliance united by the determination to pursue economic globalization. Also, territorial conquest is not the objective of war. Rather, the goal is the construction of a global security prison, in which the rules of the market are unconditionally accepted, and every alternative is ruled out. It is a security prison resembling in spirit Jeremy Bentham's Panopticon, the total surveillance regime devised to increase the prisoners-workers' efficiency. As George Caffentzis (1998) pointed out in the case of the Gulf War, in this Panopticon regime "where everything that occurs on the planet has to been seen, controlled and approved by the U.S. government (or its representatives in an international agency it controls)... the U.S. is not only aiming to be the 'cop' of the world, as it did in the 1960s, but it aspires to be the 'investigator,' 'warden' and 'executioner' of the 'world' as well at the dawn of the 21st century."

The war on Yugolsavia thus is showing us that we are entering into a new stage of imperialism where the U.S. and NATO-EU are claiming the right to violate the sovereignty of other nations for the most fraudulent excuses, and are now ready (as at the time of 19th century gunboat diplomacy) to just bomb their way to the resources or markets they want. This means that we need an anti-war movement that is now just concerned with this or that war, but with the whole "bloody neocolonial paradigm" that sustains, legitimizes and promotes each war venture. The opposition against the next wars to be fought for inhuman rights must start now with the opposition to this paradigm.

### 5. The Deadlock of the Anti-war Movement

Against this background one has to wonder why the anti-war movement has failed so far to respond to the barbaric attack that has been launched against the Yugoslavian population, including the Albanian refugees, hundreds of whom have been carbonized by NATO bombs. Could it be that people are accepting the absurd logic whereby if they oppose the war they necessarily are making a stand in support of the Milosevic regime ? If that is the case, then we encourage people to listen to the many appeals coming from those in Belgrade who have opposed the Milosevic regime, who repeatedly have said that the bombings only strengthen his position.

Or could it be that people believe that the pitiless, uninterrupted bombing of an entire population for 71 days so far, and the destruction of a century of people's work, can have some benefit after all? Then those who are tempted to take this path should consider the following.

Can the U.S. (the leader of this operation) be entrusted with the well-being and rescue of the Kosovars, or for that matter of any other population? Have we forgotten Hiroshima and Nagasaki, or Vietnam where children are still born deformed because of the thousands of tons of napalm spread over the country during the war? or Nicaragua, Angola, Mozambique, Cambodia, Chile, Guatemala, Grenada, Panama, Iraq, Somalia[e.g., for Panama see (Independent Commission on Inquiry on the U.S. Invasion of Panama 1991) and (Wheaton 1992); for Iraq see (Midnight Notes 1992) and (Clark 1994)]. What do people need to see and hear in order to distrust a power structure responsible for invading half the planet in the course of a few decades, directly or through proxies, and subverting any genuine attempt at self-determination all across the world? Again, shouldn't we be suspicious about the fact that the U.S. allegedly wishes to protect the Albanians' right to self-determination, given that all throughout its history it has never granted this right to any nation — certainly not to the Native American Indians, nor, more recently to the Palestinians, nor, to stay closer to the ground of the war, to the Serbs of the Kraina, who were brutally expelled from their homes in 1995, with a military operation comparable in its ferocity only to the Nazi invasion of Yugoslavia, amidst the deafening silence of the "international community"?

Last but not least, what would people say if Russia and China were to bomb the cities of the United States on account of the U.S. government's massive violations of human rights?

And why should we believe that the destruction of Yugoslavia was the only possible path to assure the rights of the Albanian population?

On the ground there are a million refugees who are said to support the NATO intervention. However, nobody has asked them whether, given the choice, they would have rather liked to see the billion dollars that have been and will be used to bomb Serbia, invested in Kosovo's social services, or donated by western banks, as transfer payments, to the unemployed — which in 1998 reached 40% of the labor force (RIINVEST 1998) — or devoted to reducing income differences in the region, or spent in any way that might undermine the economic roots of "ethnic cleansing." Indeed, the question that nobody is asking is this: how many ethnic cleansings are carried on in conditions of prosperity for all? How many in conditions of poverty and social uncertainty? To exit the deadlock and prevent the next war — surely to be fought for very (in)humanitarian purposes — the anti-war movement of today must start to build bridges with the anti-debt movement, the various sections of the anti-globalization movement (anti-MAI, anti-WTO, anti-IMF, anti-G7, etc.), and continue to make connections between struggles on different issues. The alternative to war is often simpler that our arrogant governments think: just put the money where your mouth is and fund human rights!

**Bibliography**

Abu-Jamal, Mumia 1999. Column #414, written 14 April 1999. *Making the World Safe for Capital*. Antifa info-bulletin, May 19.

Ash, T. G. 1999. "Europe's Endangered Liberal Order." *Foreign Affairs*., March–April.

Benderly, J. and Kraft, E. 1994. *Independent Slovenia. Origins, Movements and Prospects*. New York : St. Martin's Press.

Burbach, Roger *et al.* 1997. *Globalization and Its Discontents: The Rise of Postmodern Socialisms*. London: Pluto Press.

Caffentzis, George. 1998. "In the U.S., Dreaming of Iraq." *Midnight*

*Notes*. P.O. Box 204, Jamaica Plain, MA 02130

Chatterjee, Pratap 1998. "Scramble for the Caspian: Big Oil Looks to Divvy Up Caspian Sea Oil Riches," *Multinational Monitor*, September, pp. 16–20.

Chossudovsky, Michel 1997. *The Globalization of Poverty: Impacts of the IMF and World Bank Reforms*. London: Zed Books.

Clark, Ramsey 1994. *The Fire This Time: U.S. War Crimes in the Gulf*. New York: Thunder's Mouth Press.

Clark, Ramsey *et al.* 1998. *NATO in the Balkans*. New York: International Action Center.

Copetas, A. Craig 1999. "It's Off To War Again For Big U.S. Contractor." *Wall Street Journal*, April 14.

Dawisha, Karen 1996. "Russian Policy in the Near Abroad and Beyond." *Current History*. October.

Depleated Uranium Education Project 1997. *Metal of Dishonor: Depleated Uranium*. New York: International Action Center.

Dyker, David A. 1999. "The [Yugoslavian] Economy." In *Eastern Europe and the Commonwealth of Independent State 1999*, Europa Publications Limited.

*The Economist* 1989. *East of Eden. A Survey of Eastern Europe*. August 12.

*Financial Times* 1999, "US is Urged to Step in to Kickstart Caspian Gas Project," April 15.

Finardi, Sergio 1999. "Sporchi di oro nero." *Manifesto*, April 14, p.10.

Flounders, Sara 1998. "The War is About the Mines," *Workers World*, July 30, p. 9.

Gambino, Ferrucci 1999. "Dal Sottosuolo Alla Guerra. " *Altreragioni*, no. 8. (In Press)

Granville, Johanna 1999. "The Many Paradoxes of NATO Enlargement." *Current History*. April.

Gervasi, Sean 1998. Why is NATO in Yugoslavia? In (Clark et al. 1998).

Holbrooke, Richard 1995. "America a European Power." *Foreign Affairs*, March–April.

IMF and World Bank 1999. *The Economic Consequences of the Kosovo Crisis: A Preliminary Assessment of External Financing Needs and the Role of the Fund and the World Bank in the International Response*. Prepared jointly by the staffs of the International Monetary Fund and the World Bank April 16, http://www.imf.org/external/pubs/ft/kosovo/041699.htm

Independent Commission of Inquiry on the U.S. Invasion of Panama 1991. *The U.S. Invasion of Panama: The Truth Behind Operation "Just Cause."* Boston: South End Press.

Judah, Tim 1999. "How Milosevic Hangs On." *New York Review of Books*. June 18 .

Kinzer, Steven 1998. "On Piping Out Caspian Oil, U.S. Insists the Cheaper, Shorter Way Isn't Better," *New York Times*. Nov. 8.

Kugler, Richard L. 1996. *Enlarging NATO: The Russian Factor*. Washington, DC: RAND .

Kuzmanic, Tonci 1994. "Strikes, Trade Unions and Slovene Independence." In (Benderly and Kraft 1994).

Lenin, V. I. 1967a. *Selected Works. Vol. 1: 1987 to January 1917*. New York: International Publishers.

Lenin, V.I. 1967b. *Imperialism: The Highest Stage of Capitalism*. In (Lenin 1967a).

Levine, Steve 1999. "Oilmen and U.S., Pin Hopes on a Strike in Kazakhstan." *New York Times*, Feb. 20.

Martin, Andrew and Ross, George 1999. "The Euro and Democracy's Devaluation." *Current History*. April.

Midnight Notes 1992. *Midnight Oil: Work, Energy, War, 1973–1992*. New York: Autonomedia.

Nasar, Sylvia 1999. "GDP Growth Fails to Carry Profits With It." *New York Times*, April 1.

*New York Times* 1999a. "A New Big-Power Race Starts on a Sea of Crude." Jan. 24.

*New York Times* 1999b. "Romania Seizes Miners' Chief in Fierce Class." February 18.

*New York Times* 1999c. "Russian Anger Over Attack Tempered by Need for Cash." March 25.

*New York Times* 1999d. "Clinton Declares Most War Cleanup is Europe's Task." June 1.

*New York Times* 1999e, "The Prize: Issue of Who Controls Kosovo's Rich Mines," June 2, 1999, p. A15.

Nicoll, Alexander 1999. "Seeking a Level Battlefiled." *Financial Times*, June 3.

Petras, James and Vieux, Steve 1996. "Lethal Power Play in Bosnia. " *New Left Review*, N. 218, July–August.

Pilger, John. 1999. "Revealed: the Amazing NATO Plan, Tabled at

Rambouillet, to Occupy Yugoslavia." *New Statesman*, 17 May.
RIINVEST 1998. *Economic Activities and democratic development of Kosova.* Institute for Development Research, CIPE, September.
Shenov, Bhami V. et al. 1999. "Caspian Oil Export Choices Clouded by Geopolitics, Project Economics." *Oil and Gas Journal*, April 19.
Singer, Daniel 1996. "The Real Eurobattle." *The Nation.* Dec. 23.
*Wall Street Journal* 1999. "From Pentagon to Triangle." Editorial, May 17.
Wheaton, Philip 1992. *Panama Invaded: Imperial Occupation Versus Struggle for Sovereignty.* Trenton, NJ: Red Sea Press.

*Death (Lynched Figure)*, Isamu Noguchi

# 13

# FROM CAPITALIST CRISIS TO PROLETARIAN SLAVERY

## INTRODUCTION TO THE CLASS STRUGGLE IN THE U.S., 1973–1998

GEORGE CAFFENTZIS

> Slavery is not one type of domination and exploitation among others, not merely an aspect of one bygone phase of history. Slavery is the primary and primordial relation of exploitation, that form out of which serfdom and wage labor arise, and that form toward which the master always strives: only force can compel the master to forgo the use of slaves. Whence the many "ends" of slavery, and its many rebirths.
>
> — Pierre Dockes, *Medieval Slavery and Liberation* (1982)

AMONG MEXICAN ACTIVISTS the existence of class struggle in the U.S. is at best an hypothesis deducible from Marxist axioms, but it is one often resisted by empirical reality. Where are the anti-capitalist parties and the revolutionary workers' and peasants' armies that fill the history books in the Americas, Europe and Asia? They certainly are not to be found in recent U.S. history. Nevertheless, class struggle in the U.S. is a daily experience.[1] In this essay, I present a schematic history of this struggle during the 1973–1998 period, stressing those elements that are most important for the creation of cross-border networks of struggle and the forging of a common history uniting the U.S. and Mexican proletariat.

**The Fall**

The winter of 1998 is a time of capitalist triumphalism in the U.S. The stock market is booming, it is the seventh year of capitalist expansion, corporate profits are reaching new highs, while interest rates and unemployment are reaching lows not touched since the early 1970s. The situation is so unusual that a new species of economist is appearing on the financial pages and business journals claiming to have discovered a miracle. These "New Economy" economists hypothesize that advanced capitalist economies like the U.S. can continue to grow without igniting inflation because of the "hidden productivity" gains provided by the computerization of all areas of production and circulation. The old contradiction between growth and inflation is now history, it seems, and the new technology is being hailed as the system's healer.[2]

However, a glance at the condition of the waged working class (working with or without the computer) over the last quarter century quickly reveals the material basis for capital's triumphs. In 1973–74 the U.S. working class reached its historic peak of power measured statistically. Since then, the real wage, hours of work, security of employment, share of the total social product, capacity to strike, average level of employment have constantly and, at times, dramatically deteriorated. In 1974 the number of strikes reached a new historic high, after many years when strikes were common in most large industries. By the 1980s, however, strikes in these industries had nearly disappeared, and 1996 had the lowest level of strike activity since the early 1920s. In February 1998 unemployment reached a "historical low," 4.6%, after seven years of capitalist expansion; but it is forgotten that such a level of unemployment would have been considered a sign of recession in the 1950s and would have called for extraordinary macro-economic measures to counter its consequences. Consider also the issue of "wage dispersion," i.e., the difference between the wages of the highest and lowest paid workers, which is a rough, objective measure of working class solidarity. In the early 1970s "wage dispersion" was at one of its lowest levels in U.S. history, but the 1990s have witnessed the highest levels of wage dispersion ever in post-WWII U.S. class history. The best paid male workers in the 1970s made more than 3.5 times the wage of the least paid male workers, the ratio in the 1990s is now more than 5 to 1. The most important change, however, can been seen in the profit ratio. The 1970s saw a major, across-the-board decline in profits. Between 1948 and 1968, the U.S. rate of profit averaged about 20%, by the mid-1970s it averaged about 11%.[3]

How should we interpret these changes? For a start, it is clear that if the trends of the 1960s and early 1970s in wage increases, shortening of work hours, profits crisis, and wage dispersion had continued, capitalism in the U.S. would have collapsed. This threat of collapse was not confined to the U.S. Similar trends were developing in Europe, the major alternative place of U.S. capital's investment and profit. England and Italy in 1973–1974, especially, were the scenes of remarkably effective expressions of working class power on the highest levels of politics; for example, the 1974 miners' strike in the UK brought down the Conservative government.

A look at the condition of unwaged workers in the U.S. shows a parallel story of triumph and decline. The struggle of women against unpaid labor in the home has forced both the government and the Marxists to confront the value-productivity of the largely women's labor involved into the reproduction of labor power on a daily and generational basis. This work had historically been unpaid in the U.S., where there were not even the small "family allowances" that were experimented with by some European governments after WWII. But in the 1960s, the welfare movement largely led by black women brought together the demands of the "Black Power" movement and the feminist demands for the recognition of women's work. By the late 1960s the rights of poor, unsupported women to some form of payment for their work of raising children was being recognized as a "welfare entitlement" by the national government

In response to the struggles of women these payments grew throughout the 1960s, and by the early 1970s the Nixon Administration was discussing a plan for a "guaranteed national wage" that would regularize a nationally agreed upon bottom to all citizens' income.[4] These discussions signaled an immense crisis for capital, because one of the greatest sources of profit arises from its ability to make the working class bear the cost of its own reproduction on a daily and generational basis. The guaranteed income and the other aspects of the "welfare state" (e.g., the creation of a nationalized medical care system for the elderly, Medicare, in 1965) threatened this immense source of profit and exploitation. This development ended abruptly in the mid-1970s. By the summer of 1996 the national government had moved so far from the "guaranteed income for all" as to explicitly legislate that it was no longer guaranteeing any payment to women (poor or not) for the work they do in reproducing the labor power of the future.

The class struggle in the 1960s and early 1970s which led to a historic crisis in capitalist accumulation did not take place under the direction of a mass, ideologically identified anti-capitalist party. But it did see an immense production of theoretical and agitational literature concerning the nature of capitalism, sexism, racism in all its forms and targets (against blacks, indigenous peoples, Hispanics, Asians), homophobia, and the destruction of the environment. More crucially, it was able to express its power in the urban insurrections lead by blacks (from the Watts rebellion in 1964 to the national urban uprising after the assassination of M.L. King Jr. in 1968), as well as in the major strikes in all industries as well as in agriculture (the United Farm Workers of America strikes and the grape boycott) and government (the national postal workers' strike). To all of this we must add the incessant wildcats and slowdowns, a revolt in the army in Vietnam, strikes in the university system (including a nation-wide shut down after the invasion of Cambodia in 1970), the great prison revolts like Attica in 1971, and the revival of the feminist movement. Even capitalist apologists were beginning to despair in the early 1970s, and were writing books about workers with titles like "Where Have All the Robots Gone?"[5]

How did the U.S. working class, both waged and unwaged, which in the 1960s and early 1970s appeared to be shaking the confidence of the most powerful capitalist class on the planet, find itself, a quarter century later, more divided, with lower wages, working longer hours, and feeling more powerless and insecure? How was capital able to regain its equilibrium and then take the initiative? A thorough answer to these questions would require a book, but in the following few pages I sketch an answer.

### Recession

The first response to a period of growing working class power was instinctual to capital: depression, crisis and a refusal of investment. This did not require much planning. Any successful attack on profit will lead to disinvestment, according to the logic of the system, and the period between 1975 and 1983 included five "recessions," two of which were more severe than any since the Great Depression of the 1930s. This rapid-fire series of recessions changed what "high" and "low" unemployment rates meant. After 1983, even though there were two periods of "expansion" (1984–1990 and 1991–present), the lowest the unemployment rate reached was 4.6% — what would have been considered a "recession" rate of unemployment in the 1950s.

**Capital's Counter-strike: "Rust Belt," "Scabs," and "Union-Busting"**

In previous periods of unemployment after WWII there was never a large-scale disruption of the location of the factories and the general geographical distribution of the branches of industry. Steel was connected with Pittsburgh, autos with Detroit, rubber with Akron, coal with West Virginia, in the minds of the workers and capitalists. Even if steel, auto, rubber workers, and coal miners were laid off during a "down turn," they remained in place for the most part, expecting to be reemployed in the next "up turn." But the crisis of 1975–1983 was different. Capital physically dismantled its industrial infrastructure and moved to the southern U.S. (or even to industrialized Third World countries like Mexico or South Africa), leaving behind a "rust belt" stretching from Chicago to Boston of abandoned factories, steel mills, and working class neighborhoods. This planned "deindustrialization" of the traditional manufacturing areas of the country had a profound effect on the self-confidence of the most well paid, and historically most combative strata of the proletariat. How can you strike outside a rusty unused factory whose replacement is being built a thousand miles away? Even if northern workers, especially blacks, followed their plants south, how could they reconstruct ties of proletarian trust and cooperation with workers they met in the new plant who might have ties with the KKK or other racist groups?

Capital's campaign to terrorize the waged working class into giving up the strike "weapon" had many more dimensions beside its demonstrated willingness to respond to strikes by moving a plant thousands of miles away. Large corporations also broke one of the basic rules of "labor relations" since the 1930s: the prohibition of using "scabs," or strike-breakers, or, in the euphemistic term of the 1980s, "replacement workers." The hiring of "scabs" to break strikes had been a standard tactic of capitalists, both large and small, throughout the late 19th and early 20th century. This practice had been rejected by the larger capitalists in the era of mass factories, which required thousands of workers and were located in the midst of working class neighborhoods, as being too dangerous. But, beginning with the nation-wide strike of air traffic controllers in 1981, there was a revival of the "scab," so that today almost every category of workers' strikes, including those of meat packers, paper workers, coal miners, farm machinery assembly workers, air traffic controllers, and pilots have faced and were defeated by a campaign of scabbing. All throughout the 1980s, there were years-long sieges of factories, mines, and mills — which were operating at maximum capacity — by striking workers who impotently demonstrated on the outside. These defeated strikes taught workers a bitter lesson and have definitely reduced their capacity to reject the reduction of wages and the increase in work-time demanded by their bosses. For example, in 1974 there were 424 strikes involving more than 1,000 workers, while in 1995 there were only 31 such strikes.

Another tactic of the late 19th and early 20th century that was also revived was "union busting," in the form of capitalists' attempts to either subvert workers' efforts to unionize or to drive unions out of their factories. From the 1930s until the 1960s the large corporations had worked out an accommodation with the unions in their branches of industry, but beginning with the crisis of the mid-1970s this accommodation went into crisis. For example, when a steel mill or a coal mine was moved to a new location, the corporation often would not recognize the older union as the bargaining agent for the workers in the new location. Since companies often moved their new plants to states in the South or Southwest which had laws that hindered unionization, it was relatively easy for managers trained in "union busting" tactics (taught at a very high price by a new breed of "aggressive" management experts) to subvert their new workers' attempts to unionize and create the solidarity required to organize a strike. The result was a dramatic decline in union membership: in 1974 about 25% of the employees in the private sector were union members, in 1994 only about 12% were in unions.

Along with these planned attacks on the waged working class' most powerful weapon on the factory level, there was also an attack by the state. In the 1950s and 1960s, unemployment benefits, "food stamps" and other forms of income available to workers that were laid off were made available to waged workers who were on strike for a long time. In the 1980s and 1990s these benefits were systematically undermined. Either they were formally denied to strikers or they were severely cut. Consequently, if workers went on strike in the post-1973 period they increasingly faced immediate poverty leavened by small payments from strike funds and solidarity funds.

**The Decomposition of Work**

The attack on the waged working class in the large factories, mills and mines did not end with the elimination of its capacity to strike. Workers can refuse work (in order to demand higher wages, less work-time, and a reduction in the intensity of work) within the factory, on the "shop floor," often more effectively than by formally striking. By the 1960s, assembly-line workers had developed sophisticated techniques of slowing down the line to protest management practices and to take control of their working conditions. This quiet insurrection within the plant (called "counter-planning on the shop floor") was more terrifying to the capitalist than the picket lines outside it. Strikes are open declarations of war operating by fixed rules, but this organized insubordination within the plant was more open-ended in its threat to the sovereignty of capital. What could be done about it? Again, the first step was instinctual to capital: increase mechanization and surveillance.

As Marx wrote in *Capital,* machines are weapons in the war against the power of workers, and the immediate response to any increase of workers' power is to introduce machines to replace workers, either to reduce the skills necessary to do the work, or to subvert workers' capacity to refuse work on the job.[6] The machines and techniques have varied with the times, from the Arkwright's "mule" and the steam engine of the 19th century, to electrification and the internal combustion engine of the early 20th century, to the introduction of Computerization and Robotics in the late 20th century.

The latter innovations have led to a new source of anxiety for the worker: "downsizing."[7] In the past, one feared being laid off from a job because of a down-turn in the business cycle and a reduction in the demand for the commodity one helped produce. Normally, if "business" was good, there would be no reason to be concerned about one's job and one could use the moment to demand higher wages and better working conditions. But this "grace period" is increasingly under attack, because even during a boom time the worker can be threatened with the introduction of a computerized simulation of much of his/her work or even a completely roboticized replacement. Since the computer is a universal machine that can simulate any pattern-producing activity, almost any worker can be threatened with "downsizing," i.e., a dramatic change in or even elimination of their assigned work without a reduction in the demand for their product. Consequently, workers' power to use "good times" to make new demands and to organize greater control of their work-life is threatened. But if "bad times" are not propitious moments, and if "good times" are increasingly not propitious either, then what times are best for putting forth working class demands?

Another classical method for subverting internal worker insubordination is increased surveillance. Again this is nothing new. From the formation of the factory on the model of the prison in the late 18th century, to Taylorism in the late 19th century, to Fordism in the early 20th century, the techniques for monitoring work, controlling its motion, detecting deviations from the norm and crushing insubordination have been at the core of the capitalist science of production. Since the mid-1970s a whole set of "new" practices (often associated with Japanese management) have been introduced in all the major industrial branches. From "quality circles," to "just in time production," to "total quality control," these so-called Post-Fordist techniques are no more than new ways for the capitalists to create new forms of surveillance and spying in the process of production and to introduce a continual complicity between elements of the working class and management. As with some of the previous advances in "management science," they have proved initially successful. Conflictual class relations return to the fore as the proletariat learns to create a counter-surveillance and to subvert complicity in its ranks. But as this has been the initial period of their introduction, many of these surveillance techniques have proven effective.[8]

### Changes in the Composition of the Waged Working Class: Immigration and Gender

These changes in the location and form of work have been crucial in thwarting the militancy of waged workers. But there were other, equally important and more ambiguous factors that will help explain the collapse of many past bastions of working class strength in the U.S.

To understand these factors one must reflect on three decisive moments in the formation of the U.S. proletariat. The first two were the genocide of the indigenous people and the massive enslavement of Africans in the U.S. territory and the third was the wave of immigration from Europe and Asia in the late 19th and early 20th centuries. *The ability of U.S. capital to move large quantities of labor power is rooted in the success of the genocidal elimination of the indigenous people and in the ability to divide European, Hispanic-American and Asian immigrants, but more crucially from the historically most combative element of the working class, the descendants of the African slaves.* These moments defined the composition of the working class through WWII, but in the 1950s and early 1960s one of the most important revolutions in U.S. working class history occurred: the black working class successfully challenged and destroyed the legal apartheid it faced. This revolution opened the door for the increasing homogenization of the working class in terms of wages, because the blacks, who were traditionally on the bottom of the wage ladder, were able to increase their wages. Racism — the complex of techniques used to divide the working class according to superficial biological factors — finally began to be confronted. The years between 1965 and 1975 were "the second Reconstruction" (the first Reconstruction was the short period after the Civil War when the U.S. government intervened to extend the voting and civil rights of the liberated slaves).

A second revolution also took place at the same time: the remaining indigenous peoples began to create unified organizations and to challenge their legal status as "wards of the state." They began to demand the strict implementation of treaties concluded in the 19th century and to refuse their dependency on the state. This new presence of the indigenous peoples on the historical stage put the proletariat of European origin on trial for previous complicity in the genocide.

It was at this revolutionary moment in the mid-1960s that U.S. capital reversed its restrictive immigration policy. In the thirty years since then, almost 20 million new immigrants legally arrived from Mexico, Central America, the Caribbean, Vietnam, Cambodia, South Korea, China, India, and Africa. Driven to the U.S. by wars (from Vietnam and Cambodia to El Salvador, Guatemala, and Nicaragua), and structural adjustment policies (Mexico, the Caribbean, Africa), these new immigrants were politically sophisticated, but also desperately needed waged employment, and almost any wage would do. Since most of these immigrants were between 18 and 65 years of age, they entered directly into the U.S. wage labor force, which at the time was a little more than 100 million. Even though most of these immigrants took low-waged jobs, they inevitably added to the wage pressure, especially on the non-immigrant low-waged workers. This new immigration created new racial divisions, adding to those already separating blacks and whites.

(In the U.S. Southwest, there has long been a similar apartheid against descendents of Mexicans living in the territory seized by the U.S. in its war against Mexico in 1848.)

The new immigrants came from environments that had already confronted the most modern forms of capitalist exploitation. Thus their arrival added a new militancy and sophistication to the U.S. proletariat that will have an enormous impact in the future. But most immediately, it created the basis for the revival of low-waged "sweatshop" industry in the U.S., especially in textiles, sporting-goods assembly, and agricultural-processing industries.

The second great change in the composition of the waged working class was the increasing presence of women. From the 19th century textile mills to the airplane assembly lines of WWII, women were a crucial part of the waged working class. But just as with the blacks, they were treated as the ultimate reserve army of industry by capital and as second-class citizens by unions. "Last hired, first fired," applied to both. But beginning in the late 1960s, the rate of female labor market participation increased consistently and, over the last quarter century, has transformed all layers of employment. For example, the percentage of women in the total waged work force in 1995 was 46% while in 1960 it was 33%; similarly the labor participation rate of women in 1960 was 37% while in 1995 it was 58.9%. This too had an ambivalent impact on the wage labor market. On the one side, since women enter into the factory or the office in the face of gender discrimination, they offer an even greater opportunity for exploitation than men. Moreover, since women were still doing the housework, even though they had become waged workers, capital was able to continue accumulating the unwaged part of their working day (housework), while adding to it the surplus value extracted from their waged jobs.[9] On the other side, the introduction of a second wage in many U.S. working class households has made it possible for many workers to survive the fall of real wages. The expansion of waged work available to women has at least made it possible for many to escape the quasi-slavery of unwanted marriages, to which they previously were often doomed.

### The Internationalization of Capital: The Export of Commodities and the Export of Capital

We have been examining the most immediate determinants of the attack on wages and the length of the work day in the production cycle.

Another, less immediate, but equally effective determinant is in the circulation sphere: the export of commodities and capital. It has been given a new prominence in the 1990s as foreign direct investment throughout the world has risen from $200 billion in 1990 to $315 billion in 1995 while the growth of international trade has consistently out paced world economic growth since the 1960s (the GDPs of "high income economies" grew by 2.9% per year between 1980–1993, while their imports and exports increased by 5.5% per year). It has a new name, "globalization," which has become the "buzz" word of the decade. But the export of commodities and capital has been an age-old "escape mechanism" from the class struggle, for it allows capitalists to escape workers both physically and politically. When the export of commodities becomes a central objective of capitalists, they become less concerned with the capacity of their workers to consume their products. When the export of capital becomes an easy option and the exploitation of workers outside of the national economy is a common mode of capitalist behavior, then the quality of the reproduction of the national working class is even less of a concern.

In the period between 1973 and 1998 there was a fundamental shift in U.S. capital's focus from a domestic-national to an export-global economy. The continental size and, after the mid-19th century, the demographic growth of the U.S. has allowed U.S. capital to have its core circulatory interest in the national territorial limits up until recently. A relatively small amount of the GNP was accounted for by exports industries up until the 1980s and 1990s, and even today only about 12% of U.S. production is exported (compared with only about 5% of GDP in 1960). But the percentage of U.S. corporate profits produced in foreign facilities has grown dramatically from about 5% in 1950 to 20% in 1990. This shift has already had enormous consequences on the class struggle in the U.S.

The most obvious impact of the new export regime on the class struggle has been in the export of capital. Increasingly, when workers made demands, capitalists respond by threatening to export their plants and offices outside of the U.S. In the past these threats might have been taken lightly, but no more. There are a number of reasons for the new-found seriousness of these threats. First, there are now many more places where capital can safely be exported to (in the form of foreign direct investment). The world-wide impact of structural adjustment programs imposed by the IMF and the World Bank has now changed the legal structure of most of the nations in Asia, the Americas and Africa in such a way that the rights of foreign capital are now supreme. Second, a new continental terrain (from Berlin to Beijing) and billions of workers have become open to direct exploitation by U.S. capital since the collapse of the socialist regimes in Eastern Europe and the former Soviet Union, and the cautious "opening" to foreign capital of the nations of Asia still ruled by existing communist-parties (China and Vietnam). One can say that since the early 1980s the number of potential workers directly exploitable by U.S. capital has increased by approximately three billion. Third, an industrial proletariat has now taken shape in the majority of regions throughout the planet, consequently all the costs of producing such a proletariat do not need to be borne by the investing foreign company. Capitalists love pointing out to U.S. workers making $15 an hour in a manufacturing plant that, with little inconvenience, the plant could be exported to a country where workers are willing to work for less than $1 an hour. The reality of this threat is not lost on workers and their organizations.

There are certainly few U.S. laws that hinder the movement of U.S. capital beyond the national borders (except for the various sanctions imposed on Cuba, Iraq, Libya, and Iran) and that put an export tax on the outward flow of capital. The obsessive drive of the most powerful elements of U.S. capital on the governmental level has been to reduce any resistance to outward capital flows and any restrictions to the penetration of foreign barriers. The General Agreement on Tariffs and Trade (GATT), its progeny the World Trade Organization (WTO), and most importantly, the North American Free Trade Agreement (NAFTA), and proposed Multilateral Agreement on Investment (MAI) are all concrete products of this drive that has given to U.S. capital a legal mandate to threaten any insubordination of U.S. workers not only with a capital-strike (a halting of production), or a campaign of strike-breaking (continuing production with scabs), but with the continuation of production in a safe foreign environment where wages are a fraction of the present U.S. wage.[10]

This power to spatially move beyond the reach of working class threats is intensified by the increase of the export focus of the capital that remains in the territorial U.S. For once export-oriented industry is widespread, then a number of factors affecting the balance of class forces come to the fore. First, the old Fordist maxim — the workers in an auto plant should be able to buy an auto — is made null and void. For if the market for a capitalist's commodity is the working class or the capitalist class of a foreign country, then the purchasing power of his/her own workers is not the capitalist's concern. Consequently, the workers cannot use the old Keynesian threat that if their collective wage demands are rejected, the collective capitalists will not be able to sell their commodities and both will lose. Second, export-industrial production also de-localizes the workers themselves, for they recognize that the purchasers of the products they produce have no connection to them beyond the use value and the price of those commodities. Their relation to each other is as abstract as the mathematical space that separates them. Consequently, the locale of production is not crucial to its purchase, it could have been produced in place X, Y or Z as well. This further intensifies the message of the capitalist in the arena of wage negotiation: I do not need you in particular, therefore your particular demands are not binding on me. The capitalist can move to place X, Y, or Z, therefore threatening his/her workers without threatening the market for the produced commodity.

Export-oriented production has another side, import-oriented consumption, which has been crucial for decreasing wages and increasing profits as well. U.S. workers' real wages were reduced in the 1980s and 1990s without widespread strikes and uprisings because of the importation of clothing, shoes, electronics and agricultural products made cheap by the systematic repression of workers' organizations in Asia, the Americas and Africa. Torture chambers for union militants and concentrations camps for protesting students have become the "comparative advantage" of many Third World governments looking to attract foreign direct investment from the U.S. and to become "export-oriented." Free enterprise zones from Haiti to Indonesia now house U.S. firms that produce goods for the U.S. working class market without concern for labor or environmental standards. The reduction of the cost of clothes and food has made it possible for capital not only to reduce wages but to also increase the interest charges for credit cards and mortgages and rents for U.S. workers. This not only increases the share of surplus appropriated by capital through profit, rent and interest, it also creates a working class complicity with the exploitation of workers abroad that has only recently begun to be attacked in anti-sweatshop campaigns.

The changing composition of the waged working class, the delocalization of production, the "globalization" of production and consumption have not only affected the specific balance of forces between working class and capital. They are proceeding at such a pace that the very meaning of the terms "U.S. working class" and "U.S. capital" are becoming problematic. For example, *if "U.S. capital" means "capital owned by a U.S. citizen" and "U.S. working class" means "someone being exploited by U.S. capital," then much of the capital in the U.S.*

*national territory is not U.S. capital and an enormous part of the U.S. working class are citizens of other countries.* There were definitional problems of this sort before, of course, because the localization of capital and exploitation is intrinsically difficult. However, these problems are now becoming critical and demanding a new strategy to deal with the actual class composition of the working class and the concrete threats of contemporary capital. Not surprisingly, however, at this very moment a new "nationalist" ideology (full of race hatred, capitalist toadying, and anti-immigrant) is becoming the rallying cry of much of a proletariat that cannot find a way to effectively counter the tremendous forces arrayed against it without tearing itself apart.

### The State and the Working Class: the End of Keynesianism

In such an environment of class tension, one might expect the state to mediate more forcefully. However, there has been a profound change in the relation among the working class, capital, and the state since the early 1970s. The state has traditionally been concerned with the reproduction of capital and, as its necessary condition, the reproduction of the working class. This concern with the working class, beyond merely repressing its desires, became especially important with the rise of Keynesianism in the U.S. "Keynesianism" is a form of political economy named after the famous 20th century English economist John Maynard Keynes. His thinking influenced the U.S. government's economic policy of the 1940s through the 1960s. It rejected the view that capitalism, left to itself, will lead to a low unemployment, high growth economy. These objectives required that the state try to plan the major variables of a capitalist economy, from the money supply and the wage rate, to the GNP and the profit rate. Keynesianism, combined with the commitment of U.S. capital to the development of a national market, created a set of mediating mechanisms between capital and the working class, from the formalization of national wage negotiations and unionization, to welfare policies for poor women and their children, to education policies to train future workers and the management of U.S. apartheid (called "racial segregation"). One of the most important functions of the Keynesian state was the management of a parallel growth of wages and productivity, via its control of the money supply and the interest rate. If wage increases out-ran productivity increases, then an increase in the money supply with its inflationary impact followed by an interest rate increase and its recessionary consequences, would reduce the value of the wages in line with productivity. But in the late 1960s and early 1970s this cybernetic strategy began to fail. A sure sign of this failure was the lack of correlation between inflation and unemployment (the first went up the latter was down, and vice versa) called "the Phillips curve" in economics. The 1970s was a period of high unemployment and high inflation (sometimes called "stagflation") whose most important impact was the dramatic decline of real wages in the U.S. after 1973. The commitment to keeping wages growing in line with productivity growth, a central maxim of Keynesianism in practice, was rejected in the crisis.

The new political economy hostile to wage increases was euphemistically dubbed "inflation fighting," since it would not have been politic to call it what it really was: "wage hating" and "profit loving." The theorists of this policy, however, could afford to be more open, because they were more abstract. They defined an acceptable level of employment to be that level which does not increase inflation. In other words, acceptable unemployment rates had nothing to do with workers' needs, or even the national interest. In practice, any increase in wage demands from any part of the proletariat was immediately used as a pretext to impose higher interest rates that would further weaken the bargaining power of workers even in a boom, because the real interest rates would reduce the pace of business expansion and the demand for labor power. Real interest rates (i.e., nominal interest rates minus the inflation rate) remained at historic highs throughout the 1980s and 1990s. The result: inflation was reduced from 12% per annum in the late 1970s to less than 3% in the mid-1990s, while the hourly manufacturing real wage was reduced by almost 20% in the same period. This decline in wages and increase in hours took place in two major business expansions (roughly 1984–1990 and 1992–to the present [1998]).

The end of Keynesianism could be seen not only in the inflation-fighting "macro-economic" policy outlined above, it also involved a successful tax revolt by capital and capitalists. Corporations began a campaign in the 1970s to reduce direct taxes on their profits, which eventually led to a dramatic reduction of the corporate "income tax." For example, in 1957, U.S. corporations paid 45% of local property taxes, but by 1987, they paid only 16%, even though they are legally considered individuals and have all the rights of individuals. There has also been a steep decline in the corporation's share of all taxes (state, local and federal). In the 1950's for every one dollar paid by families and individuals, corporations paid about sixty-five cents, while by the 1980s corporations were paying twenty cents.

Individual capitalists also began a campaign to lower their own income tax rates in the 1970s. They succeeded as decisively as corporations. As of the mid-1990s, individuals whose income is $250,000 and higher pay about 30% of their income in taxes, whereas in the mid-1970s they were paying almost 50%. This tax revolt of the rich has not only meant a redistribution of income to the already wealthy. This upwards redistribution was paid for by deficit financing. These budget deficits from the 1980s on were partly financed by government borrowing from (not taxing) the wealthy of the U.S. and the planet who bought U.S. Treasury bonds at very profitable interest rates. Government interest payments now form the third largest expense of the national budget, after defense spending and social security (national old-age pensions). They grew from 8.9% of the national budget in 1980 to 15.2 % in 1995.

Interest payments are, in effect, a direct reduction of U.S. working class income in favor of the capitalist class of the planet. Besides shifting the "tax burden" to reduce wages, capital's tax revolt also rejected another Keynesian axiom — investment in the reproduction of the working class is essential to capitalism in an "advanced" stage.

Capital's successful tax revolt put an enormous stress on the national budget, since it meant that the private and corporate owners of the social surplus would not be taxed. This loss could only partially be compensated by new taxes (which were, in effect, generalized wage reductions) on the proletariat. As a result, "austerity budgets" have become commonplaces in the midst of two economic booms of the 1980s and 1990s. "Austerity" when applied to money was the dignified Protestant name for "poverty" in the 19th century, but in the late 20th century it is a cant phrase hiding a grim reality: U.S. capitalism admits that it can not solve the basic human problem of poverty even in its own territory. The anti-poverty programs introduced in the 1960s and early 1970s, occasioned by the struggle against racial apartheid and the revolt of women (which had at its center single women with children and the descendants of the slaves), were met with one "austerity" budget after another, at all levels of government, in the 1980s and 1990s. In the midst of stock market booms, "healthy profit reports," and the usual signals of capitalist vitality, the evident growth of poverty, the segregation of social life, and despair accumulated for all to see on the streets of the metropoli. In the face of this evidence, politicians said time and again, "There is no money," as they spent millions seducing any wandering capitalist with a few dollars to invest.

The result of the fall of real wages, the transformation of the tax burden, the increase of corporate profits and stock prices, the "austerity" budgets which ended the redistibutive efforts of government, and the rise of interest payments on the national debt has created a dramatic income disparity within U.S. society. The gap between high- and low-income families has widened every year since 1980 so that, according to former U.S. Secretary of Labor Robert Reich, "[The U.S. has] the most unequal distribution of income of any industrialized country in the world."[11]

**The Return of Slavery in the U.S.**

This is not a pretty picture. And it is rather one sided, for this essay has largely dealt with capital planning in its struggle to escape the crisis which threatened it in the early 1970s. The working class has not been passive in this period of retreat and decomposition. But the ingenuity and toughness demonstrated by working-class struggles between 1973 and 1998 (which require a chronicle of their own) have not been enough to turn the tide. The great strikes of the 1980s (e.g., the 16-month long strike of paper workers in Jay, Maine) and the Los Angeles "no peace without justice" insurrection in 1992 were important moments in a long series of episodes of resistance, but in the last two years there have been legislative changes that have laid the basis for the return of slavery in the U.S. on a mass scale.[12] In effect, the U.S. Congress has redefined what it means to be a human being. It is now possible that at the dawn of the new millennium there were 8 to 10 million adults — which would constitute about 7% of the "economically active population" of the U.S. — in a slave-like status.

This does not imply a return to the "chattel" slavery of the pre-Civil War period, where the slave was the property of private individuals and could be sold at will. But there are many forms of "unfree labor" — e.g., debt bondage, serfdom, prison labor, and corvee. These near-slave forms of labor were used in the U.S. South for almost a century after slavery was abolished and the First Reconstruction was scuttled.[13] The ending of the Second Reconstruction — practically in the late 1970s, and formally in 1995, with the Supreme Court decision to void Affirmative Action — has paved the way for a second round of near-slavery regimes which prey on the traditional source of slaves: the poor woman, the prisoner, and the stranger. For if slavery is, as Orlando Patterson suggests in his broader definition, "the permanent, violent domination of natally alienated and generally dishonoured persons," then these people fit the description of the dominated. The existence of an "information-driven," "cyber-spaced" capitalism will not save us from a revival of slavery. As Dockes has put it in the opening epigraph, the development of capitalism will never automatically lead to the end of slavery. On the contrary, as long as capitalism continues to exist there will be an inevitable tendency to reintroduce slave-like forms of labor. If waged and unwaged workers do not have the force to resist this tendency, then many of our number will be doomed to slave status at whatever the level of productive forces the capitalists command.[14]

In 1996 three separate laws, directed at single mothers, prisoners and strangers, were passed in the U.S. Congress. They formalized the collapse of proletarian resistance to this tendency to the slavery inherent in the capitalist system and facilitated a new era of enslavement and low wages in the U.S.

The first of these three laws is the "Anti-Terrorism and Effective Death Penalty Act." On the surface, this law is directed against two different groups of people (which, however, the state wants the public to identify as the same): the U.S. supporters of revolutionary groups around the world (from the Zapatistas, to the Palestinians, to the IRA); and the people convicted of capital crimes who are on death row. This law has very severe provisions for both, but included in this law is a fundamental denial of one of the most basic civil rights, habeas corpus, that is, the right to petition a higher court to show just cause why s/he is being kept prisoner. This has been used by thousands of prisoners who had reason to believe that they were being held on false charges and being treated in a discriminatory way. It is the ultimate right of a prisoner to protest his/her imprisonment.

What does the abolition of habeas corpus have to do with the return of slavery in the U.S.? First, there are about two million adults in prison in the U.S., and this number is growing. The prison population has increased in line with the fall of wages. Prisons became the "growth industry" of the 1990s, and the portion of some states' budgets (e.g., California) is larger than that spent on higher education. This growth has come from the criminalization of the cocaine, heroin, and marijuana industry and the "mandatory sentencing laws" that assign people convicted of particular crimes to long sentences with no possibility of parole. As a result, if one is poor, young, male and black, he has a one-in-three chance of going to prison sometime in his 20s. Given the "austerity" budgets that have continued into the boom years of 1990s (and the still virulent racism and classism of the U.S.), there is a capitalist demand for using these prisoners profitably to "make them pay for their crimes." Hence, prison industries are being instituted throughout the U.S. even faster than the prisons are being built, and increasingly prisons are being built as part of an industrial complex.[15]

*But slavery — especially profit-making slavery in the prisons — cannot be reintroduced without a death penalty "effectively" threatening the physical elimination of any rebellious imprisoned workers.*

Prisoners have always worked in prisons, of course, but this work was either directed at the prison's housework (e.g., the laundry or building maintenance) or for the benefit of the state (e.g., the famous auto license plates or highway signs). In prison industries, the prisoners work for private, profit-making companies which pay them a non-negotiated wage from which their living expenses in the prison and a payment into a "victim fund" is deducted. They are slaves, not because they are forced to work (for that is every proletarian's fate), but because they have no right to organize and negotiate their wages.

The second pro-slavery law of 1996 was the "welfare" law, the "Personal Responsibility and Work Opportunity Act," which in effect eliminated the U.S. government's guarantee to provide minimal benefits to every indigent person in the U.S. This law puts a limit of five years on the federally-funded welfare support they receive, and stipulates that in order to get it they must join a "workfare" program. "Workfare" requires that people receiving benefits report for work or training at assigned places (usually in government agencies) or they will be cut off. In effect, the welfare benefit is transformed into a wage. But again, this is a non-negotiable wage. Consequently, people on workfare are placed in a quasi-slave condition, a form of debt bondage.[16]

Finally, we come to the immigration law of 1996, the "Illegal Immigration Reform and Immigrant Responsiblity Act." This law has many draconian penalties for documented and undocumented immigrants even though the U.S. is a society that is largely peopled by immigrants. Most crucial for our theme are the provisions that make a transition from an "undocumented status" to a "documented status" next to impossible. This creates a permanent sector of workers in the U.S. who have no rights nor even a possibility to petition for them. This stratum is immediately placed into a slave-like status because people in this situation have great difficulty in negotiating a wage. Moreover, while an employer of an undocumented worker faces a small fine if s/he is discovered, an undocumented worker faces financial catastrophe or even death.

Prisoners, single mothers, and undocumented workers are all entering into a new legal status: that of waged workers who cannot legally negotiate their wages. In other words, millions of adults in the territorial U.S. are finding themselves in situations reminiscent of the 19th century, with its plantation slavery in the South, coolie workers in the West, and indentured servants in the East of the U.S. This revival of slavery constitutes a major defeat for the U.S. proletariat, for how can one launch a major wage struggle knowing that there are millions of people in slave-like situations undercutting wages? Slaves, not computers, are the somber basis of U.S. capital's "bright prospects" in the winter of 1998.

### Conclusion: "The Force to Compel the Masters"

Surely any story that ends with the revival of slavery is a story of working class defeat. It is important for Mexican comrades to know the grim facts, but we cannot end here. Especially not in an article meant to begin a discussion about "the force to compel the masters to forgo the use of slaves" in the common history and future of the U.S. and Mexican proletariats.

A good place to begin this discussion is with NAFTA itself, the official document by which the masters of Mexico and the U.S. have agreed to structure relations between themselves and "their" proletariats in the coming decades. The NAFTA principle is: free the flow of capital and commodities across the borders and highly restrict the passage of labor power, allowing capital to easily escape wage struggles while making it difficult for workers to escape wage defeats. NAFTA has definitely been successful for U.S. capital. Since 1994 real wages both in Mexico and the U.S. have fallen, while trade, capital flow, and profits have increased dramatically in the U.S.

But NAFTA is not yet a perfect capitalist tool. A major debate among capitalists in the U.S. since NAFTA became operational in 1994 has been over how restricted should be the passage of labor between Mexico and the U.S.? The far right has been demanding "an immigration moratorium" while the center of the political spectrum is satisfied with creating a class of immigrants in a quasi-slave status who would neither be able to access government services nor negotiate their wages. The "Illegal Immigration Reform and Immigrant Responsiblity Act" of 1996 was a tentative compromise between these two groups, but the sparring between openly racist hard-cops like Pat Buchanan, the Republican presidential candidate, and neo-social democrat soft-cops like Robert Reich, Clinton's former Secretary of Labor, will continue far into the future. For this politics is used to manipulate the quantity of labor power moving across the borders and to divide Mexican and U.S. workers from each other in accordance with the needs of the labor market. Moreover, this vicious debate allows the Mexican government to appear as a concerned protector of immigrant Mexican workers (and their remittances) in the U.S.

But this NAFTA debate is an exercise in futility for the North American working class, forever enclosed by the rhetoric of racist exclusion, efficient slavery, and Machiavellian paternalism. NAFTA must be turned upside down and revised in the interest of the North American proletariat. This revision would require putting new restrictions on the movement of capital and freeing the movement of workers. This strategy began to be discussed in the struggle against NAFTA in 1993 by different cross-border alliances of labor unions and was forcefully put on the working class agenda by the EZLN in the Revolutionary Law they proclaimed on January 1, 1994.

The Zapatistas self-consciously chose that date to begin their uprising as a blow against NAFTA.[17] They called NAFTA a "death sentence" for the indigenous of Mexico and demanded that the NAFTA-inspired revision of Article 27 of the Mexican Constitution be annulled and that any foreign company coming into Mexico pay the same wages to Mexicans that they pay at home. But the Zapatista's demand for legal and economic autonomy for indigenous regions of Mexico, if successful, would undermine the effect of NAFTA on the whole North American proletariat. Indeed, this rebellion has already helped to halt the expansion of NAFTA to Chile, Argentina, Costa Rica and other parts of the Americas. In this sense, the revolt in Chiapas poses the problematic of the North American working class in its sharpest contours. This explains why the U.S. government has been so diligent in arming and training the Mexican Army (under the cover of a phony "drug war") and why the Mexican government has been so harsh in its rejection of the San Andreas accords by claiming that it would "Balkanize Mexico."

The problem of indigenous autonomy for capital is not that it would bring about the breakup of Mexico, but that it would provide a model for workers (both waged and unwaged, both U.S. and Mexican) to restrict and control all capital that flows into its vicinity. Though not anti-capitalist in itself, this autonomy would have revolutionary consequences in the contemporary era of totalitarian neo-liberalism. Consequently, an important condition for the common proletarian future in North America is the survival and success of the struggle for indigenous autonomy in Chiapas.

Can the search to find "the force to compel the masters to forgo the use of slaves" end in the *ejidos* of Chiapas, the poorest (and richest) region in all of North America? This would not be surprising. In the decade after the defeat of the 1871 Paris Commune, Marx turned his attention to the revolutionary possibilities stemming from the communal lands and peoples of the world. He found them in the Russian *obshchina*, "a form, albeit heavily eroded, of the primitive communal ownership of land" similar to the *ejido*. In one of his last published writings, the "Preface to the Second Russian Edition of the *Manifesto of the Communist Party*" (1882), he laid his considerable prestige on the concluding sentence: "If the Russian revolution becomes the signal for proletarian revolution in the West, so that the two complement each other, then Russia's peasant communal landownership may serve as the point of departure for a communist development."[18] These were prescient words, but they were certainly "off color" for those committed to the vanguard role of the industrial proletariat in 1882. Let us learn from history, especially our history, to question our assumptions and dismissals.

Mexico City–Parma–Newport–Brooklyn
July 1997–March 1998

*(Mexican comrades asked me to write this essay for a Mexican audience in the summer of 1997. I thank them for their patience and inspiration.)*

**Notes**

[1] There were periods when there was much political cooperation and communication between Mexican and U.S. proletarian organizations. The involvement of the Industrial Workers of the World (IWW) in the 1906 strike of Mexican miners in Cananea and with the Magon brothers' "desert revolution" in Baja California was well known. During the Mexican Revolution, the American Federation of Labor (AFL) organized contacts with La Casa del Obrero Mundial and many other newly formed Mexican unions. The Congress of Industrial Organization (CIO) supported the

Cardenas government's expropriation of the oil companies and collaborated with the Confederacion de Trabajadores de Mexico (CTM) in the 1930s. These organizational ties began to fade in the 1940s and are only being revived in the 1990s, under the pressure of North American Free Trade Agreement. For a discussion of the relation of U.S. and Mexican working class organizations from 1906 to the 1940s see Harvey A. Levenstein, *Labor Organizations in the United States and Mexico: A History of their Relations.* (Westport, CT: Greenwood, 1971). A good handbook for the post-NAFTA renaissance of relations between U.S. and Mexican labor unions is Harry Browne (ed.), *Cross Border Links: A Directory of Organizations in Canada, Mexico, and the United States.* (Silver City, NM: Interhemispheric Resource Center, 1997).

2 A review of the "New Economy" literature would include articles like Alan B. Krueger's "How Computers Have Changed the Wage Structure: Evidence From MicroData, 1984–1989." *Quarterly Journal of Economics* 108 (June 1993): 33–60, John R. Cranford's "Economy Will Benefit from Deregulation: Question Is, How Much?" *Special Report, The Information Arena, Congressional Quarterly,* supplement to no. 19, May 14, 1994, and Michael Rothschild, "The Coming Productivity Surge," *Forbes ASAP,* March 29, 1993. But these technology boosters need to confront "the productivity paradox," i.e., labor productivity grew by 3% annually between 1960s and 1973 but it has fallen to 1.1% between 1973 and the present. The latter period has seen an elephantine investment in computer hardware, software, and personnel, but it produced a productivity mouse! For a discussion of this paradox see Daniel E. Sichel, *The Computer Revolution: An Economic Perspective* (Washington, DC: Brookings Institution Press, 1997), and Thomas K. Landauer, *The Trouble with Computers: Usefulness, Usability, and Productivity* (Cambridge, Massachusetts: MIT Press. 1993).

3 See Fred Mosley, "The rate of profit and economic stagnation in the U.S. economy," *Historical Materialism,* Autumn 1997.

4 Daniel P. Moynihan, *The Politics of the Guaranteed Income: The Nixon Administration and the Family Assistance Plan* (New York: Random House, 1973).

5 Harold L. Sheppard and Neal Q. Herrick, *Where Have All the Robots Gone? Worker Dissatisfaction in the '70s* (New Year: Free Press, 1972).

6 Karl Marx, "Machinery and Large-Scale Industry," *Capital: A*

*Critique of Political Economy*, Vol. 1, Chapter 15 (Harmondsworth: Penguin, 1976).

7 For a thorough journalistic account of "downsizing" and workers' reaction to it see The New York Times' Special Report, *The Downsizing of America* (New York: Times Books, 1996).

8 For a positive discussion of "Post-Fordism" see A. Lipietz, *Mirages and Miracles: The Crisis of Global Fordism* (London: Verso, 1987); and for a critique of the thematics of "Post-Fordism" see Ferrucio Gambino, "A Critique of the Fordism of the Regulation School," *Common Sense: Journal of the Edinburgh Conference of Socialist Economists* No. 19, 1996.

9 For statistics on the increase of the total work day of U.S. women since the early 1960s, see Juliet B. Schor, *The Overworked American: The Unexpected Decline of Leisure* (New York: Basic Books). Schor shows that there has been an extraordinary constancy of the U.S. housewife's working hours throughout the twentieth century. For example, even though the average U.S. home has much more capital equipment and "labor-saving" appliances in 1990 compared to 1925, there has been virtually no decrease in the housewife's working hours: in 1925 she worked 51 hours per week, while in 1990 she worked 49 hours (pp. 86–87).

10 The literature on "globalization," "neo-liberalism," "liberalization," "the New International Division of Labor," "The New Enclosures" and other terms used to describe the post-1973 history of planetary capitalism is immense. I merely suggest a short list: Midnight Notes, "Introduction," *One No, Many Yeses* (Boston: Midnight Notes, 1997); Silvia Federici, "Reproduction and Feminist Struggle in the New International Division of Labor." In M. R. Dalla Costa and G. Dalla Costa (eds.), *Women, Development, and the Labor of Reproduction: Issues of Struggles and Movements* (Lawrenceville, NJ: Africa World Press, 1999); Jerry Mander and Edward Goldsmith (eds.), *The Case Against the Global Economy and For a Turn Toward the Local* (San Franscico: Sierra Club Books, 1996); Roger Burbach, Orlando Nunez and Boris Kagarlitsky, *Globalization and its Discontents* (London: Pluto Press, 1997); Kevin Danaher (ed.), *Corporations Are Going to Get Your Mama: Globalization and the Downsizing of the American Dream* (Monroe, Maine: Common Courage Press, 1996). For a more sceptical treatment of these descriptions see Paul Hirst and Grahame Thompson, *Globalization in Question: The International Economy and the Possibilities of Governance*

(Cambridge, UK: Polity Press, 1996).

11 Quoted in Kevin Danaher, *Corporations Are Gonna Get Your Mama*, p. 29.

12 The story of the epic strike in Jay, Maine was told by David Riker in Midnight Notes (ed.) *The New Enclosures* (New York: Autonomedia, 1990).

13 An important set of articles on slavery and its horrendous cousins was edited by Leonie J. Archer, *Slavery and Other Forms of Unfree Labour* (London: Routledge, 1988); see especially G.E.M. de Ste. Croix's "Slavery and Other Forms of Unfree Labour" and Robin Blackburn's "Slavery — its Special Features and Social Role."

14 Orlando Patterson, *Slavery and Social Death: A Comparative Study* (Cambridge, MA: Harvard University Press), p. 13; and Pierre Dockes, *Medieval Slavery and Liberation* (London: Methuen & Co. Ltd., 1982).

15 For a discussion of the "prison-industrial complex" see Section One of Elihu Rosenblatt (ed.), *Criminal Injustice: Confronting the Prison Crisis* (Boston: South End Press, 1996).

16 There has been a major struggle against the 1996 welfare law's provisions concerning the non-negotiablity of the wages and working conditions in workfare. For example, one activist group, Association of Community Organizations for Reform Now (ACORN), has created a union of workfare employees in New York City and is demanding recognition. The Clinton Administration has responded to such efforts by placing a provision in the 1997 Budget bill requiring that workfare workers employed by state governments should receive at least the minimum wage.

17 For a discussion of the complex conjuncture of forces that led to the decision to start the Zapatista insurrection on January 1, 1994 see Subcommendante Marcos with Yves Le Bot, *Il sogno zapatista* (Milan: Mondadori, 1997), pp. 133–149.

18 The Preface is reprinted in an important collection of essays and documents concerning Marx's last decade: Teodor Shanin (ed.), *Late Marx and the Russian Road: Marx and "the peripheries of capitalism"* (New York: Monthly Review Press, 1983). The quote is on p. 139.

*Rod Thurton*

# 14
# EULOGY FOR RODERICK THURTON (1938–2000)

SILVIA FEDERICI

RODERICK CRISPIN THURTON was born in Trinidad on October 25, 1938. He grew up in a supportive environment surrounded by family and kin. He used to joke that as a child there was nothing he could do without a member of his family noticing it. But he was especially close to his mother, a religious woman of Chinese descent, who was his first inspiration and teacher. It was from her that Rod acquired his sense of justice, self-discipline, and commitment to people. She was also the one who gave him his first lessons in communalism. Rod remembered with admiration how, at Christmas time, she opened the house to everyone, so that for days people would come and no one would leave without getting some food or some punch. Her death, after months in coma, while she was visiting the United States, was one of the greatest sorrows in Rod's life.

Rod began his education in Trinidad. It was an education he was proud of. He liked to describe how tough were the exams in his high-school, and how the school always scored high points compared with its equivalent in England; and he took great pleasure reciting poems or essays he had memorized. It was in high-school that his interest in politics developed. At this time, he learned about the Chinese revolution from a man in the Chinese community he had befriended. He also began to forge a lasting relationship with C.L.R. James, who Rod always considered his mentor. When James and others founded the Workers and Farmers Party, he joined them, and in 1966 when the Party contested the elections against the ruling People's National Movement (PNM) he was the only candidate who did not loose his deposit.

The relationship with James was something very special in Rod's life, a turning point. Through him Rod acquired not only an internationalist perspective and a political network that stretched from Detroit to Toronto and Turin, but also a view of revolution as a collective process, the result not of party politics but workers' self-organization. This enabled him, throughout his life, to understand the inseparable connection of race and class, colony and metropolis, and the crucial role of immigration in the international circulation of struggle. This is why when he came to the U.S., in 1967, to pursue a medical career, he could continue to do political work he had begun in Trinidad and, at the same time, avoid the trap of exile politics.

Six months after arriving in the U.S., Rod returned to Trinidad to get married to Crystal. On that occasion, a friend of his dedicated to him a poem which he gave him together with a tray of various Trinidadian woods — God's bits of wood in the African tradition — probably knowing how much Rod treasured his country, and how ready he was, despite the fact that he was now moving to the U.S. to give what he had to defend its people and its resources.

Back in the States, Rod realized that medicine was not his calling. He was already very politicized when he came, and then these were the times of revolution; and soon he began the life of intense activism through which most of us have known him. In the early 1970s, he participated in the foundation of the New Beginning Movement, and organized public forums in Brooklyn, to discuss current political issues especially concerning the Caribbean. He also enrolled in a political science program specializing in Caribbean and African Studies and International Relations, subjects which he then taught for more than 15 years at a number of universities in New York, including Queens College and City College.

Rod was a great teacher, because he had a deep knowledge of international history and politics, and was determined to have a democratic relation with his students. Those who have worked with him remember how critical he was of teachers who walk into the classroom with syllabi ready-made. As for him, he believed that students had to be involved in shaping the courses they took with him, and he did his best to treat them like peers, often helping them with their personal problems.

Rod was a teacher also in his political work. For years he ran classes on Caribbean history and politics at the Marxist School. He also did educational work through the many programs he contributed to WBAI; and even after he had returned to Trinidad, he continued to make plans for organizing workshops, or making videotapes, to help the younger generations understand the world, and break away from the materialism and cynicism by which he saw them surrounded.

Above all Rod was one of those rare persons who teach as they speak. Whatever the occasion, he always had such powerful analysis and spoke so eloquently that when he would say "let me tell you something" you set yourself to listening because you knew that your consciousness was about to be expanded. Certainly this was because he came from a great political tradition — the tradition that produced James, Eric Williams, the Mighty Sparrow, the role models of his youth — and he had so much confidence in what people can do, he trusted so much that history, in the end, is going to come out on the right side, that whatever he discussed, he gave you a sense of the new society that is in the make, and the broader struggle to which we are connected.

Rod also taught through his political commitment and courage. Convinced as he was of the importance of theory in the revolutionary process, he never for a minute doubted that you have to put your body on the line, and do what you can, starting from now, to better people's lives. Thus, in 1992, he participated in the caravan that broke the embargo against Cuba. In the same period, he began a campaign, through the Caribbean-American Action Committee and the Pan-Caribbean Research Institute, both of which he founded, to expose the fraudulent ways in which the Trinidadian government was planning to sell out BWIA, the national airline.

This struggle was very important for Rod. He knew very well that if BWIA was lost, Trinidadians in the U.S. would be personally and politically cut off from home. But it was also a dangerous challenge to the schemes of the Trinidadian government and its American allies, and the revenge was swift. Shortly after his return from the caravan, in November 1992, Rod was assaulted by four men who did not take his money but made it a point to break his eyes, which forced him to be home-bound and stay in the dark for many weeks. Nevertheless, his determination to expose the BWIA fraud was not lessened. In fact, he proceeded to complete a report that detailed all the aspects of the fraud being attempted, and had it published and publicized in Trinidad, after making it available to the airline's unions, with the result that the BWIA sell-out was prevented.

In 1996 when Basdeo Panday who had previously been a comrade of his in the Workers and Farmers' Party and, later, the head of the Sugar Workers Trade Union, was elected president of Trinidad, Rod decided it was time for him to go home. He believed that Trinidad now had a chance to become a center of resistance to the IMF, World Bank, and globalization in the Caribbean. But he was bitterly disappointed, and in fact shortly after his return he began taking his distance from the government, after observing how all his proposals fell on deaf ears, and his trust in the government's will to steer an independent course was misplaced. He was especially embittered by the concessions the Panday government made to the U.S., and its usage of the death penalty, against which Rod spoke on a panel at the Socialist Scholars conference, exactly one year ago.

Rod, however, remained in the post to which he had been appointed as member of the boards of directors of BWIA (British West Indian Airways), Leeward Island Air Transport (LIAT), and TANTEAK, hoping to contribute to block any privatization and sell-out attempt, and build a different relation between these companies and their workers' unions. His very untimely death struck him down in the middle of this most important battle in his life — a battle that would certainly have had profound consequences on Trinidad's economic and political life.

Rod's task now remains to be completed, and it is something to which each of us, here, must contribute, aware that with Rod's death we have lost a great ally in the struggle we now have to fight against the new forms of colonization and proletarian enslavement worldwide.

With Rod's death we have also lost a very beautiful man, who despite his busy agenda always made the time to follow closely the life and progress of his three children; who nursed his brother ill with cancer day-after-day, not sparing any effort to relieve his pain, and to investigate new treatments; a man who gave his family and friends many happy memorable hours, talking, playing, laughing, maybe around a bottle of rum, all the while looking for the political lesson in everything.

We mourn his loss, but with the knowledge that his spirit will always be with us, and that it will now be our mission to continue his work, and to ensure that others can share the great political and spiritual wealth that he brought to us.

*Fernando Lopez Isunza*

# 15
# EULOGY FOR FERNANDO LOPEZ ISUNZA (1973–1999)

DAVID RIKER

FERNANDO LOPEZ ISUNZA was born in the town of San Marcos, in Tlascala, Mexico, on July 15, 1973. In 1994, at the age of twenty one, Fernando joined a growing exodus of young Mexican immigrants traveling north to the United States in search of work. He found work in New York City's garment district, and for the next five years, until his tragic and premature death, he dedicated himself to building an immigrant workers' movement both in and outside of the sweatshops.

Within a year of arriving in New York's garment district, Fernando had become an active member of the Garment Workers Justice Center, a strategic initiative by UNITE, the Union of Industrial and Textile Employees, to organize new immigrant workers outside of the sweatshops. Fernando's considerable organizational and communication skills were quickly recognized, and brought him first into the press and propaganda committee, and later led to his being elected head of the organizing committee. Also while at UNITE's Workers Center, he helped found two theater groups, Mascaras and Sin Fronteras, and volunteered as a GED teacher, instructing garment workers after work.

When, in the winter of 1997, UNITE expelled the coordinator of the Workers Center, Fernando left the center with other activist members. Together, in a meeting of several hundred workers in the basement of a church, they constituted a new organization, the Garment

Workers Solidarity Center, which remains an autonomous, worker-led, grassroots organization in New York's garment district.

Fernando was both a teacher and a student, and his dedication to acquiring knowledge in order to empower himself and others in the fight for social justice was unwavering. As a GED teacher, he represented the best of the tradition of worker-teachers. Always carrying a bag full of books and papers, Fernando moved through the garment district carrying his enormous passion for ideas. He saw in every worker the capacity to think freely, a capacity without limits. And though he would arrive at class tired after the long days in the sweatshops, and often without having eaten, he insisted that his students, themselves equally exhausted, push themselves to study literature and mathematics. He brought great patience, humor, and clarity to all of his teaching.

In 1999, after being arrested in an INS raid at the sweatshop where he worked, Fernando refused to reveal his country of origin, and was as a result jailed for more than a month. At his court hearing, when the judge ruled that he be deported, Fernando answered that he still had a great deal to do and would be back. In the INS detention facility in Elizabeth, New Jersey, he worked to help fellow inmates from Africa, China, Guatemala and El Salvador. Fernando often said that the only border that existed was his skin.

Beyond his efforts to build a movement among garment workers, Fernando crossed the city from one side to the other, building bridges between groups who rarely worked together. In his short time in New York, he helped build the new movement for immigrant rights, joined the struggle against the death penalty and to free Mumia Abu Jamal, and worked with the New York Zapatistas to support the indigenous movement in Chiapas.

When he learned that he would have to return to Mexico after his arrest, he started making arrangements to travel to Chiapas, to witness first hand the struggle of the Zapatistas and to see how he could become involved. Sadly, Fernando died days before leaving for Mexico, falling under a moving subway train. His friends and family could not help but feel that his tragic death was connected to his imminent deportation.

Fernando often wrote poetry for his friends. Here is one of his poems, read at his memorial service in the garment district.

> Espero vivir mil anos
> Para poder comprender esto mundo

*Eulogy for Fernando Lopez Isunza*

En este juego de la vida
Solo hay dos caminos
El de la vida facil,
y el de los grandes sacrificios
Espero tener la dicha
de caminar por el segundo
Para que al final de mi existencia
Me encuentre lleno de satisfaciones

The following is a rough translation:

[I hope I live a thousand years,
to be able to understand this world.
In this game of life,
there are only two paths.
One of the easy life,
and one of great sacrifices.
I hope I have the chance
to travel down the second,
So that at the end of my existence
I'll find myself filled with satisfaction.]

Para siempre y por siempre, Fernando Lopez presente.

The Tyger

Tyger Tyger, burning bright,
In the forests of the night;
What immortal hand or eye,
Could frame thy fearful symmetry?

In what distant deeps or skies,
Burnt the fire of thine eyes!
On what wings dare he aspire?
What the hand, dare sieze the fire?

And what shoulder, & what art,
Could twist the sinews of thy heart?
And when thy heart began to beat,
What dread hand? & what dread feet?

What the hammer? what the chain,
In what furnace was thy brain?
What the anvil? what dread grasp,
Dare its deadly terrors clasp?

When the stars threw down their spears
And water'd heaven with their tears:
Did he smile his work to see?
Did he who made the Lamb make thee?

Tyger Tyger burning bright,
In the forests of the night:
What immortal hand or eye,
Dare frame thy fearful symmetry?

# 16
# REVOLUTIONARY TYGERS IN THE NIGHT

PETER LINEBAUGH

Tyger! Tyger! burning bright
In the forests of the night,
What immortal hand or eye
Could frame thy fearful symmetry?
—William Blake

ONCE AGAIN, it is an Africa / America story that we have in Blake's tiger. It is a revolutionary story, and it is a story about the commons, as I shall prove with additional evidences, mainly from Captain Stedman, the soldier who fought four years in Suriname against the maroons and against the slaves, most of whom were state-of-the-art forest dwellers. Captain Stedman lived to tell his tale by writing, which took him about fourteen years to do. He submitted his "narrative" to Joseph Johnson, the publisher, in 1790. Johnson was a "liberal" publisher, doing Wollstonecraft, Blake, Erasmus Darwin, &c., but also cautious, and when the firing started he quickly withdrew as Paine's publisher. He hired an "editor," to tone down and racialize a bit more, Stedman's narrative, which wasn't published until 1796. Those dates are important: in 1790 the revolution in the Caribbean had not begun; by 1796 England was at war against the Haitian uprising, determined to exterminate the freedom-fighting slaves, and sacrificing thousands and thousands of young English boys and men in the futile effort. In terms of Blake's poetry, these are the years in which (a) he developed his own revolutionary energy, and (b) he was gagged and feared to publish.

Stedman also painted water colors and submitted more than a hundred to Joseph Johnson. The pictures have been lost, but eighty of them became the basis of engravings in the published *Narrative*. Johnson hired William Blake to help with this work. Blake was one among several engravers, some having more prestige than he, although Stedman profusely thanked Blake for his renderings, and to us now, Blake's are clearly the more interesting. We know that for two or three years Blake studied these images, because engravings with his signature appeared in 1794, though most of Blake's are dated 1793, and with some in 1792. From sometime in 1791 until 1794 William Blake bore down, his elbow grease mixed with the burin and copper plate, on these images of an American slave revolt. He imbued most successfully the knowledge contained in the pictures and the text, knowledge which was going to influence his writing, politics, and poetry.

*Stedman's "The Tiger-Cat of Suriname"*

Take the tiger. There is an engraving of the tiger cat and the jaguar but not by Blake, at least not that is known. Stedman's soldiers captured a jaguar in the chicken coop and drowned it. He describes for a couple of pages this, the cougar, and the tiger cat. Stedman describes a "Tiger-Cat Which is Extremely Beautiful ... The Tiger Cat is a Very Lively Animal With its Eyes emitting flashes of Lightning; — But ferocious, Mischievious, and not Tameable like the rest" (359), or, the "Red Tiger... the head is small the Body thin the Limbs Long with tremendous whitish Claws The Teeth are Also Very Large, the Eyes prominent, and Sparkling like Stars..." in the nighttime forest. After the tiger has gorged upon its prey, they become cowards, says Stedman, and take to flight at a dog or a fire, of which they are mortally afraid, "which is the best bulwark to keep them at a distance, and as such every night made use of by the Indians in Guiana."

*British painter George Stubbs "Tiger," probably known to Blake*

What would the Zapatista think of this tiger? What would the Black Panther Party think of this tiger? What do we? It lives in the forest. It is untameable, and ferocious. It is a creature of the commons. Its depredations upon the fowl and livestock of the soldiers, villagers, or planters is not much recounted by Stedman. But it is clear that he was fascinated by the tiger's eyes, just like he was by the eyes of the giant python that he attempted to slay, and failed twice, before at last succeeding.

In what distant deeps or skies
Burnt the fire of thine eyes?
On what wings dare he aspire?
What the hand dare seize the fire?
And what shoulder, & what art,
Could twist the sinews of thy heart?
And when thy heart began to beat,
What dread hand? & what dread feet?

What the hammer? what the chain?
In what furnace was thy brain?
What the anvil? what dread grasp
Dare its deadly terrors clasp?

Blake is thinking of the creator of the tiger. Stedman, of course, as a hunter, respected the creature but only to kill it. Blake expressed a dialectical relation, wondering that the creation was composed of antagonists, not just between hunter and prey, but between oppressor and oppressed. These he understood as social forces. In *Marriage of Heaven and Hell* (1793) he inveighs against priest and tyrant and merchant in his "Song of Liberty." In the same year he published *America; A Prophecy*, which begins with a "Preludium" showing red Orc spread-eagled by wrist and ankles to the ground. It is a terrible image. A young virgin brings him food and water. He bursts his bonds and passionately embraces her. She cried:

> I know thee, I have found thee, & I will not let thee go; Thou art the image of God who dwells in darkness of Africa.

Thus the redeeming energy that propels the American revolution is figured as African. This corresponds with recent scholarship of the American War of Independence, which has emphasized the autonomous struggles of the slaves, whether fleeing to north or south, to Canada or the Caribbean, and had this in common: the rejection of slavery. Blake, too, saw the American revolution as a slave revolt. But there is more.

Commentators are agreed that Orc as here depicted bears resemblance to an engraving in Stedman, probably by Blake, called "The Execution of Breaking on the Rack." From pages 544 to 550, Stedman tells the remarkable story of Neptune and of slave resistance to the tortures and mutilations that plantation society visited upon those who resisted it. His left hand is chopped off. With an iron bar the executioner, also a Black, of course, "smashes to shivers every Bone in his Body." He begged that his head be chopped off. This was refused. "However you Christians have mis'd your Aim, and I now Care not were I to lay here Alive a month longer," and he sang two songs. He demanded that a Jewish debtor repay him five shillings. He asked the sentinel on guard, "how it came that he a White Man should have no meat." "Because I am not so rich," said the soldier. "Then I will make

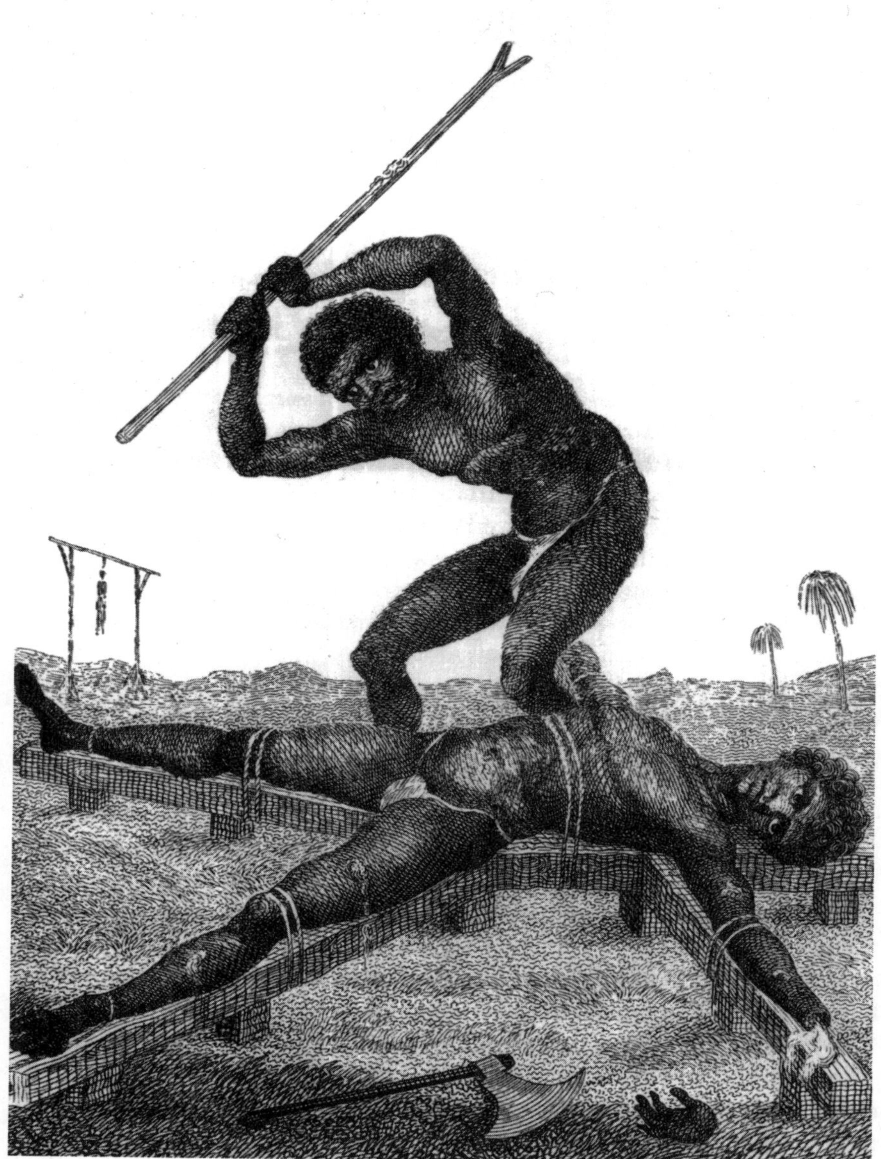

"The Execution of Breaking on the Rack"

you a Present first pick my Hand that was Chopt off Clean to the Bones Sir — Next begin to myself till you be Glutted & you'l have both Bread and Meat which best becomes you," and he laughed again. Stedman reflected that in 1789 thirty two hanged in Demerara, without a single complaint. Stedman is moved to quote from *Daniel*:

> And in those times there Shall many Stand up Against the King of the South, Also the Robbers of thy People shall exalt Themselves

and then,

> After this shall he turn his face to the isles and shall take many — but a prince of his own behalf shall cause the reproach offered by him to Cease ...

In other words, Stedman is suggesting that Neptune, who suffered most, be compared to the redeeming savior prophecized by Daniel. Blake takes this theme and draws the red Orc as Neptune.

> When the stars threw down their spears,
> And water'd heaven with their tears,
> Did he smile his work to see?
> Did he who made the Lamb make thee?

Throwing down the spears, according to David Erdman, is Blake's way of saying military defeat, and this defeat referred to here is that of England by America.

> Tyger! Tyger! burning bright
> In the forests of the night,
> What immortal hand or eye
> Could frame thy fearful symmetry?

The poem concludes once again with the opening quatrain, the famous invocation and the equally tremendous question at the end; or is it a challenge? *The Songs of Experience* were composed (I think) in 1792 or 1793. I should find out, because it makes a difference in another argument. All I want to say here is that this is the time of the cotton gin and the steam engine; it is the time of the formation of the English working class and the Black church in America and the

*"Europe supported by Africa & America"*

Resistance of Blood on both sides of the Atlantic. That is the tyger. Ten years later Blake's anthem — *Jerusalem* — ends with England's green and pleasant land. Not so at this high point of revolutionary energy against slavery and for the commons in 1792.

Stedman's *Narrative* concludes with another picture of Blake's, one hand-tinted with water colors. "Europe supported by Africa & America" shows three beautiful nude women standing, arm in arm, upon a green, with mountains in the distance. Stedman calls it an emblematical picture "accompanied by an ardent wish that in the friendly manner as they are represented they may henceforth & to all eternity be the prop of each other; I might have included Asia but this I omitted as having no Connection with the Present Narrative — we all only differ in the Colour but we are Certainly Created by the same hand & after the Same Mould ..." lines which, it seems, were on Blake's mind in composing his first draft of the "Tyger."

Could fetch it from the furnace deep
And in thy horrid ribs dare steep
In the well of sanguine woe?
In what clay & in what mould
Were thy eyes of fury roll'd?

Stedman was a soldier against the freedom-fighters. I don't forget this. Blake's acquaintance with him — (it was more, they dined togther, they exchanged presents, and Stedman entrusted to Blake some business affairs) — however, brought the revolution of the Americas to Blake in a way that saved Blake from the condescension of the sentimental abolitionism of the 1780s. It enabled Blake to move right into revolutionary energy, a revolutionary politics, and a revolutionary vision that was sparked by the slave revolts of the western Atlantic.

"Then All the Slaves from every Earth in the wide Universe Sing a New Song, drowning confusion in its happy notes," he wrote in 1797 in *Vala, or the Four Zoas* but not published for fear of prosecution until 1804 (I think). The "New Song" refers to *Revelations* 4, where the Lion of Judah opens the seals, or it may refer to *Isaiah* 42 where the captives are freed. Blake puts this revolutionary deliverance in a composition of an African Black.

# ACKNOWLEDGEMENTS

We would like thank the following for permission to reprint and/or translate the following articles:

Ana Esther Ceceña, the editor of *Chiapas*, gave permission to translate and publish: "Interview by Ana Esther Ceceña with Adelina Bottero, Luciano Salza, Friederike Habermann, Marc Tomsin, Massimo de Angelis and Ulrich Brand: Zapata in Europe," and "Interview by Ana Esther Ceceña with Adriana Lopez Monjardin, Carlos Manzo and Julio Moguel: Civil Society and the EZLN." These articles were originally published in Spanish in *Chiapas*, number 4, 1997, pp. 111–134 and pp. 135–154 respectively. The journal *Chiapas* is produced by the Institute of Economic Research of the National Autonomous University of Mexico (UNAM).

Peter Linebaugh's "Revolutionary Tygers in the Night" was originally part of a birthday letter to George Caffentzis, a member of the Midnight Notes collective.

David Riker and Victor Sira gave permission to reprint their photos of the immigrant garment and construction workers in New York City and the stills from *La Ciudad*.

Monty Neill's "Encounters in Chiapas" was first printed in *Industrial Worker*, December, 1996.

Parts of Olivier de Marcellus' "People's Global Action: Dreaming Up and Old Ghost" were originally published in *Race & Class*, April–June 2000.

Claudia von Werlhof's "Upheaval from the Depth" was originally printed in the *International Journal of Comparative Sociology*, vol. xxxviii, n. 1–2, June 1997. Thanks to Pat Lauderdale and the IJCS for permission to reprint parts of the piece.

**e-mail:** anti_theses@hotmail.com

# Reading Capital Politically

by Harry Cleaver

Karl Marx wrote *Capital* to put a weapon in the hands of the working class. Our understanding of the term 'working class' has altered over the last century but *Capital*'s usefulness as a political weapon is as great as ever. In *Reading Capital Politically* Harry Cleaver presents a detailed study of the first chapter of *Capital* and suggests how the rest of the work can be read as a political document.

Cleaver shows how we can directly apply Marx's categories to study in depth first the various ways in which the capitalist class seeks to dominate us, and second the methods we ourselves use to struggle against that domination. He shows how reading Marx can provide a guide both to understanding and opposing capitalism. The book's introduction includes a brilliant overview of working class struggles in the past century and the development of ideas of autonomy.

First published in 1979, this second edition includes a new Preface by the author.

**184pp paperback**
**ISBN: 1 902593 29 4**

**Available from good bookshops for £8 or US$15, or direct from Anti/Theses, c/o Cardigan Centre, 145–149 Cardigan Road, Leeds LS6 1LJ, UK for £6 or US$12, including postage/shipping air mail. Sterling cheques/POs payable to ANTI/THESES; cheques in US dollars payable to M. RANSOM**

## THE BLUE LINE
## A NOVEL IN 26 MILES

*DANIEL DE ROULET*

Max, a French architect, is running in the mammoth New York City Marathon. And, like the first Greek marathoner Pheidippides, the French communard Gustave Courbet, or the Italian autonomist Giangiacomo Feltrinelli, Max has run before... At war.

Daniel de Roulet, who has run the New York City Marathon three times, was born in Switzerland in 1944. An architect and information worker, he is the author of many novels in French and German, and the winner of the 1994 Prix Dentan. This is his first novel published in English.

## CALIBAN AND THE WITCH
## WOMEN, THE BODY, & PRIMITIVE ACCUMULATION

*SILVIA FEDERICI*

*Caliban and the Witch* is a history of the body in the transition to capitalism. Moving from the peasant revolts of the late Middle Ages to the witch hunts and the rise of mechanical philosophy, Federici investigates the capitalist rationalization of social reproduction. She shows how the struggle against the rebel body and the conflict between body and mind are essential conditions for the development of labor power and self-ownership, two central principles of modern social organization.

## CONVERSATIONS WITH DON DURITO
## THE STORY OF DURITO AND THE DEFEAT OF NEO-LIBERALISM

*SUBCOMANDANTE MARCOS OF THE EZLN*

This book began in 1994, when Zapatista Subcomandante Marcos replied to a 10-year-old girl from Mexico City who had sent him a drawing. "*Sub-comandante Mariana Moguel: I greet you with respect and congratulate you for the new rank acquired with your drawing. Permit me to tell you a story which, perhaps, you will understand someday. It is the story of... DURITO.*" The ensuing collection of related fales about the warrior beetle, narrated by his pipe-smoking, black-ski-masked human squire, is an extraordinary account for the general reader of current global political struggle.

## AN EXISTING BETTER WORLD
## NOTES ON THE BREAD AND PUPPET THEATER

*GEORGE DENNISON*

Editors Geoffrey Gardner and Taylor Stoehr present the late author's intimate reflections on Vermont's Bread and Puppet Theater, arguably the most important politically-inspired American performance artists of our time. Profusely illustrated.

## DIGITAL RESISTANCE
## EXPLORATIONS IN TACTICAL MEDIA

*CRITICAL ART ENSEMBLE*

Essays in culural politics from the collective authors of *Electronic Disturbance, Electronic Civil Disobedience and Other Unpopular Ideas,* and *Flesh Machine.* Chapters in this new volume include "Electronic Civil Disobedience and the Public Sphere," "The Mythology of Terrorism on the Net," "The Promissory Rhetoric of Biotechnology," "Observations on Collective Cultural Action," "Recombinant Theater and Digital Resistance," "Contestational Robotics," "Children as Tactical Media Participants," and "The Financial Advantages of Anti-Copyright."

## DR. PENETRALIA
## A NOVEL

*TH. METZGER*

Scabrous, mystical, vulgar, drenched in hormones and ecstatic angst — *Dr. Penetralia* is a pilgrimage through the rancid backwaters of Th. Metzger's nightmare America. Filth and beauty, lust and spiritual secrets, tainted pleasure and pain's lost treasures: descend pilgrim, come with us to the place where the gods whisper all night and the flesh dissolves into smoke and light.

## EXTENDED MEDIA OBJECT

*VLADIMIR MUZHESKY, EDITOR*

Essays on new media, culture and techno-logy from many hands, including "ADILKNO" (Foundation for the Advance-ment of Illegal Knowledge), Alan Sondheim, Bart Plantenga, Bob Dobbs, Bruce Sterling, Dietmar Offenhuber, Douglas Rushkoff, Geert Lovink, Konrad Becker, Lev Manovich, Masaki Fujihata, Mark Amerika, Natalie Jeremijenko, Oliver Frommel, Pauline van Mourik Broekman, Peter Lamborn Wilson, Ricardo Dominguez, RTMARK, Tim Boykett, Vladimir Muzhesky and Vuk Cosic.

## FORBIDDEN SACRAMENTS
## THE SURVIVAL OF SHAMANISM IN WESTERN CIVILIZATION

***DONALD P. DULCHINOS***

The indigenous practice of shamanism has been under siege for as long as Western European societies have practiced colonialism and Christian missionary work. Only very recently has there been a backlash condemning the cultural chauvinism that labels indigenous shamanism "primitive." Increasingly, shaman-centered cultures are respected for values of community, environmental consciousness, and first-hand spiritual experience. What is not widely known is that Western civilization itself, beneath layers of Christianity and industrialism, stands upon its own shamanic foundation.

## HACKTIVISM
## NETWORK_ART_ACTIVISM

*ELECTRONIC DISTURBANCE THEATRE*

The definitive insider's history of electronic civil disobedience, from its first appearances to the present, with contributions from an immense cast, including Stefan Wray, Ricardo Dominguez, Harry Cleaver, Fran Ilich, Cult of the Dead Cow, Federation of Random Action, Alex Galloway, Manuel de Landa, Sadie Plant, Keith Sanborn, Diane Ludin, Sandy Stone, Arthur & Marilouise Kroker, Chris Gray, doll yoko, the HongKong Blondes, many more.

## I'M STILL THINKING
## CONFLICT, CONTROL, COLLAPSE: ART FROM THE BALKAN WAR

*MIRO STEFANOVIC*

Piercing, witty, heartbreaking editorial cartoon art from the Balkan War. From a dissident Serbian perspective, Stefanovic documents the political machinations and atrocities of Europe's latest war, from the beginnings of the conflict until the overthrow of Milosevic, casting a jaundiced, sardonic, ecology-conscious eye in all directions.

## NIGHT VISION
## A FIRST TO THIRD WORLD VAMPYRE OPERA

*FRED HO & RUTH MARGRAFF*

"Low and behold it moves, the world moves first to third world, third to first world as we take our little turns... Affix me centrifugal to my so-called self." Inspired by Hong Kong action cinema, Iraqi desert songs, Crusader art, and Times Square erotica, Night Vision is a bloodcurdling transfusion of Fred Ho's operatic "jazz" and Ruth E. Margraff's neo-biblical libretti. *Night Vision* tracks a 2000-year-old female vampyre who rises to pop music superstardom, hyped up by a Renfield-like diabolical techno-genius, The Spin Doctor. Libretto & double CD set.

## LAB USA
## ILLUMINATED DOCUMENTS

*KEVIN PYLE*

Electromagnetic mind-control, open-air biological testing in New York City subways, and clandestine dosing of citizens with psychotropic drugs are all part of America's little known, yet well-footnoted, history of medical abuse. *Lab USA* chronicles and illuminates these and many more events through the medium of comix. Employing declassified documents, court testimony, and interviews, *Lab USA* contrasts objective facts with powerful images to reveal the role of language and authority in the implementation of these dark deeds.

## SURREALIST SUBVERSIONS
## RANTS & OTHER WRITINGS FROM *ARSENAL*

*RON SAKOLSKY, EDITOR*

Vast anthology documenting the "Chicago School" of Surrealism in the United States, with contributions by Franklin and Penelope Rosemont, Paul Garon, Nancy Joyce Peters, Robin D.G. Kelley, Ted Joans, Jayne Cortez, Philip Lamantia, Leonora Carrington, David Roediger, Herbert Marcuse, Paul Buhle, more.

## NIETZSCHE & ANARCHISM

*JOHN MOORE, EDITOR*

Eleven essays on Nietzsche and anarchism, libertarianism, Emma Goldmann, Ananda Coomaraswamy, politics, aesthetics, humor. Contributors include Daniel Colson, Leigh Starcross, Allan Antliff, Guy Aldred, Andrew Koch, Franco Riccio, Salvo Vaccaro, Max Cafrad, John Marmysz, John Moore, and Peter Lamborn Wilson.

## HELP YOURSELF!

*THE UNBEARABLES*

Send-ups of self-help literature by Samuel R. Delaney, Robert Anton Wilson, Sparrow, Jim Knipfel, Arthur Nersesian, Carl Watson, Doug Nufer, Richard Kostelanetz, Tsaurah Litzky, Denise Duhamel, Christian X. Hunter, Michael Carter, Jill Rapaport, Bob Holman, Ron Kolm, Susan Scutti, and more.

## GRASS
## A COMPANION BOOK TO THE DOCUMENTARY FILM

*RON MANN*

This book accompanies "Grass, the Movie," the award-winning (and briefly-banned) documentary by Canadian filmmaker Ron Mann. Heavy color visuals throughout, including archival stills, artwork by Paul Mavrides, text by Ron Mann, an introduction by Woody Harrelson, and essays by Keith Stroup of NORML, film critic Jonathan Rosenbaum and Dr. John Morgan.

## DREAMER OF THE DAY
## FRANCIS PARKER YOCKEY &
## THE POSTWAR FASCIST INTERNATIONAL

*KEVIN COOGAN*

Francis Parker Yockey, a U.S. lawyer and former war-crimes prosecutor, was one of the most enigmatic figures inside the far right in both Europe and America. Best-known today for his book *Imperium* — the *Mein Kampf* of Neo-nazism — his life as an international figure in the post-WWII fascist underground has remained a mystery. Coogan's vast biographical investigation takes us into the heart of a Shadow Reich composed of spies, conspirators, theorists and occultists.